IMPLEMENTING THE LEXICAL APPROACH

Putting Theory into Practice

Michael Lewis

with Classroom reports by

Cherry Gough
Ron Martínez
Mark Powell
Jonathan Marks
George Woolard
Heinz Ribisch

LTP
TEACHER
TRAINING

Language Teaching Publications

35 Church Road, Hove, BN3 2BE, England

ISBN 1 899396 60 8
© LTP 1997

The Author

Michael Lewis taught English in Sweden at all levels from primary school to adult. In 1981 he co-founded LTP. He has lectured on language and methodology in most European countries, Japan, the States and Central America. He is the author of *The English Verb* and a number of student texts and co-author of *Business English* (with Peter Wilberg) and *Practical Techniques for Language Teaching* (with Jimmie Hill). The highly acclaimed *The Lexical Approach* appeared in 1993. His current professional interest lies in integrating lexis, grammar and phonology and in the ways in which language is stored in the mental lexicon.

A Note on Dictionaries

The four principal dictionaries designed for non-native learners referred to in this book, usually by abbreviations which are in fairly wide use, are:
CIDE   Cambridge International Dictionary of English (1995 edition)
COBUILD Collins Cobuild English Dictionary (new edition, 1995)
LDCE   Longman Dictionary of Contemporary English (Third edition 1995)
OALD   Oxford Advanced Learner's Dictionary (Fifth edition 1995)
In some cases the earlier editions are very different, and some of the remarks made in this book apply only to the 1995 (or later) editions.

Acknowledgements

I am grateful to all who responded to *The Lexical Approach* with comments, letters, suggestions and criticisms. I hope they got as much out of the debate as I did. I am particularly grateful to the colleagues who have contributed classroom reports for this book, to Heinz Ribisch's pupils who kindly lent me their notebooks, and finally to my colleagues Jimmie Hill, who proved a demanding but helpful editor, and Mark Powell, who provided some valuable insights.

Cover Design by Anna Macleod.
The drawing on page 148 by Jonathan Marks.
This is just to say by William Carlos Williams, Collected Poems, Carcanet Press.
Horse by George Mackay Brown, Scottish Poetry 1, used by permission of John Murray (Publishers).

Printed in England by Commercial Colour Press, London E7.

Implementing the Lexical Approach

The Lexical Approach can be summarised in a few words: language consists not of traditional grammar and vocabulary but often of multi-word prefabricated chunks. Teachers using the Lexical Approach will, instead of analysing language whenever possible, be more inclined to direct learners' attention to chunks which are as large as possible. This book provides a detailed discussion of the implications of this change of mindset.

Implementation may involve a radical change of mindset, and suggest many changes in classroom procedure, but the methodological changes are small:

*   Recording adjective + noun rather than noun alone
*   Highlighting certain expressions as having a special evocative and generative status
*   Exploring the environment in which certain kinds of words occur
*   Emphasising the pronunciation of lexical chunks, not individual words.

Implementing the Lexical Approach in your classes does not mean a radical upheaval, likely to upset colleagues, parents and learners. On the contrary, if introduced with thought and sensitivity, its introduction will be almost invisible, involving perhaps 20 or even 50 small changes in every lesson, each in itself unremarkable, but the cumulative effect will be more effective teaching and more efficient learning.

At the other end of the scale, the Lexical Approach may yet provide more radical challenges to much that is standard in course content and methodology. Although this book is primarily concerned with how to take our present understanding into class immediately, the final chapter suggests ways in which the theory and practical applications continue to develop as each informs the other as we try to discover the best way to help learners.

This book is based on the reactions of many teachers to *The Lexical Approach* and is a contribution to the continuing debate.

Terminology

This book is primarily for language teachers and I have tried to avoid unnecessary jargon. The term *text* is used in a slightly technical sense to refer to any piece of continuous language, whether written or spoken. When used in the technical sense of 'type of lexical item', the words *collocation, word,* and *expression* appear with an initial capital letter. I have also used an initial capital when I distinguish classroom Activities from Exercises.

Michael Lewis, Hove, 1997

Contents

Recording and revisiting
Practising in the Lexical Approach
Learner participation
The value of repetition
Noticing
Consciousness-Raising
The importance of negative evidence
The central strategy: Pedagogical chunking

Translation is inevitable
Learning L2 is not identical to learning L1
Translation and lexis
Translation and collocation
The value of translation
Interference can be helpful
L1 awareness as a resource

Principles
Notebooks
Formats

Exercises designed on lexical principles
Basic Exercise Types
Sample Exercises

Adapting activities to provide a lexical focus
Sample activities

Report 1: Introducing Collocation – Cherry Gough
Report 2: Developing Awareness of a de-lexicalised verb – Ron Martínez
Report 3: Sound Scripting – Mark Powell
Report 4: Pronunciation in the Lexical Approach – Jonathan Marks
Report 5: Using Literature – George Woolard
Report 6: Lexical Notebooks – Heinz Ribisch

Chapter 1

What is the Lexical Approach?

INTRODUCTION

When *The Lexical Approach* was published in 1993 it stimulated wide and lively debate. Many reviews appeared, and an enormous number of colleagues have written with queries, disagreements, support, and practical suggestions for taking the Approach into the classroom. It is particularly gratifying that most of the comments from teachers working in regular language classrooms have been positive and show how they believe they can incorporate lexical insights into their day-to-day teaching. *The Lexical Approach* was intended to be a practically applicable methodology book. It stands or falls on the simple criterion of whether or not it can be implemented in everyday language classes. Readers familiar with *The Lexical Approach* may prefer to begin at Chapter 2, as this first chapter provides a brief summary of the central ideas of *The Lexical Approach*, together with some reactions to it.

TASK

Look through a good modern EFL dictionary: how are the contents different from a simple pocket dictionary?

The good EFL dictionary contains better definitions, more examples and more information about the grammar of the headwords, but perhaps the single most striking difference is that it contains a much larger range of items. In addition to single words, it contains phrases, idioms and even complete expressions. The lexicon of the language is considerably larger than any list of the "words" of that language. This simple insight is the basis for a lexical view of language, and a lexical approach to teaching.

WHAT IS LEXIS?

The standard view divides language into grammar (structure) and vocabulary (words); the Lexical Approach challenges this fundamental view of language. Instead, the Lexical Approach argues that language consists of chunks which, when combined, produce continuous coherent text. The chunks are of different kinds and four different basic types are identified. One of these consists of single words while all the others are multi-word items.

1. Words

This category is familiar; it is old-fashioned vocabulary, and is found listed and explained in even the most unsatisfactory dictionaries. Words which can stand alone *(OPEN, Certainly!)* are lexical items, as are words where a single substitution produces a totally new meaning: *salt/pepper* in *Could you pass the ...., please?* Unsurprisingly, this category is by far the largest of the four categories in the lexicon. The most fundamental linguistic insight of the Lexical Approach is that much of the lexicon consists of multi-word items of different kinds. Words are the largest and most familiar category, but it is the other categories which provide the novelty and pedagogic challenge which is the subject of this book.

There is a relatively small group of lexical items which sit somewhere between words and the major multi-word categories. *By the way* is conventionally written as three words, while *nevertheless* is written as one; *on the other hand* has no similar expressions **on the other arm/finger/leg* etc; only one of *once in a blue/red/green/new moon* is standard English. Combinations such as *to and fro, bread and butter,* are, despite logical considerations, not normally reversible: **fro and to, *butter and bread*. This may be different in different languages – the Swedish equivalent of *bread and butter* is literally *butter and bread*. These multi-word items are polywords, arbitrary combinations, a sort of mini-idiom.

2. Collocations

One of the two central specifically linguistic ideas of the Lexical Approach is that of collocation. Collocation is the readily observable phenomenon whereby certain words co-occur in natural text with greater than random frequency. We all know which is the more common in each of these pairs: *chase/miss the bus, make/do a mistake, slump dramatically/gracefully*. But do we really know? Are our intuitions reliable? And, even if they are, what part does collocation play in standard classroom activities? Is it a simple extension of vocabulary teaching, or can we find patterns and paradigms which move it towards word-grammar, and hence towards the generative pole of the vocabulary-grammar spectrum?

Collocations range on a spectrum from fully fixed (*a broken home, to catch a cold*), through relatively fixed, to totally novel. It is by no means the case that because two words co-occur, they collocate. This complex idea is fully explored in the next chapter. Those collocations which are most fixed closely resemble words; indeed David Brazil describes chunks as 'word-like objects'. Many of the most interesting collocations, however, are not fully fixed, but are partnerships with a slot which can be filled by a limited number of partner-words. This allows us to identify partnership patterns. Far from being of only theoretical interest, collocations can be taken into the classroom immediately. Fixed idioms have long been recognised; most readers will see only one way of completing these: *It was a case of the tail wagging the .... , You can't pull the .... over my eyes,* but it is now clear that many more phrases than previously recognised, while not fully fixed, are very likely to be completed in a relatively small number of ways, a phenomenon which can be put to excellent pedagogic use.

TASK

Complete each of these in three different ways if you can:

1. absent from ......   7. She's better at ......
2. guilty of ......   8. It consists of ......
3. a bar of ......   9. It was very ...... equipped.
4. suspicious of ......   10. Prices fell ......
5. It's not relevant to the present ...... 11. Things went ...... wrong.
6. We had a ......time.   12. Could you turn the ...... off, please.

Did you find three completions easily? Do you think someone else would choose some of the same words? Do you think your choices are unusual, common or even more-or-less fixed standard expressions?

EFL currently teaches certain adjectives with their associated preposition: *suspicious of, relevant to,* etc, but chunks are bigger than that. The Lexical Approach emphasises combinations which are not only possible but highly likely. It is a small but significant improvement to direct learners' attention to slightly larger chunks: *suspicious of people who..., relevant to our discussion/problem/needs.* The change may seem so small as to be trivial but this is not so. We store much of our mental lexicon in complete, fully-contextualised phrases. In the past, teaching, in an effort to make learning easier, broke things down into chunks which were quite simply too small.

3. Fixed Expressions

The Lexical Approach highlights a second major category of lexical item – Expressions. These have a special status in the language. The category is sometimes usefully divided into those Expressions which are fully fixed, and others which are semi-fixed 'frames' with 'slots' which may be filled in a limited number of ways.

Language teaching has always recognised some types of Fixed Expressions. Those which have featured most often in teaching materials are:

a. Social greetings:

Good morning; It's a lovely morning, isn't it?; Happy New Year.

b. Politeness phrases:

No thank you, I'm fine; I'll have to be going.

c. 'Phrase Book' language:

Can you tell me the way to ...., please?

I'd like a twin room for .... nights, please.

Although this is often mocked, everyone recognises the value of some 'useful expressions' for predictable tourist-type situations.

d.   Idioms – especially of the more picturesque kind:

Hang on, you're putting the cart before the horse there.

You're making a mountain out of a molehill.

This language has, however, been seen as relatively marginal to learners' needs – the first three categories have only been considered important for learners in a native speaker environment such as private language schools in Britain or ESL students in the US, while the last category is usually seen as the icing on the cake for learners who can already 'say what they mean'. It has also frequently been easy to criticise the actual language taught in these categories as dated, not what people really say, inappropriate for non-native users, ethnocentric and for a host of other, often valid, reasons. It is time for us to revise our view of Fixed Expressions in the light of evidence from modern corpora based on what David Brazil has aptly termed 'used language'.

TASK

Rearrange the following to make natural expressions.

1.   How it long will take?
2.   What do you size take?
3.   Don't to things home your forget take.
4.   I'll for responsibility full happens what take.
5.   I'll to a just have chance take.
6.   Nobody the of parents your can place take.
7.   I more any can't take!
8.   If you you'll my it with do to nothing have advice take.

Three points are worth noting:

• You do all these examples except the last by quickly scanning the component words. This allows you to recognise and recall prefabricated wholes. These are stored as Fixed Expressions in your mental lexicon.

• All the examples contain the verb *take*, a word which in itself has little meaning but which, like the other so-called de-lexicalised verbs, is often a component of many such Expressions and accordingly can be used as an organising principle for some lexis.

• The last example is simply too long to be done in the same way. It is, in fact, two lexical items: *If you take my advice* (5 words); *you'll have nothing to do with it* (7 words). The significance of this is discussed in the next chapter.

Modern analyses of real data suggest that we are much less original in using language than we like to believe. Much of what we say, and a significant proportion of what we write, consists of prefabricated multi-word items. Fully fixed expressions must be acquired as wholes in precisely the same way as individual words or very strong collocations. The final category of lexis is, however, much more useful and significant.

4. Semi-fixed Expressions

Fully Fixed Expressions are comparatively rare, and many are short, often verbless expressions in the spoken language for managing everyday situations. The following is a perfectly believable response, made up of three fully fixed expressions: *Not too bad, thanks. By the way, many happy returns.* In contrast, there is a vast number of Semi-fixed Expressions and these occur widely in both spoken and written language. Many different types deserve attention, for example:

• Almost Fixed Expressions, which permit minimal variation: *It's / That's not my fault.*

• Spoken sentences with a simple slot: *Could you pass ......, please?*

• Expressions with a slot which must be filled with a particular kind of slot-filler: *Hello. Nice to see you. I haven't seen you* + time expression with *for* or *since.*

• Sentence heads, which can be completed in many ways: *What was really interesting / surprising / annoying was ... .*

• More extended frames such as those for a formal letter or the opening paragraph of an academic paper. For example:

There are broadly speaking two views of .... . The more traditional, usually associated with ... and his / her colleagues, suggests that ...., while the more progressive view, associated with .... suggests .... . In this paper I wish to suggest a third position, which, while containing elements of the view proposed by .... also takes account of recent developments in .... which have produced evidence to suggest.... and so on.

As the last example shows, the Semi-fixed Expression category contains items which are hardly covered by the informal use of the word 'expression'. This is a large and important category which contains a spectrum, from very short to very long and from almost fixed to very free. An important consequence of viewing language from a lexical point of view is that the traditional distinction between 'fixed' vocabulary and 'generative' grammar is recognised as an invalid over-simplification. Language consists of items which occupy all points on the spectrum between these two extremes.

SENTENCES WITH SPECIAL STATUS

Traditional linguistics has concerned itself with possible sentences, but, as we shall see, not all possible sentences have the same status.

TASK

Do you consider the following sentences:
a. correct, possible sentences of English?
b. different from each other in any way(s)?
If so, what differences seem important?

1. I'll see you on Monday.
2. It takes a while to settle into a new house.
3. Are you all right? You don't look very well.
4. I'm going to buy the blue one even if it is a bit more expensive.
5. It's clouding over.
6. We need to do something about the broken pane in that window.
7. It's time we were on our way.
8. She tried to warn them, but they went ahead and did it anyway.
9. Don't worry. I'm sure it'll turn up.

All are correct possible sentences, but the odd numbers 1,3,5,7,9 are much more high frequency, typical examples. A glance at many ELT materials, particularly grammar books, shows that there is a tendency to treat all possible sentences as of equal status. While linguists may be concerned with the possible, language teaching can more usefully direct learners' attention to highly probable examples. The Lexical Approach consciously highlights certain examples as having a special status because they are Fixed, Semi-fixed or prototypical. All of these ideas are discussed in detail later.

REACTIONS TO 'THE LEXICAL APPROACH'

While reaction to the linguistic analysis of *The Lexical Approach* was broadly positive, reaction to the pedagogical implications was decidedly more mixed, ranging from an enthusiastic: "Yours is far from being yet another 'approach', but a quantum shift", to the dismissive: "So what?" Here are some of the comments which have appeared in print, together with my initial reaction to each. The ideas raised are fully discussed later, in the relevant chapters.

> Michael Lewis in *The Lexical Approach* would like to completely change the way teachers think about ELT.
> *TESOL Quarterly Winter 94*

That is true, if taken absolutely at face value – completely change the way teachers **think about** ELT, yes; but change what they actually do in the classroom only in comparatively modest ways.

To begin with, the lexical approach does not require returning to square one and starting from scratch. Much of what the book suggests is – or rather should be – standard practice already. On the other hand, it has to be acknowledged that following Michael Lewis' ideas and giving lexis such a prominent place in ELT requires more than making only a few minor adjustments in one's teaching. It touches the very core of what we do in class and questions the attitudes which are central to our understanding of the role of the teacher.
Heinz Ribisch, ELT News No. 28 February 1996

Absolutely – many small practical changes, both additions and subtractions from present practice, but all informed by a major shift in the teachers' perception of their own role. In many ways it would be easier to argue for radical paradigm shift, for then at least the issues would be clear and the debate easier to stimulate. In fact, as already mentioned, implementing the Lexical Approach involves a big change in the teacher's understanding of language, but only small, consistent changes in the classroom so that the Approach can be introduced without serious upheaval.

Simply put: if we seriously understand how lexis works in real-world communication, we will naturally make sense of the lexical approach. But without that deeper understanding, we will trivialise again, and just replace one set of jargon terms with another. This is the challenge [The Lexical Approach] sets out so elegantly – a serious book by a serious teacher. Just how far forward do we want to go?
Andrew Barfield, The Language Teacher Feb 95

I have some sympathy with all these reactions. On the one hand, 'weak' implementation of the approach is a comparatively modest affair, involving little more than changing conventional vocabulary teaching activities to take account of the wider concept of lexis. Revising the fundamental way in which we see the constituent elements of language – viewing language as lexis rather than a combination of grammar and vocabulary – can, on the other hand, provide a catalyst for a much more radical reappraisal of content, materials, methodology and, most importantly of all, the attitudes of teachers, trainers, and even examining boards and curriculum designers. The possibility exists for more radical change – what might be called 'strong' implementation. The range of possibilities, and the danger of being seduced into much more radical changes than you initially foresee is neatly captured by this extract from a review:

The central tenet "Language consists of grammaticalised lexis, not lexicalised grammar" may not strike the reader as very radical or revolutionary, but the consequences of its consistent application to teaching and learning processes turn out to be sometimes outright 'heretic', questioning practically all traditionally accepted principles of language teaching.

> The whole structure of the work, starting from theory and general ideas and developing those to reach much more practical and very concrete points of view in the later chapters, makes for a nice build-up in reader reaction: at first the reader is (metaphorically) nodding in agreement, be it sometimes with certain reservations, but half way through the book eyebrows are being raised, wrinkles appear in the forehead, and finally mouths drop open in astonishment or even plain indignation.
> *Raf Erzeel, review VVLE Newsletter 3/96*

This book tries, as the review suggests, to apply the theoretical standpoint outlined in *The Lexical Approach* consistently. The implications for the classroom are discussed and many examples of exercises and activities re-orientated to take account of a lexical view of language are given. The implications for both the content of language courses and teacher training are also discussed. New, or at least radically modified, exercises and activities are described in detail. Many of the suggestions have been generously contributed by teachers in feedback sessions and letters.

I hope this book seems cautious enough for those seeking weak implementation, and radical enough for those favouring strong implementation. I urge both groups to remember that implementing, like learning, is a process. We need a constant openness to revision in the light of research and experience. My own views on implementation develop constantly and will, I know, continue to do so. As the philosopher Don Cupitt has observed, we do not need new dogma or orthodoxy; the truth, such as it is, is in the movement.

Michael Swan in a plenary address at the 1996 IATEFL Conference commented:

> A few weeks ago somebody told me 'We've all gone over to the Lexical Approach now – we hardly do any grammar at all.' I doubt if Michael Lewis would have been pleased to hear that his ideas have been allowed to fill somebody's horizon in this way.

Michael Swan was quite right; *The Lexical Approach* was concerned primarily with the nature of language; only then did it address pedagogical questions. But it is a gross misreading of the text to pretend that asserting the pedagogic value of lexis is in any way to deny the pedagogic value of grammar. While stressing the importance of lexis and probable language, *The Lexical Approach* fully recognises that without a generative element, novelty and innovation – possible language – become impossible. I totally dissociate myself from any suggestion that *The Lexical Approach* denies the value of grammar and, as Michael Swan correctly assumes, any suggestion that 'Lexis is the answer', or even that there **is** an answer. Both explicitly contradict my belief in our dynamic, ever-evolving understanding of both language and learning.

WHAT CHANGES CAN WE EXPECT?

Like Krashen's Natural Approach, and in the tradition of the Communicative Approach (as conceived by applied linguists, not the bowdlerised version which publishers incorporated into coursebooks), the Lexical Approach places communication of meaning at the heart of language and language learning. This leads to emphasis on the main carrier of meaning, vocabulary. The concept of a large vocabulary is extended from words to lexis, but the essential idea is that fluency is based on the acquisition of a large store of fixed and semi-fixed prefabricated items, which are available as the foundation for any linguistic novelty or creativity. Grammatical knowledge permits the creative re-combination of lexis in novel and imaginative ways, but it cannot begin to be useful in that role until the learner has a sufficiently large mental lexicon to which grammatical knowledge can be applied.

SUMMARY

It may be helpful to provide a checklist of some of the changes in both content and methodology which implementing the Lexical Approach involves. These ideas are all extensively discussed later but it is immediately apparent that taking a lexical view of language impinges on almost every aspect of current practice, sometimes in potentially disturbing ways.

More attention will be paid to:

* Lexis – different kinds of multi-word chunks
* Specific language areas not previously standard in many EFL texts
* Listening (at lower levels) and reading (at higher levels)
* Activities based on L1/L2 comparisons and translation
* The use of the dictionary as a resource for active learning
* Probable rather than possible English
* Organising learners' notebooks to reveal patterns and aid retrieval
* The language which learners may meet outside the classroom
* Preparing learners to get maximum benefit from text

Less attention will be paid to:

* Sentence grammar – single sentence gap-fill and transformation practices
* Uncollocated nouns
* Indiscriminate recording of 'new words'
* Talking in L2 for the sake of it because you claim to use 'a communicative approach'

Finally, we ask why does Raf Erzeel, in the review quoted above, suggest that the implications of the Lexical Approach can make the jaw drop? There is, perhaps, one basic reason: emphasising lexis necessarily reduces the role of grammar. Many distinguished linguists have pointed out that vocabulary carries more meaning than grammar. David Wilkins memorably wrote: *Without grammar little can be conveyed; without vocabulary nothing can be conveyed.* At IATEFL 1996 John Sinclair stated unequivocally: *A lexical mistake often causes misunderstanding, while a grammar mistake rarely does.*

However unpopular it is with teachers, language which contains grammatical errors is unlikely to be misunderstood in context, but with lexical errors misunderstanding, incomprehension, or in rare cases even offence, are quite likely. Recognising the lexical nature of language, and the centrality of lexis to the creation of meaning, and consequently to communicative power, demotes grammar – and in particular, the often unnatural, inaccurate grammar of standard EFL – to a subsidiary role. This single change is enough to leave many teachers scandalised and resistant to the changes implicit in strong implementation of the Lexical Approach. Without a clear understanding of the different kinds of lexis we cannot begin to look at classroom implications, so we turn in Chapter 2 to a closer analysis of the kinds of chunks which are the building blocks of all natural language.

Chapter 2

Understanding Lexis

No teacher can begin to implement the Lexical Approach without a clear understanding of lexis; this involves one important theoretical principle, but principally it means a clear view of the essential concepts of Collocation and Expressions. This chapter explores these essential topics.

ARBITRARINESS OF LEXICAL ITEMS

Every teacher is familiar with the difficulty when a student asks *Can you say . . . ?* and you reply *Well, you could say that, but you wouldn't.* The student asks *Why?*, only to receive the apparently unsatisfactory answer *It just doesn't sound right.* However unsatisfactory that answer seems in class, it is the correct answer and lies at the very heart of a lexical understanding of language. A clear understanding of why this is so is indispensable for all language teachers; it is also helpful if learners themselves gradually develop an understanding of why it is that their apparently simple question receives such a seemingly unhelpful answer. *You could, but you wouldn't* could almost be a slogan for the Lexical Approach. Why?

The single most fundamental principle of linguistics is the arbitrariness of the sign. The importance of this principle cannot be over-emphasised. A particular thing is called a *pen* in English, while another thing is called a *book*, but you cannot usefully ask **why** these particular words are used for these particular objects. What is conventionally called a pen could be called a book, but then that name would be unlikely to be used in the way we now use it for books, as too much confusion would almost certainly result. Homophones do occur – *sole, soul* – but the meanings are usually so widely separated that there is little danger of any misunderstanding in context. When they ask *What is the English for ...?*, learners are usually content to record the word in their vocabulary notebook; they do not ask *Why is that the word for ...?* But when we consider multi-word items, the classroom becomes more difficult for the teacher unless she has truly internalised the concept of the arbitrariness of the sign. When learners ask why, teachers have an understandable desire and tendency to explain – but that leads to difficulties if the explanation is theoretically unsound.

All lexical items are arbitrary – they are simply the consensus of what has been institutionalised, the agreed language which a particular group do use, selected from what they **could** use, actual language as opposed to theoretically possible language. *Pat, pet, pit, pot* and *put* are all English words, with totally different meanings; *sat, set, sit, sot* are also English words, but *sut* is not a standard item in the lexicon; it could be used as an English word, but it isn't. *Happy Christmas, Merry Christmas, Happy Birthday* are all standard but * *Merry Birthday* is not.

Many important linguistic phenomena are arbitrary, for example, irregular plurals (there is nothing wrong with * *childs,* but *children* is standard), or past tenses (*went,* but we could accept * *goed).* Students frequently ask why the language behaves in a certain way, and are unhappy to be told *English is like that,* but unfortunately that is the only accurate answer.

The tendency to seek explanations affects teachers too. Most readers probably suspect they know why a bus stop is so called – probably because buses stop there. But the so-called explanation is an illusion – taxis stop not at a * *taxi stop,* but on a *taxi rank*; trains do not stop at * *train stops,* but at *stations. Bus stop* is as arbitrary as *taxi rank*; by coincidence it looks as if it can be explained, and no doubt the coincidence makes it easier to recall, but, and this cannot be stressed too strongly, its construction is **not** susceptible to explanation; it is as arbitrary as *pen* or *book,* and attempts to explain will in the end cause confusion rather than help. Learners need to be taught that some questions are helpful, but others are not, as 'answers' to them simply do not exist. Etymology, for example, may reveal the sources of some words or patterns, but the explanations are never more than of details. Language remains essentially arbitrary.

This uncomfortable fact most obviously affects vocabulary but arbitrariness affects collocation too:

• A *relative* can be *close, near* or *distant* while a *friend* can be *close,* but neither *distant* nor *near,* although a *close friend* may be one of your *nearest* and *dearest.*

• You can *want* something *badly* (a lot), which in no way corresponds to the standard meaning of *badly* in other contexts.

• An amusing example of the arbitrariness of language can be found in the unlikely world of the dirty joke; such jokes are common in many languages. As any English-speaker will tell you, such jokes are *blue* – which comes as a surprise to Spanish speakers, who are convinced they are *green.*

The Lexical Approach claims that many multi-word items are word-like in quality, and share the arbitrariness of words. Apparently similar items may vary in similar, or totally different ways:

I hope so.   >   *I hope not.*
I think so.   >   *I don't think so.* (Possible, but less likely: *I think not.*)

While a negative sentence may be acceptable as a Fixed Expression, it is by no means certain that the 'positive equivalent' is also sanctioned:

> *I won't wait.*   >   *I'll wait.*
> *I won't bother.*   >   **I'll bother.*

Even the superficially more flexible 'grammatical variations' may be constrained by conventional lexical criteria, so that the following are effectively pragmatic opposites:

> *This'll take ages.*
> *This won't take a moment.*

The existence of lexical constraints – which select from possible English sentences those which actually occur, has long been a source of irritation to teachers, but its theoretical base is not always understood. Arbitrariness extends to all kinds of lexical item – Collocations and Expressions as well as individual words. Some items are sanctioned and some are not. This is not, however, a matter of unalterable fact; new Expressions do become part of the standard lexicon in the same way as new words, but, as already suggested, the answer *You could say that, but you wouldn't* is central to understanding lexis.

THE SIZE OF THE MENTAL LEXICON

Recently, while reading an article in a professional journal, I needed some obscure 'vocabulary': *ontological, metaphorical inference pattern, conceptual metonymy, epistemic mapping,* but, curiously, these are not 'difficult words' to someone interested in the topic about which I was reading. Indeed, it would be difficult to talk about the subject without these lexical resources. The same applies to anyone who uses a language for vocational or professional purposes, or enjoys a particular sport or hobby. This has considerable implications for anyone involved in English for Special or Academic purposes.

If you are a native or near-native speaker of British English, and want to feel the enormous size and limitations of your mental lexicon, buy a real American newspaper and turn to the sports section. Unless you have taken a keen interest in baseball and basketball over a number of years, the match reports are incomprehensible – they are, as we sometimes say, 'written in a foreign language'. The individual words may be familiar, but the collocations, fixed phrases and idioms provide a real bar to understanding. This experience parallels that of acquiring the lexical knowledge necessary to take up a new job, or begin studying an unfamiliar discipline. Similarly large lexical fields cover every area of our everyday lives – family relationships, cooking, travel – so it is abundantly clear that a basic vocabulary of individual words is wholly inadequate to make you functionally effective in talking and reading about any area of life. Our mental lexicon is larger than previously recognised, although very few of the lexical items we know were consciously learned. Krashen has observed that a vocabulary of 100,000 items does not imply either 100,000 fill-in exercises, or 100,000 trips to the dictionary. We have, in his term, acquired rather than formally learned most of the vast mental lexicon which we carry prefabricated and ready for use.

'Vocabulary' is more than Words

The understanding that language does not consist of grammar and words, and that much of our mental lexicon is stored as prefabricated multi-word 'chunks' is far from a trivial observation. It means a revision of some cherished beliefs. Nation, writing as late as 1990, suggests:

> . . . evidence from the few frequency counts of spoken English indicates that in spoken English a small number of words accounts for a very large proportion of spoken language. . . . The first 2000 words covered almost 99 percent of the material. About 5 percent of these very frequent words in spoken English were not among the most frequent words in written English. Clearly, to speak English it is not necessary to have a large vocabulary. In developing learners' spoken English vocabulary it is best to give learners practice in being able to say a lot using a small number of words.
> (*Teaching & Learning Vocabulary*)

This passage deserves comment, for it contains a spectacular misjudgement, and raises an important question. Most speech consists of certain highly-frequent words – true. *Clearly, to speak English it is not necessary to have a large vocabulary* – false! Nation (and this represents a widely-held view) equates 'a large vocabulary' with 'knowing a lot of words'. But this cannot be true; educated speakers can talk fluently and effectively about most things, including highly complex topics. If my spoken lexicon was so small, there would be great areas of experience about which I could write, but not speak. Although this may be true for emotional reasons, we do not meet people who say, for linguistic reasons *I can write about it, but I can't talk about it.* To speak English well you do need a large lexicon. That lexicon is different from the comparable lexicon of the written language, which consists largely of (relatively) rare words. The spoken lexicon consists of many prefabricated, but arbitrary chunks, apparently made of the most frequent words of the language. But why 'apparently'?

Sinclair pointed out (IATEFL symposium 1996) that although we make use of words in compiling dictionaries, this is a convenient fiction, which does not reflect the true nature of language. It is true, but singularly unhelpful, to be told *You don't need many sounds to speak English.* English, like other languages, is made of sounds, and there are only 40 or so of them; but a knowledge of the sounds is in no way to be equated with a knowledge of

English; English is not the sounds, but the myriad combinations of those sounds. Not, notice, the combinations which **may** be made from those sounds, but the actual combinations which exist. The sounds are a possible way of breaking the language **down,** not building it **up.** We can break language into sounds, morphemes, words, sentences; but words are no more the basic units out of which English is 'built' than sounds, letters or morphemes. Words are simply one possible analytical tool, admittedly one which proves exceptionally useful for many purposes. But words are in no sense the basic components.

Nation urges us: *In developing learners' spoken English vocabulary it is best to give learners practice in being able to say a lot using a small number of words.* While we can endorse the suggestion, it inevitably poses the question: *How?* Two implications are:

1. You cannot learn to speak English well from exclusively written input materials, nor to write well from spoken input materials. The languages of speech and writing are simply too different from each other for this to be possible. This endorses the view expressed by Carter and McCarthy:

> There is little point in agonising over interactive features of informal spoken British English grammar if such features simply do not occur in the target variety. This goes alongside our view that there is equally little point in basing grammar teaching exclusively on written models if the goal is to encourage speaking skills.
> *(Applied Linguistics vol. 16/2)*

2. You will not learn to speak well by practising the words, as Nation seems to suggest; learners need input rich in the prefabricated chunks, which they notice as items deserving special attention. Some combinations of words have a different status in the language from other superficially similar combinations. This is not obvious to learners, and is frequently not remarked upon by teachers. A more developed awareness of the special status of certain chunks is intrinsic to the Lexical Approach.

WORDS

The largest, and in one sense most basic, category of lexical item is the familiar one of Words. Although the others are more novel, and correspondingly take more space in our discussion, it remains true that a central task for learners is the acquisition of a sufficiently large vocabulary in the traditional sense of that word. Competent users of a language have, at a minimum, several tens of thousands of words at their disposal, at least for receptive purposes. Although we shall not have much new to say about words, a few points are worth closer scrutiny.

Contractions

How many 'words' do you think these sentences contain?

I can't tell you anything more about it.
Don't wait for me!

There are good reasons for saying that *can't* and *don't* are independent lexical items, that is, they are single words. If that is so, they should be treated linguistically, and perhaps even pedagogically, without direct reference to *can* and *do*. Notice, for example, in both cases, simply substituting the so-called 'positive equivalent' for the supposedly negative *can't* and *don't* will not produce sentences which are plausible and natural 'correct opposites' of the originals.

Polywords

And what about these: how many 'words' do you think these contain?

By the way, have you got your results yet?
We've collected over £500 up to now.

Expressions such as *by the way* and *up to now* allow no variation. In some contexts *way, route* and *road* are closely synonymous, but there is no expression * *by the road / route* which approximates to *by the way*. Similarly, expressions such as * *down to / from now* are not items in the English lexicon. Clearly, items such as *by the way* and *up to now* are invariable, indivisible word-like units. They are 'words-with-spaces-in-them'. These polywords have exactly the same status in the language as individual words. Some applied linguists, notably Nattinger and DeCarrico, treat polywords as a separate class of lexical item; we prefer to treat them as so similar to simple 'Words' that they are at best a sub-category. What matters for the teacher is an awareness of polywords. They are nearly always very short 2- or 3-word phrases which are obvious units. They are often, but by no means exclusively, adverbial phrases of different kinds. Here are some examples:

Sentence adverbs:	*On the other hand, In some ways,*
Expressions of time:	*the day after tomorrow, every now and then,*
Prepositions of place:	*on either side of, upside down*

A further important and familiar category is compound nouns, where two words have been so closely bound to each other that dictionaries list them as single items, sometimes even according them headword status: *prime number, nativity play.*

Speakers do not construct these items, but simply recall them, direct from the memory, as learned wholes. Good dictionaries provide a source of polywords, and language teachers need to draw special attention to their word-like quality. The sentence adverbials, for example, are of particular importance in ensuring fluency in speech and coherence in writing. This discourse marking language is discussed again in Chapter 9.

Information content

Some grammatical categories such as nouns, seem to carry more meaning than others, such as prepositions. The same applies to individual words; some words carry more meaning than others.

TASK

Which in each of these pairs seems to carry more meaning? Can you explain why?

mansion – house	*stagger – walk*
assiduously – carefully	*egregious – calm*

Mansion and *stagger* are more specific than *house* and *walk*; they carry connotational as well as referential meaning. Such cases are easily explained, but even when there is no apparent relationship between the words, as in the other two pairs above, one is in no doubt that *assiduously* and *egregious* carry more meaning than *carefully* and *calm*. The reason is so simple that it is easy to overlook – the words are rarer. We think certain words carry more meaning precisely because we do not meet or use them so often; familiarity breeds contempt. Events which are rare in our lives are invested with more significance than everyday events; your wedding anniversary is not just another day, the cup final is not just another game. As with events, so with words: special uses carry more significance or meaning.

The vast majority of the lexicon of English (or any other language) consists of nouns. In addition, there are relatively few verbs, adjectives and adverbs, and a minute number of words from the grammatical closed classes, determiners, pronouns, prepositions etc. These small classes contain highly frequent words – *which, on, this, then* – which carry almost no referential content out of context. They derive their meaning anew on each occasion of use almost entirely from the context in which they are used. At the opposite end of the spectrum are relatively rare words, usually nouns, which carry so much meaning that they rarely require qualification, so they rarely occur with adjectives except in very specialised texts: *penicillin, cactus, submarine*. That leaves the centre of the spectrum, words which carry some meaning, but not too much: it is a good general rule that the more meaning a word carries, the rarer it is and the fewer strong collocates it has; the converse – less meaning, more common and more collocates – is also true.

Common words

Common words, other than those from the grammatical closed classes such as pronouns or prepositions, are common precisely because they occur in so many Expressions. Some examples make this clear:

mind
It went right out of my mind.
My mind's gone blank.
I can't get it out of my mind.
Sorry, my mind just wasn't on what I was doing.
I'd go out of my mind if I had to ....
Why don't you .... It'd take your mind off things.

All those examples and many others for *mind* are under a single entry in CIDE.

way
He didn't go out of his way to help me.
There's two ways of looking at this...
I looked the other way.
Get out of the way!
Summer's still a long way off.
He was hurt in more ways than one.

All from Cobuild, and six of the enormous number of examples under *way*.

In the Introduction to the new (1995) edition of the Cobuild dictionary, John Sinclair writes:

> The word or phrase being defined in each paragraph is printed in bold face. . . . The commonest words of a language have many uses, and to explain them in a dictionary results in very long entries. . . . We have tried to print more words in bold face to help you to find the sense you are looking for. For example, the entry for **thing** is long, and many of the meanings of the word are difficult to explain and recognize. Notice how often there are one or more other words in bold face in that entry. – senses 3 and 5 indicate some variable expressions, and then from sense 18 to the end [sense 38] there are a large number of relatively fixed phrases.

It makes little sense to ask learners *Do you know the word ...?* with words such as *mind, way, thing*. Such words hardly have an existence independent of the multi-word phrases and expressions in which they occur. These phrases are mini-idioms, where the meaning of the phrase is not transparent from the component words, so, unless the teacher specifically draws them to learners' attention, they may not be noticed. L1 conversational fluency does not come from the use of a lexicon of difficult words, nor from simply the most common words of the language, but from a repertoire of phrases and expressions made of the most common words. Pedagogically such language has been given scant attention. Courses which aim at oral competence need materials and procedures which develop the lexicon in precisely this way. The pedagogical treatment of common words, including sample exercises and activities, is discussed later.

De-lexicalised words

Many common words carry little meaning in themselves: *thing, point, way, put, have.* Such words may have one or more content-bearing uses: *Don't point! I need something with a sharp point. I had a Volvo at the time. They had three children,* plus several so-called de-lexicalised uses. In these the individual word carries little or no meaning, and the expression in which it occurs has an idiomatic quality: *I don't know the best way to deal with it. I don't think there's much point.*

A major sub-group of de-lexicalised words is the de-lexicalised verbs: *put, take, make, have, keep, call.* Such words usually have one fully lexical use: *have = possess, take = transport, make = manufacture* etc. but in addition they are elements in large numbers of multi-word mini-idioms: *take your time, to have a ball, to make your mind up.* Vocabulary teaching tends to be noun-orientated (unsurprisingly, as the class of nouns is by far the largest word class), while the teaching of verbs has tended to concentrate on their structure, i.e. the tense system. The de-lexicalised words sometimes have one or more discernible meaning-patterns; if so, these can be used in a generative way which more resembles traditional grammar than vocabulary. Two extended examples based on the use of *get* and *have* are discussed in detail in Chapter 8.

COLLOCATIONS OR WORD PARTNERSHIPS

Collocations are those combinations of words which occur naturally with greater than random frequency. Collocations co-occur, but not all words which co-occur are collocations. We need to explore the idea of collocation more precisely.

Collocation is linguistic, not thematic

Collocation is about words which co-occur, not ideas or concepts. An example helps to make this clear. In Britain people drive cars and drink coffee, but in English they do not, or at least not very often. Confused? Consider these examples of dialogues:

So, how did you come this morning?
> *Oh, I brought the car. / I drove.*
> * *Oh, I drove the car.*
Would you like a coffee?
> *No thanks, I've just had one.*
> * *No thanks, I've just drunk one.*

In each case the last answer is very unlikely, if not impossible. This is not to deny the possibility of examples such as *Driving my car always leaves me with a bad back these days,* but we need to be more aware of partnerships such as *bring/take the car, have a coffee.* Such examples are not unusual, while many ELT examples popular for their apparent clarity *(to drink coffee, to ride a horse)* are unlikely in actual use precisely because they are too explicit. Teachers need to focus on collocations which do occur, rather than combinations which 'ought' to exist, or which are easy for learners to understand.

Arbitrariness of collocation

Collocation is, as we have already seen, arbitrary: *high/tall building, tall boy* but not * *high boy. Prices rise and fall;* you can *rise to the occasion* but not **fall to the occasion.* You can *look at* a person or problem; you can *gaze at* a person but not at a problem. This non-generalisability clearly indicates that we meet and store words in the prefabricated chunks upon which the Lexical Approach is based.

Collocations in text

Look at this opening paragraph from a newspaper report:

> *All pupils should carry out compulsory community service as part of a radical approach to promoting moral values in schools, a Government advisory group is expected to recommend. The group suggests that public service, such as assisting the elderly or hospital work, would strengthen children's sense of social responsibility.*

Notice the collocations, both explicit and implicit – *to carry out a service, to promote values, moral values.* We immediately realise that these groups of words, far from being creatively combined, are items we recognise as familiar. This text seems to consist of little except collocations combined with each other. Although this type of text is more collocation-rich than many, chunks of different kinds are characteristic of texts from different genres. The following example is taken from a newspaper business report:

> *Since March, the group has announced the closure of Wellcome's main research site in Beckenham, the proposed sale of Wellcome's London headquarters and the closure of its own head office in the West End. The new headquarters will be at Glaxo's office in Greenford, and in America manufacturing of prescription medicines will be concentrated on Glaxo's North Carolina factory.*

Obvious partnerships are *research site, proposed sale, prescription drugs;* but notice *announce a closure / sale; to concentrate production on* (slot filled with expression of place). Identifying the latter two partnerships immediately suggests useful classroom work – what other words most frequently follow *announce*? Is there a pattern? What else which is similar to *production* collocates with *concentrate?* What sort of expressions can fill the place-slot? Seen in this way, collocations are not just an extension of the concept of 'words'; they provide learners with a powerful organising principle for language.

Partnerships and Relationships

From time to time we all meet people we have never met before; such people sometimes become close friends, sometimes we never see them again. Occasionally we even find ourselves in the company of someone we would prefer not to be with at all. We also have regular acquaintances, friends and partners. Individual words are very similar. Some words are frequently found in the same textual environment. Such co-occurrences may be frequent or rare, strongly or more loosely bound.

The parallel between word partnerships and human relationships provides a powerful and revealing metaphor. Our human relationships differ, and differ in different ways; the same applies to word partnerships. Some people have a small circle of close friendships, but relatively few acquaintances; some gregarious but perhaps fickle folk have a large circle of 'friends', but seem incapable of serious, stable, sustained relationships; some fortunate people have a strong stable family life and a few trusted friends, but also another range of perhaps mutually incompatible friends with each of whom they share a particular interest. Most, but by no means all, people have a wide range of comparatively casual acquaintances. None of these people is odd or peculiar; although their 'fields of relationship' differ widely, all are quite 'normal'. The parallel between words and people is close, and the corresponding range of collocation types surprisingly, and revealingly, similar.

If I commute to work daily, I may meet the same travelling companion twice a day or ten times a week, but our friendship may remain superficial. At the same time I may only meet a particular close friend infrequently, but that friendship is intrinsically closer. What matters is not the frequency of our meetings, but the closeness and quality of the relationship; in a certain set of circumstances it is precisely, perhaps uniquely, to this particular friend that I turn. A computer which recorded all the meetings of my life over a given period could easily give a completely false impression of me and the relationships which are important to me. Basing conclusions on frequency of meeting alone – in linguistic terms, collocation – gives a wholly false picture. Frequency alone does not reveal quality. Raw frequency of collocation reveals the typical patterns of a word. But typicality is not necessarily the same as strength or importance. For language teaching, frequency is undoubtedly of interest, but strength may provide a more powerful organising principle.

Non-reciprocity of collocation

The two words of a two-word partnership may be related to each other in different ways, and typically the relationship is not equally strong in both directions. Again, human relationships differ in similar ways. As the playwright Robert Bolt perceptively but rather disconcertingly puts it: "Loves are never equal". Typically, one word suggests the presence of the other more strongly than the reverse: *non-alcoholic* suggests *drink* more than *drink* suggests *non-alcoholic*; *premature* suggests *baby*, *awake* suggests *wide*, *flatly* suggests *contradict* or *refuse*. Such collocational strength relates closely to the general rule that nouns tend to call the shots.

Intuitively, the noun is usually 'what the sentence is about', the verb tells us 'what happens' to the noun, and the other elements are optional, adding details. We shall see the power of the sequence: noun > verb > adjective > adverbial when we consider translation in Chapter 4. In general, it is the noun which dominates collocations, but this is by no means always the case. Two words may be so strongly bound that they are to all intents and purposes inseparable: *raving lunatic, blithering idiot.* Such items are closer to being polyword compound nouns than collocations.

Many nouns, even out of context, naturally suggest a field of potential verb collocates:

bill: *pay, foot, receive, present, reduce, submit*

Similarly many nouns naturally suggest a field of adjective collocates:

accident: *serious, slight, unfortunate, tragic, fatal, terrible*

And some verbs naturally suggest lists of probable adverbial collocates:

check something: *properly, quickly, regularly, automatically, carefully, closely, meticulously, again and again*

The same applies to adjectives:

acceptable: *perfectly, widely, mutually, readily*

Such lists are in no way definitive. For a whole host of legitimate reasons – new situations, wit, humour, the advertiser's urge to grab attention – unlikely, even apparently impossible (i.e. internally contradictory) co-occurrences are common in used language. Nonetheless, the lists above give words which are statistically much more likely to occur together than random choice suggests. That is precisely the definition of collocates.

Information-content and collocation

Most of the most meaning-bearing words of the language are comparatively rare nouns. Their very rarity means they often carry so much meaning that adding an adjective to them is redundant, or at least the range of possible adjectives with which they co-occur is very small. It is intuitively obvious that more general nouns like *character, job, issue, plan* tend to be qualified by adjectives and the evidence of data based on used language supports this. It is these words which teachers may need to explore with a concordance program as we discuss elsewhere. (See page 112).

TASK

How many different words come readily to mind to complete these gaps? (You need a single word for each gap.)

1. (S)he's got rather a .... accent.
2. I don't really want to .... a decision until I have more information.
3. I know you haven't had time to think about it yet, but what's your .... reaction?
4. I'm .... convinced that things will work out for the best.

---

1. Data based on used language suggest that the adjectives which collocate most strongly with *accent* are *strong, slight, French / German / northern.* Above, only *strong* seems highly likely, and was probably the choice of most readers. Other words are possible, and perfectly correct: *cute, pretentious, tricky*; but not *glazed, tough,* or *spacious.* Examples like *weak, delicate* are doubtful; while not sounding 'wrong', they have a feeling of unnaturalness. Collocation is about degrees of likelihood. We recognise a spectrum between pairs of words which we expect to find together and words which we are surprised to find together. Collocation is not determined by logic or frequency, but is arbitrary, decided only by linguistic convention.

2. In the second example above, *make a decision* is almost the only choice. English has many such lexical items consisting of a de-lexicalised verb and a noun. This suggests learners should learn such nouns from first meeting them as part of the collocation. It is easy to dis-assemble a collocation and use a component word in other contexts. If you learn the word in isolation, you can only guess its potential partner-words. Word partnerships where the verb is de-lexicalised are particularly likely to produce translation mistakes. This is because the chunk is *make a decision* and it is chunk-for-chunk not word-for-word translation which is successful. (See Chapter 4).

3. Example three strongly suggests *initial reaction*, though *first* and a few other words are possible. The presence in a text of a number of collocations where neither word is very common or very rare, but where the collocation is fairly strong, makes such a text easier to understand, particularly when listening. Hearing only one of the words in such strong cases suggests the presence of the other. Hearing only imperfectly, the listener can often reconstruct the missing element. This clearly demonstrates the importance of these medium-strength collocations.

4. The last example is similar; *absolutely convinced* is highly likely, but also *firmly, almost,* but not **solidly* or **approximately* while *nearly convinced* leaves us in some doubt. This shows us that *(. . .) convinced* has a small group of words which can fill the slot. It is efficient to teach those words as a group when learners first meet *convinced.* Words of similar meaning which are not acceptable collocates should also be mentioned as impossible. Examination

of learners' written texts clearly shows that mis-collocation is a common source of errors. This means taking time to explore the collocations of a word rather than indiscriminately listing new words. It is just such small changes which are the discrete but effective implementation of the Lexical Approach.

Strong and frequent collocation

We recognise strong collocations as partnerships which are so tightly linked they behave almost as single Words. Strong collocations may be frequent or comparatively rare; it is far from true that those words which co-occur most frequently are the strongest collocations. Weak collocations *(a nice day, a good chance)* occur between two common words, each of which may co-occur with many other words. Collocations may be any combination of strong and frequent, strong and infrequent, weak and frequent, or weak and infrequent, though this last category is of little interest.

If strong collocation is not a matter of frequency, what makes us so sure that a particular, relatively infrequent partnership is almost a single, fixed item?

TASK

Write a short definition of the word *golden*.
Now list six nouns which you think very commonly occur with *golden*.

Almost certainly your definition would be something like *made of,* or *looking like gold.* Equally certainly your collocations probably include *opportunity, wedding, age, mean, boy/girl, handshake*; the strong collocates are not literal uses and none is particularly frequent. What is important is that they occur more often than is statistically likely – a higher than expected proportion of all uses of *golden* involve the words we think of as strong collocates.

Frequency alone is only a poor guide to the strength, and corresponding pedagogic usefulness. Teachers need to be aware of both strength and frequency when directing learners' attention to collocations.

The idea of collocation is a very powerful one in helping learners maximise the value of the language to which they are exposed, but they need help in identifying the powerful and useful partnerships in a text. Some are much more useful to the language learner than others. A major problem is that the fact that two words are next to each other in text does not ensure that they are a collocation, and conversely many collocations do not occur in text as immediately adjacent words.

In *He's got an accent just like mine* the words *accent* and *like* co-occur but this is a matter of almost pure coincidence. Similar sentences are *He's got a car / job just like mine;* the key pattern is about comparing; accents can be compared – true but of no real pedagogical interest. The sentence frame *(S)he's got a .... just like mine* may be of pedagogic interest, but the co-occurrence of *accent* and *like* is simply a distraction. The more we explore, the more we see that co-location and collocation are very different, hence the importance of the teacher actively directing learners' attention to the language in the texts they meet which is most useful to them.

Collocation and grammar

The collocations *drug addict* and *business letter* are both made using two words usually thought of as nouns, but instinctively one feels some difference between the two pairs. While it is difficult to think of *drug* as an 'adjective' describing a kind of addict, there is a much greater tendency to feel that *business* is 'a noun being used adjectivally' to describe the letter. Is there a sound linguistic basis for the feeling, or is it just another unreliable, and potentially misleading, intuition?

There is a sound linguistic reason. Try to find other words which will fill the slot occupied by *drug* in *drug addict;* probably you have chosen *coffee, cocaine, heroin, chocolate*; now try to find words to fill the slot occupied by *business*. This time you have a wider choice and you have probably got at least some of these: *personal, urgent, registered, love, (in)formal*. Notice in the first case **all** the collocates are normally used as nouns, while in the second case only one – *love* – is used as a noun. So you were influenced not only by the particular words in a collocation, but also, subconsciously perhaps, by the **class** of words which typically fill any variable slot.

A strong collocation like *drug addict* in which there is very little potential variation is best treated in the same way as words like *umbrella* or *lawyer.* Although variations such as *alcohol addiction* are possible, they are too unusual or rare to justify drawing attention to any potential pattern.

TASK

The collocations that a particular word makes with other words may be quite different from those of a closely related word.

1. Find word partnerships for *economy* and *economist*. Are the two collocational fields similar or different?

2. Can you think of three words which can have *little* in front of them, where the meaning does not remain the same if *little* is replaced by *small*?

3. A *mess* can be an untidy physical state: *This room's in a terrible mess.*
   A mess can be a difficult situation: *What can we do? We're in a real mess.*
Find as many verbs as you can which form strong collocations with *mess:*
get into a mess, clear up the mess.
Divide them into three groups:
• *mess* meaning an untidy state
• *mess* meaning a difficult situation
• those which are used for both

Collocation is an arbitrary linguistic phenomenon. This means we cannot assume that a pattern is generalisable or that words which are similar in one way will behave similarly in other ways. Implementing the Lexical Approach means learning to look at how words really behave in the environments in which they have been used. Chapter 7 suggests ways of doing this in class.

Pedagogic value of collocation

Two simple observations make clear the value of noticing, recording and learning words together with partner-words. Firstly, words are not normally used alone and it makes sense to learn them in a strong, frequent, or otherwise typical pattern of actual use. Secondly, it is more efficient to learn the whole and break it into parts, than to learn the parts and have to learn the whole as an extra arbitrary item. Joanna Channell asked learners to mark collocations in a grid such as the following:

	a bill	somebody's papers	a school	the headlines	what someone said	the meaning of a word	a patient	the records	
check									
examine									
inspect									
scrutinize									
scan									

One feature of her research results is of particular interest: learners averaged only three wrong collocations in such an exercise, but they missed an average of 14 possible partnerships. Consciously heightening learners' awareness of collocation, and encouraging them to explore is, therefore, useful in encouraging learners to make better use of language they already partly 'know'.

Benson and Benson report that learners who had been introduced to using *The BBI Collocation Dictionary* had considerably increased scores on collocation tests. This supports Channell's research. Raising learners' awareness of collocation may be one very efficient way of increasing their communicative power – that is, the ability to say more of what they want to say with the limited language resources at their disposal.

EXPRESSIONS

Although Fixed and Semi-fixed Expressions can be distinguished, much of what follows applies to both. Nattinger and DeCarrico point out that: "while some lexical phrases such as *by the way* or *on the other hand* are set phrases allowing no variability, the majority are more like skeletal frames that have slots for various fillers". Sinclair has pointed out that the vast majority of fully Fixed Expressions are phatic social phrases – what EFL has sometimes called 'politeness phrases'. The main emphasis, then, is on Semi-fixed Expressions, which includes frames such as *That's not as ... as you think*, sentence heads such as *What really surprised me was ...*, and the more extended frames which are used to structure discourse, such as a company report or academic paper.

The importance of Semi-fixed Expressions cannot be overestimated; some critics have suggested that the Lexical Approach has a strongly behaviourist streak, and that lexis is non-generative. The contrary is the case. Although the lexicon is larger than we suspected, and the learning load in some ways consequently greater, Semi-fixed Expressions reveal previously unsuspected patterns which help organise what McCarthy once called 'the chaos of the lexicon'.

Seven – the magic number

Several linguists who have studied and classified Expressions have come to the conclusion that they consist of between two and seven words and, most interestingly, they do not normally exceed seven words. Here are some examples:

I'll see you soon.
It takes two to tango.
It wasn't my fault.
If you take my advice, you'll have nothing to do with it.

As we saw in Chapter 1, the last looks like an exception until we recognise it as two lexical items juxtaposed: *if you take my advice* and *you'll have nothing to do with it*. Research on short term memory bears out this limit, which remains speculative, on the length of individual lexical items.

Frames, slots and fillers

Like patterned collocations, many Expressions have one or more slots which can be filled in only a limited number of ways. The constraints on how the slots may be filled may be real-world or strictly linguistic. In *I've got a stone in my shoe,* another nominal can replace *a stone: a pebble / something / some sand*; linguistically, the slot can be filled by *a banana*, but real-world knowledge tells us it is extremely unlikely that the sentence *I've got a banana in my shoe* ever actually occurs. This rather bizarre example reminds us that the Lexical Approach concentrates on actually-occurring or probable language and not – as has been the tendency – on all the possible sentences of English most of which have not occurred, and, we suspect, never will occur. The possibility of novelty, humour and originality are, of course, not denied; the generative power of what is traditionally thought of as grammar is recognised, but I suggest it is pedagogically more valuable to direct learners' attention to highly probable, and often more immediately useful, language.

The slot in *I've got a (plane) to catch* permits the obvious alternative *train,* but not *taxi* or *post*, although *I've got to catch the post* is sanctioned. Here we see linguistic rather than real-world constraints on the slot-fillers. It is another example of the arbitrary way in which lexis is, or is not, socially sanctioned.

In general, Semi-fixed Expressions consist of a pragmatic (or 'functional') frame, which is completed by a referential slot-filler. This applies to much more than simple conversational expressions such as *Could you pass (my book) please*. Here are the first two sentences of a newspaper report:

> A meteorite that fell to earth after being ejected from Mars contains evidence of fossilised primitive creatures, providing the first traces of extra-terrestrial life. The question of life on Mars has fascinated scientists, philosophers and writers for millennia.

Despite the apparently original writing, there are two frames: *X contains evidence of Y.; The question of* (topic) *has fascinated* (group of people) *for* (long time period).

The first – *X contains evidence of Y* – is buried by two complex noun phrases, most notably the grammatically complex subject. Pedagogically it might be best to teach collocations of *evidence: gather/collect/present evidence for..., show/contain/reveal evidence of ....* . The second example, however, has wide applicability: *The question of (the real reasons behind the German invasion*

of Poland) has fascinated historians for decades.
The question of (the existence or otherwise of the ether) fascinated physicists for years until the Michelson-Morley experiment settled the matter.

The slots can be filled in different ways, and it may even be possible to alter or distort the frame itself slightly; finally, of course, a writer may break the mould completely and produce novel language; in that case grammar rather than lexis creates the new combination, though even then parts of it are likely to be prefabricated, as with *primitive creatures, extra-terrestrial life* in the above example.

Suppression

The importance of such frames was recognised years ago with books teaching business correspondence, but the wider applicability to other text-types and parts at least of many different kinds of text, was underestimated. The key idea is that text can be crudely separated into two quite different parts: a frame which structures the discourse, and slots filled with content-bearing language. This has great potential for choosing and using language materials for learners who need to write essays, read or write academic materials or contribute to such spoken 'events' as seminars or business meetings. Consider this text:

> In this paper we examine two intonation rules which are commonly found in standard textbooks, namely those for intonation in lists and intonation in questions. We begin by arguing that the standard rules are inadequate descriptions of what actually occurs in recorded natural data. We then go on to offer an alternative analysis, using a discourse model based on that originally proposed by Brazil (1984,1995). In conclusion we suggest the implications of the alternative description for materials writers and modifications to classroom procedures.

While the content may be of interest to an applied linguist, the text seems to have little relevance to a chemist, but this is not so. The content is subject-specific, but the frame is function- and genre-specific; it is the standard frame for providing the introductory summary of an academic paper. This is readily apparent if we separate it into two parts, which is very easy to do, and if necessary re-do, with a word processor:

> In this paper we examine ...... which are commonly found in standard ....., namely those for .... and .... We begin by arguing that the standard rules are inadequate descriptions of what actually occurs in .... We then go on to offer an alternative analysis, using a .... model based on that originally proposed by .... (year). In conclusion we suggest the implications of the alternative description for ...., and modifications to ....

.... two intonation rules .... textbooks .... intonation in lists .... intonation in questions .... natural recorded data .... discourse .... Brazil ...... materials writers .... classroom procedures.

One can quibble over exactly which words are frame and which are content (which do *standard rules* and *procedure* belong to?), but by simply deleting the main content words we are left with a powerful extended frame which is as much a standard element of English as *Could you pass ... please*, and, for some learners, at least as important. The principle of suppression – delete the content-bearing words and examine what is left with care – is a powerful lexical tool for teachers working in ESP and EAP. It reminds us that texts differ considerably in the type of lexis they contain. Selecting texts, and matching text-types to learners' needs is an important facet of implementing the Lexical Approach, and needs to be taken up in teacher preparation.

Expressions and grammar

Many natural sentences of the spoken language exhibit a strange linguistic phenomenon. Consider these examples:

1. *I don't think so, but I hope so.*
2a. *It's OK. Don't bother to ring me.*
2b. *I won't bother to ring.*
3. *I'm sorry. It'll take quite a long time.*
4. *I'm sorry I'm late.*

What is remarkable is that supposedly elementary 'transformations' on these produce language which is bizarre, unacceptable or odd:

1. **I think so, but I don't hope so.*
2a. **It's not OK, so please bother to ring me.*
2b. **I'll bother to ring.*
3. *Don't worry. It won't take long.* but not
      *It won't take (quite) a long time.
4. **You're sorry you're late.*

Language which is apparently grammatically possible is not, in practice, lexically sanctioned. Again we are reminded of the arbitrariness of all lexical items. These bizarre sentences are something of an embarrassment to those who maintain the importance of the generative power of grammar, for, while grammar can generate many original and useful utterances, it can also **over-**generalise and appear to sanction language which is not accepted by the speech community.

A modified idea of idiom

To most people an idiom is a picturesque expression which is marginal to natural language use; nothing could be further from the truth. Idioms are relatively-fixed Expressions where the meaning of the whole is not transparent from the meanings of the constituent words. Curiously, this means many traditional idioms are less problematic for learners, at least receptively, than we might imagine, while many comparatively everyday expressions are more difficult than has usually been recognised. A few examples make this clearer.

He was running around like a headless chicken is a graphic image and thus comparatively easy to understand, though most learners will sound strange if they incorporate it into their active vocabulary. What makes it 'an idiom' is that it is non-literal and rigidly fixed – it is not a reference to chickens and a headless duck or goose does not qualify as 'correct' English. It is, however, comparatively transparent; if you understand the meanings of the individual words, the expression as a whole, used in context, should cause few problems, despite its non-literal quality.

Expressions which are more common, more central to the spoken language, and much more useful for learners, are those made of common words where the meaning of one or more of the key words is in some sense metaphorical rather than literal:

1. *I see what you mean.*
2. *I'll get back to you as soon as I can.*
3. *It took my breath away.*
4. *Take your time, there's no hurry.*

Few of the individual words are difficult, and the meaning of each lexical item is itself straightforward – if you know it. But why are these not acceptable synonyms?

5. **I grasp what you mean.*
6. **I'll return very soon.*
7. **It winded me.*
8. **Use the moment, there's no hurry.*

The answer is that lexical items are arbitrarily sanctioned independent units and, at least in the British native speaking community, 1 – 4 are sanctioned but 5 – 8 are not. Expressions 1 – 4 are just as much idioms as the picturesque *It's raining cats and dogs* which we all know but which we so rarely use or hear. Many common and useful expressions, which will not sound inappropriate in the mouths of intermediate learners (see Chapter 9), must play a more central role in language courses, at least those which claim to target spoken English.

Semi-fixed idioms

It is usual to think of idioms, even in the extended meaning of that term as (almost) Fixed: *(S)he threw in the towel, I'll get it, There's no (not much) point.* This view needs to be somewhat modified if we consider certain common metaphorical phrases which 'sum up' many different sets of circumstances:

The number of cases which are coming to court are thought by police to be only the tip of the iceberg.
If we let them get away with this, it could turn out to be the thin end of a very expensive wedge.

The idioms here are *It's the tip of the iceberg* and *It's the thin end of the wedge,* but these expressions, rather than appearing in the simple fixed form, are frequently used as frames for novel expressions. The novelty, however, is always constrained by the underlying expression, which may occur only rarely in its supposedly fixed form.

Presenting Expressions

Fixed Expressions should be taught without internal analysis. Learners should, however, be introduced to the idea that such expressions exist in their own language. On occasions they should be asked to find equivalents in their own language for the Expressions they meet in English. This suggests a revised role for the learners' own language (L1), which is discussed more fully in Chapter 4.

Teaching materials should contain dialogues containing Fixed Expressions, Exercises and Activities which practise them but also straightforward lists. In these, Expressions may be glossed in dictionary-like fashion with the suggestion that learners should look for equivalents in their own language. A major departure from traditional methodology is the explicit suggestion that the teacher should not dictate what is then done with the list. *That's fine, but what do you do with these expressions? How do you ensure that they learn them?* teachers ask. The simple answer is that you can't. Writers and teachers should ensure the accuracy of carefully chosen expressions, grouped in ways likely to aid retention; writers can ensure suitably sized, well-chosen and well-arranged lists; teachers can manage the time devoted to the lists, both in class and by suggestions of out-of-class activity; they can arrange class activities to generate and maintain interest while meaning is explored, often through the search for L1 equivalents and the importance of contextual restraints – then it's up to individual learners, who may or may not wish to learn particular expressions, and may or may not succeed in retaining them. Accepting learner autonomy also means accepting that teachers cannot guarantee what is learned. The teacher must be content and fulfilled by the role of learning-manager.

LEXICAL AWARENESS HELPS

Many teachers have commented on the immediate applicability of

Expressions to their ESL and EFL classes. Valerie Whiteson, contributing to the TESL-L internet group, comments:

> I'm very impressed by many things about the lexical approach. We have included chunks in most of the lessons in our new book . . . Students are really grateful. They have no idea that these chunks actually go together and are not just ordinary English sentences.

This is an important insight – not all sentences in the language have the same status; some are one-offs, some are frames, some are fully fixed. This is far from obvious, so learners need help if they are to extract maximum benefit from the language they meet, both in and out of class.

In similar vein, Alistair Banton writes:

> I have long held the view that Functions are essentially lexical. In fact, this is one of the things I liked about the Cobuild English course. It dealt with these things very economically, in little boxes with appropriate titles like Inviting, Accepting, Refusing. This made a welcome change from (attempts) to stretch them into whole units.

As an example of Cobuild's 'little boxes', this one presents reactions with *That's:*

That's	great. dreadful. exciting.
That sounds **That must be** **That must have been**	terrifying. interesting. marvellous. awful. wonderful. good fun.

Note that *That's ..., That must be ..., That must have been* ... are presented together without grammatical analysis. The organisation is lexical, not structural.

George Woolard describes a new awareness which immediately influenced his teaching in an important, but easy-to-introduce way:

> Since reading *The Lexical Approach* I almost automatically started incorporating Semi-fixed Expressions, particularly sentence heads, into my teaching. I've been acutely aware of institutionalised expressions and these are finding their way into

my lessons. I am now much more aware of how much of this natural language use is missing from lower level courses. These phrases are now weaving their way into my roughly-tuned input. It's amazing what a little awareness can do!

He proposes supplementing the standard coursebook with chunks:

> Many of the exercises in TEFL coursebooks involve the production of sentences, the content of which is 'bare fact'. In natural discourse speakers often signal or focus what they are going to say with an introductory chunk. These have often been considered structurally complex, and so they are omitted from many coursebooks. If, however, they are seen as chunks and presented unanalysed, they pose little difficulty, even for learners at lower levels.**

Teachers can supplement the coursebook by extending existing practices with natural lexical alternatives which exist for many traditional EFL structures:

Expressing likes and dislikes:
I like John's sense of humour.
The thing I like about John is his sense of humour.

Giving reasons and explanations:
I'd like to be a teacher because I like working with children.
The main reason I'd like to be a teacher is I like working with children.

In place of the traditional functional exponents for giving advice, learners can be given the sentence head *The best thing to do is ...* and encouraged to use:
The best thing to do is make an appointment to see the doctor.
The best thing to do is go to bed.

This can be extended to: *The worst/only/easiest/most important/thing to do.* In this way the lexical pattern becomes generative.

One of the bonuses of this approach is that it is efficient and economica,l as meaning, lexical phrase, and intonation are always dealt with together.

George's observations, based on classroom experience, are taken up again later, when we discuss phonological chunking in Chapters 5 and 8, and the importance of discourse-structuring language in Chapter 9. Expressions frequently reveal previously unsuspected patterns in the lexicon. In addition, they bring together elements of grammar, vocabulary and pronunciation which have previously been treated separately, and thus in less efficient and less accessible ways.

** This exactly mirrors what happens with *That must have been terrifying* in the list above.

SO WHAT EXACTLY IS LEXIS, THEN?

My colleague, Mark Powell, discussing the nature of lexis, proposed the following summary: *Grammar tends to become lexis as the event becomes more probable.* More detailed examination makes this clearer – the probability may be based on simple frequency, or it may be that when a particular word is used, even if infrequently in absolute terms, it tends to co-occur with another word with much greater than random frequency – hence strong collocation; or when one situation arises another typically co-occurs – hence two-clause items such as *I would if I could,* which give rise to the innovative double-gapping exercises discussed in Chapter 6. Broadly, we may say that grammar helps us to use novel language – (relatively) new combinations of lexical items – to talk about (relatively) unusual situations, while lexis helps us handle highly probable events fluently and effortlessly by providing us with prefabricated ways of dealing with them. There is nothing new in that except that lexical language is seen to cover a much greater area of the totality of language, particularly speech, than has usually been acknowledged.

LEXIS IS NOT ENOUGH

We have just seen there is a strong tendency for lexis to be associated with probable things or events. But life also includes new ideas, unlikely situations, humour and other experiences which are not things we individually or as a community have done or said many times before. Language is not only the history of its previous use; as traditional studies of grammar have always emphasised, language has generative, creative potential. New things can be said, ideas which have never been expressed before can be formulated. The Lexical Approach suggests the content and role of grammar in language courses needs to be radically revised but the Approach in no way denies the value of grammar, nor its unique role in language. While the Lexical Approach emphasises probable language, based on observation of 'used' language, it recognises clearly that lexis is not enough and that courses which totally discard grammar are doing learners a serious disservice.

Highly unusual language may occur because the writer has a humorous or literary intent, but often highly unusual language occurs precisely because of the rarity of the event itself; unsurprisingly, novel or unusual situations give rise to novel and unusual language. Here are a few examples of surprising language, which was appropriate to the unusual event reported or the unusual circumstances in which it was used. They are all examples of used language which I came across serendipitously while writing this book:

> In the future, one can change the future past.
> (Physicist, speaking on a TV documentary)

A transsexual, whose marriage was declared null and void after
17 years when his wife found out he was a woman, had his claim
for financial support rejected by the Court of Appeal yesterday.
(Newspaper report)

The ideal observer sees a streaming stillness in which
everything is unchangingly transient.
(Don Cupitt, *The Last Philosophy*)

. . . the town has decided that eternity will not last forever.
(Newspaper report)

Self-evidently language of this kind, none of it particularly remarkable,
cannot be produced without knowledge of a grammatical system; no amount
of prefabricated lexis would be enough.

EVOLVING UNDERSTANDING

This book treats lexical items as belonging to four categories, but there is
nothing definitive about these categories, which are no more than a
convenient tool. Sinclair has remarked that we are only just beginning to
understand lexis, and perhaps all we have understood so far is that the 'word'
is no more the basic unit of language than the 'letter'.

Among those who have written extensively about lexis slightly different
emphases can be discerned:

Willis is perhaps unique in keeping the word as basic. He sees enormous
generative power in the most common words of the language. He tends to
group individual words according to form (all uses of *light*) or discoursal
function (all reporting verbs). The results highlight certain areas which have
been unjustly neglected, but can cause confusion, and do not address the
multi-word nature of many chunks.

Nattinger and DeCarrico place more emphasis on short items which they
term 'lexical phrases'. In this book these are referred to as polywords. I
suspect these items remain the Cinderella among lexical items, and deserve
more attention in language classes than they currently receive.

Nattinger and DeCarrico, together with Sinclair, recognise the relatively low
proportion of truly fixed expressions, and emphasise the semi-fixed, frame-
like quality of many items. This is an important insight, as it rescues lexis
from a behaviourist methodology. Three insights can perhaps be identified as
uniting writers on lexis, but in each case we see only general trends within
the theoretical framework:

• The units of language – chunks – are both larger and more numerous than we thought.

• There is an important category of semi-fixed items, frames with slots, which fits somewhere between traditional fixed words and generative grammar. This category may be central to understanding how language is acquired and stored in the mental lexicon.

• From a pedagogical perspective, these new insights into the nature of language highlight the inadequacies and even, at times, inappropriateness and inaccuracy of parts of the traditional syllabus.

Both theoretical work and classroom implementation continue to develop. Nothing in this book is intended to be definitive. Its aim is to suggest where recent developments have already taken us and point forward to further developments.

SUMMARY

This chapter has provided a closer look at Collocations and Expressions, the two most important types of lexical item in addition to the familiar Words. Our concern has been largely descriptive, and it is not self-evident that the description can or should be taken into the classroom. Two things are, however, clear: if the idea of lexical chunks is to be of real help to learners, we need to identify a powerful strategy which will inform the teacher's mindset and pervade **all** the activities of the lexical classroom and, as the linguistic features we have discussed occur in other languages, we need to re-consider the role the learners' mother-tongue (L1) plays. The role of lexis in the classroom, and the implications that has for the revised role for L1 are the subjects of the next two chapters.

Chapter 3

Lexis in the Classroom

We have seen that language consists of prefabricated chunks of different kinds, but describing a language and teaching it are two very different things, and we must ask whether lexis can usefully be taken into language classes, and if so what changes are needed to materials, methods and, most importantly, the teacher's mindset.

The most efficient language learning must be based on the real nature of both language and learning. This simple observation means we do need to reflect the lexical nature of language in the classroom. As well as knowledge of enough Words, a 'good vocabulary' means an adequate phrasal lexicon as well. Efficient language learning means learners turning a high proportion of the input to which they are exposed into intake; for that they need to observe that input and notice the units, the lexical items, from which it is constructed. In this chapter we will see the importance of skills, learner training, repetition and revisiting, and most importantly, the central role played by 'noticing', sometimes called consciousness-raising, and the learner's ability to chunk successfully any text which they meet. These strategies will mean learners derive greater benefit from the language they meet both in and out of class. Although the individual changes in classroom procedure are small, they offer significant benefits.

SKILLS AS WELL AS LANGUAGE

There is a strong case to be made that although languages can be learned, they cannot be taught, at least not in ways in which there is a one-to-one relationship between what is taught and what is learned. Skehan observes: *We can be sure that learners will make use of the language they experience; we cannot be sure how they will make use of it.* Some language teachers see this as deeply threatening but, far from making them redundant, it broadens and deepens their role. Instead of deriving their status from their knowledge of the language, they derive status from their ability genuinely to assist learning. Once this is accepted, the supposed advantage of the native speaker teacher (NST) against the non-native (non-NST) is more easily seen as the myth it always was. Knowledge of the language is an important element of a language teacher's necessary knowledge, but it is a smaller part than has often been assumed; knowledge of teaching, learning, and interpersonal skills are at least as important. Here are some of the questions which teachers need to consider before going near the classroom:

TASK

1. Do you think your learners will learn most of their vocabulary (in the extended sense) in class or outside?
2. How will you use valuable class time to make learning vocabulary less daunting, more enjoyable and more efficient?
3. Will you concentrate on the quality or quantity of learners' lexicons?
4. What proportions of class time will you spend on vocabulary and grammar respectively?
5. How will you decide which lexical items deserve special attention in class?
6. How will you encourage learners to use their dictionaries to help build their lexicon? What activities will you use to develop their dictionary skills?
7. How will you decide what items are worth recording in learners' notebooks?
8. Will you follow up what has been recorded in (a) later lesson(s)? How?

SELECTING

A major decision facing teachers on a daily basis is how best to use the limited time available in class. Although many teachers rely heavily on coursebooks to provide a basic framework, there are always questions of what to concentrate on, omit, or expand. The Lexical Approach suggests more time devoted to multi-word items, and, as we shall see, to awareness-raising receptive activities and efficient recording of new language; this does not mean ignoring attention to form, traditional grammar or undervaluing novel and creative use of language. We need to keep the baby and the bathwater constantly in mind.

Teachers have to select both in and out. It is not sufficient for something to be unknown and useful; the ideal is to select what is most useful. Teachers must not abdicate this responsibility; Swan observed in his 1996 IATEFL plenary:

> It is of course true that only the learner really knows exactly what he or she wants. It is, however, equally true that only the teacher knows what there is to be learnt. In other branches of teaching we are not usually so diffident about imposing direction and constraints on the learners. I would not, for instance, encourage my seventeen-year-old son to adopt a discovery approach to learning to drive my car ... . Strangely, the 'instruction versus natural acquisition' debate has concentrated

almost exclusively on the learning of grammar, and on the question of how grammar is learnt. In fact, it seems to me, that this question is almost irrelevant to a comparison between instructed learning and natural acquisition. The crucial difference between the two, surely, has to do with vocabulary, and far more with what is learnt than with how it is learnt.

The choice of basic materials is sometimes not the teacher's, but every teacher introduces supplementary materials and directs learners' attention to some parts or feature of the materials rather than others. Such decisions need to be based on lexical, as well as grammatical, principles.

A word of caution is necessary in choosing material to develop the learners' lexicon even for a group of learners with a specific ESP or EAP objective. Reading student texts on economics or chemistry does not require the same language as that used by someone working as an economist or chemist; similarly, my colleague Mark Powell has pointed out the language needed to describe your job in English in a needs analysis is very different from the language required to do that same job in English. If teachers are to choose maximally useful input they must think of the language necessary to perform rather than to describe the tasks.

EXPANDING THE LEARNERS' LEXICON

The single most formidable task facing the learner is mastering a sufficiently large lexicon. This is particularly so with English, with its combination of two separate source lexicons, Germanic and Romance. The Lexical Approach suggests the task is even greater than we have recognised in the past. Estimates vary, but moderately competent users of English must have a good knowledge of the 2000 most common words *(sic);* the next thousand are met comparatively infrequently, but are essential for intermediate level comprehension. Any even moderately specialised use requires another substantial vocabulary. Nation provides a list of words from West's *General Service List* which research shows are frequently unknown for many learners. He provides another list of several hundred words which research shows are essential for university students of any discipline who study in English but which are frequently unknown from their earlier studies.

This situation produces two mutually contradictory responses – intensive vocabulary programmes, and a view that, if language classes are generally well-organised, vocabulary will 'take care of itself'. Examination of word counts, classroom materials and a little elementary statistics prompted Swan, in that same IATEFL plenary, to observe:

> Vocabulary, then, will **not** take care of itself. If students with limited time available for study are to learn high-priority lexis, this needs to be deliberately selected and incorporated into

learning materials or activities. If this is not done, students will not be exposed – even once – to numerous important vocabulary items, and they will finish their courses with serious gaps in their knowledge.

Although Swan's primary concern was with the construction of materials to ensure that they covered an adequate lexical syllabus, the challenge of ensuring learners develop an adequate and appropriate lexicon constantly faces teachers.

One major new emphasis in the Lexical Approach is the potential as a learning resource of a good L1/L1 dictionary. There have been great developments in lexicography over the last few years, and modern dictionaries have many new features which can form an important resource for awareness-raising activities. Teachers could usefully devote additional class time to dictionary-based activities, where the emphasis is on exploring lexical items of different kinds, perhaps at the expense of traditional vocabulary or grammar practices. Some are discussed in Chapter 7.

LEARNING STRATEGIES

Teaching has tended to take a one-brick-at-a-time approach to input, emphasising the need to master one bit before proceeding to the next. This is misguided, as all the evidence suggests that at any point the learner's lexicon contains items which are fully available for recognition and production, items which are understood in context but are not fully acquired, and others which are known, but actually misunderstood in some way. The mental lexicon, as with intergrammar, is a muddle of items 'known' to different degrees; both the lexicon and the intergrammar develop not linearly, but holistically. We cannot say precisely what the student has learned at any particular moment.

Class time is best used to maximise the likelihood of learners turning input into intake. This means class time is better spent helping learners develop strategies for dealing with unknown items they meet when listening or reading, particularly the ability to guess on the basis of context, situation or lexical clues, rather than laborious practice aimed at consolidating individual items. Similarly with the learners' active lexicon: class time is better spent raising awareness and encouraging effective recording of patterns, rather than too much concentration on individual items. This is particularly so as some efficient learning strategies are counter-intuitive and so unlikely to be used by learners unless encouraged by the teacher. Among such initially unappealing but genuinely helpful strategies which teachers need to ensure learners understand and use are:

• Don't worry if you don't understand everything when listening or reading; a lot of listening and reading, partially understood, will help you much more than a small quantity where you have understood every word.

• Don't worry about confusion and mistakes; they are a positive sign that you **partly** understand, not a negative one that you didn't understand everything.

• You make some 'grammar mistakes' because you don't know enough vocabulary; if you want to avoid grammar mistakes, building your vocabulary will help you more than lots of grammar practice.

• Try to learn whole expressions containing useful words, rather than just the words, even though that seems much more difficult.

• When you record a new lexical pattern in your notebook, consciously try to think of other examples similar to those of the pattern. It is not wasting time to explore certain words slowly and carefully.

Schmitt and Schmitt *(ELT Journal April 1995)* have suggested that words which are very familiar should not be taught at the same time for fear of causing confusion in the learner's lexicon. They give examples such as the pairs *left/right, effect/affect*. The difficulty they fear arises from teaching such words de-contextualised; if learners met and recorded full examples such as *In France we drive on the right; The changes won't really affect me* there is little possibility of confusion. De-contextualised vocabulary learning is a legitimate strategy, but it is best restricted to words with high information content, particularly less common nouns. In general, the more de-lexicalised a word is, and the wider its collocational range, the more important it is to meet, acquire and record it in a Collocation or Expression.

It is this kind of non-intuitive insight which the teacher should regularly provide. Although this emphasis on skills re-defines the teacher's role, it in no way diminishes it.

Teachers need a well-developed awareness of certain very specific language items which they can pass on in manageable pieces to learners, more through frequent short comments and regular activities often lasting only a minute or two, than through formal teaching. The objective is not to expand learners' knowledge about English, but through the comments help expand their knowledge of English, principally by helping learners expand their (particularly phrasal) lexicons.

Key linguistic and pedagogical targets in these on-going comments are:

• different kinds of collocation, both fixed and free
• fully fixed expressions
• sentences with a special status
• the patterns in text of de-lexicalised verbs
• other important de-lexicalised words
• other common words
• actively looking to widen collocational patterns and expression slot-fillers

RECORDING AND REVISITING

Learners need to be directed away from listing every 'new word', and from listing crude *L1 word = L2 word* translations. The concept of a Lexical Notebook (see Chapter 5) needs to replace the traditional 'vocabulary book'. This is another aspect of the shift from simply teaching the language to helping learners to develop their learning skills.

Research evidence shows new items need to be recycled if they are to be fully acquired. This may occur naturally through reading and listening but most teachers will also wish to be more pro-active in managing learning. It may simply be enough for the teacher to ask after a few days *What was the word you recorded for ... ?* or *Can you use three expressions you put in your notebook last week?* What is important is to encourage learners to look back at the language they have recorded and do something – perhaps anything – with it. Schmitt and Schmitt suggest the teacher enlarges a completed page of a learner's notebook onto an OHP transparency and asks the rest of the class to question the owner of the page about its contents. They also suggest some learners may wish to supplement their notebooks by recording some of the items, particularly Expressions, on a cassette tape, encouraging out-of-class revisiting of the new language.

PRACTISING IN THE LEXICAL APPROACH

I shall distinguish Activities – usually classroom-based, group-orientated and often with both linguistic and non-linguistic outcomes – and Exercises, usually individual, reflective and with a purely linguistic focus. Many examples are given in Chapters 6 and 7, but we look first at some general principles and identify a central strategy.

Learner participation

The Lexical Approach values both the quantity and quality of input. A corollary of it is that it is less concerned than some communicative methods with output. This is an important methodological shift, with which teachers need to feel comfortable. It certainly does not mean a return to chalk-and-talk teacher-dominated classrooms, but some sacred cows are slaughtered on the way. *Increase student talking time* is dismissed as a principle; learners are encouraged to participate fully in lessons, but we recognise that although they may participate through speaking, they can also do so, perhaps sometimes more effectively, by listening, noticing, and reflecting.

At lower levels, teachers are encouraged to talk extensively to their classes, while requiring little or no verbal response from learners. This mirrors L1 learning, and has been successfully used by followers of Asher's Total Physical Response (TPR) and Krashen's Natural Approach. The quality of the teacher's talk should ensure learners' active, albeit non-verbal, participation, and acquisition. Gradually, learners are encouraged to produce what Krashen has termed Random Volunteered Responses (RVR); the teacher's talk provides opportunities for speech, by, for example, including rhetorical questions – *And what do you think the man said? What do you think he said....(pause) He said...* . If learners respond, they are encouraged by the teacher's body language, eyes, and perhaps words – *Yes, that's right, he said, What are you doing?* – but they are in no way pressurised to speak, nor does the teacher evaluate the responses in any way. If some learners respond and others remain silent, this too is accepted without comment or evaluation.

It must be emphasised that this is not irresponsible or lazy; if we genuinely believe that it is input which aids acquisition, then classroom activities must reflect that understanding. The challenge for the teacher is to keep learners fully involved, without resorting to productive exercises or activities which can be at best inefficient and at worst counter-productive. In the lexical classroom learners will, particularly in the early stages, meet a lot more language than they are expected to produce; this represents an important methodological change for some teachers.

Older teachers may remember when any use of *would* was impossible until Book 4 on the (spurious) grammatical grounds that it was "the conditional": the communicative approach, by providing functional labels such as Offering and Refusing allowed examples such as *Would you like a cup of coffee / to go to the cinema this evening* to move to a much earlier and more appropriate place in the syllabus. In a similar way, the Lexical Approach encourages the introduction of powerful patterns as lexical items – that is without analysis of their internal structure – appropriately early in the syllabus. If learners know *Do you (live in Vienna)?* there is no reason why they cannot meet *Did you (see ... on TV last night)?* in their first few weeks of studying English. This increases the possibilities for natural teacher-talk (input), and makes the L2 learning closer to the natural exposure of L1 learning. From the earliest lessons learners can be introduced to such language as:

Expressions
Sorry, I don't know.
Sorry, I can't remember.
Sorry, I've forgotten.
Could you (say that again) please?
Sorry?

Sentence Heads
Do you... ?
Did you ... ?
Have you ever ...?
All the main question words

Many teachers already provide such language in the roughly-tuned input of the informal language they use talking to the class, but I urge them to add a little more, and any teachers who believe their learners should master everything they meet to broaden the language they use in classes at all levels, including beginners. Both George Woolard and Heinz Ribisch report in Chapter 8 how an understanding of lexis has encouraged them to go further than they did earlier in introducing language which lies outside the formal syllabus set by the coursebook.

Two conditions are essential for this strategy to be effective: firstly, the item must be taught lexically, without analysis, and secondly, teachers must, in the early stages, expect only comprehension, not production, of this language. A lexical view of the phrase differs from traditional structural analysis: the lexical chunks are the fully fixed head *Did you* and a slot. Structural analysis has always proposed *Did you see... ?* as a "Do-question". The lexical analysis is not only more helpful in the early stages of L2 study, but more accurately mirrors how L1 learners acquire such language.

The value of repetition

The remnants of Present-Practise-Produce (P-P-P) methodology are more pervasive than we sometimes recognise. It encouraged the belief that learning was a sequence of small steps and that what learners met, they must master. Teachers said both *They haven't done that yet*, and, more worryingly, *They've already done that.* That *done* in that context meant *met,* not *mastered,* was frequently ignored. While both theoretically and practically discredited, one aspect of the methodology remains relatively unquestioned, namely that you improve your language level by learning new things, and doing new texts, activities and exercises. 'Doing the same thing twice' is still widely considered time-wasting and potentially boring. But research evidence shows the opposite is true; repeating certain kinds of activity such as summarising a text orally one day and again a few days later may be the most efficient way of improving learners' language. This applies to both lexical and grammatical knowledge.

Many researchers have concluded that we acquire an individual word by meeting it a number of times; typically they suggest you are likely to have acquired a word after meeting it seven times. This does not mean the word needs to be explicitly taught seven times; indeed, according to some linguists, meeting it frequently with no explicit teaching is both a necessary and sufficient condition for its acquisition. The broad consensus is that each time you meet a word in context and (at least partly) understand it, you understand more of its meaning, and gradually integrate it into your lexicon for immediate access.

Although such research was done on vocabulary or 'new words' there is every reason to suppose that exactly similar considerations apply to multi-word lexical items, **providing** they are perceived as single lexical items. Some implications are obvious:

- coursebooks should deliberately recycle lexis
- consciously 'learning the new words' in each unit is unlikely to be sufficient for them to be fully acquired without some revisiting
- teachers should consciously recycle Collocations and Expressions in the roughly-tuned input they provide through talking informally to the class. A new motto emerges: *Increase carefully-controlled teacher-talking-time.*

While no teacher can impose a methodology successfully on an unwilling class, it is an important part of the teacher's job to guide learners towards the best ways to efficient acquisition. Persuading learners to 'do the same thing twice' is an important part of that process.

Noticing

The key idea of 'noticing' informs all Exercises and Activities in the Lexical Approach. While agreeing with Krashen's main proposition in *The Natural Approach*, namely *We acquire language by understanding messages*, the Lexical Approach differs in one important respect. The Natural Approach claims conscious learning has no influence on acquisition. If Krashen is right, then all formal instruction is pointless, or even impedes acquisition. While this is more often the case than many teachers admit, it is not **always** so. Teaching helps, precisely when it encourages the transition from input to intake. Meaning and message are primary, but Exercises and Activities which help the learner observe or notice the L2 more accurately ensure quicker and more carefully-formulated hypotheses about L2, and so aid acquisition which is based on a constantly repeated Observe-Hypothesise-Experiment cycle. The Exercises and Activities of Chapters 6 and 7 raise learners' awareness of the lexical features of L2; they encourage noticing which, as Skehan observes, "forms an important preliminary to internalisation".

Consciousness-raising

A similar view, called Consciousness-Raising (CR), which closely resembles that of noticing, has been extensively discussed, particularly by Dave and Jane Willis, who encourage teachers to use CR activities rather than traditional practices:

> If we believe that the successful learner is actively involved in looking for regularities in language data and in drawing conclusions from those regularities then we have an obligation to encourage this process. If we are successful in this we will not only succeed in making specific generalisations about language available to learners, we will also succeed in inculcating learning habits which will pay valuable dividends wherever and whenever the learner encounters language. CR can be seen as guided problem-solving.

They propose this taxonomy of CR tasks, the outcome of which they suggest will be 'an increased awareness of and sensitivity to language':

1. Students search to identify a pattern or usage and the forms associated with it.
2. Students classify according to similarities and differences.
3. Students are asked to check a generalisation about language against more data.
4. Students are encouraged to find similarities and differences between patterns in English and those of their own language.
5. Students manipulate language designed to reveal underlying patterns.
6. Students recall and reconstruct parts of a text, chosen to highlight a significant feature.
7. Students are trained to use reference works.
Challenge and Change in Language Teaching, Heinemann.

Something of a buzz-word in recent years, CR activities apply to many parts of the language curriculum. Jonathan Marks, who looks at the intersection of grammar, lexis and phonology in Chapter 8, in reviewing Brazil's *Pronunciation for Advanced Learners of English, CUP 1994* writes:

> The pronunciation work is based on an inductive approach, and proceeds from perception to production. Learners therefore have valuable opportunities to make their own observations and draw their own conclusions, which will stand them in good stead not only for developing their own pronunciation, but also, and perhaps more immediately, for processing and interpreting native speech – the 'receptive' aspect of pronunciation work whose importance is, I think, often overlooked by learners as well as teachers.

David Brazil himself writes:

> It is not so much a question of whether good pronunciation is best taught or caught: it is rather a matter of making the catching process more effective and efficient – of enabling learners to make the best use of such experience as comes their way.

A primary purpose of teaching is to help learners make better use, for acquisitional purposes, of all the language which they meet. Accurate noticing of lexical chunks, grammatical or phonological patterns all help convert input into intake, and provide, as we shall see, the central strategy of the Lexical Approach.

The importance of negative evidence

The Lexical Approach, like Krashen's Natural Approach, emphasises input and exposure; in one important respect, however, natural input, although necessary, is not sufficient. Learners formulate hypotheses about language patterns by making (conscious or unconscious) generalisations on the basis of the input. Inevitably they make some over-generalisations, assuming combinations are possible which are not sanctioned by general use. Yip observes *When a learner's state of L2 knowledge leads her to overuse a rule, construction, and so on, there is nothing in the input to tell her not to use it.* Although natural input provides alternatives, these may not be noticed and over-generalisations may become fossilised. Someone has to say what is not possible and this is clearly a task for the teacher. Nothing could be worse, however, than an obsession with errors or teacher-dominated correction. What is needed is reformulation, perhaps with *Did you notice ...?* comments, provided in a supportive way in a positive learning environment.

Swan recognises the importance of negative evidence concerning grammar patterns in *Practical English Usage* where he warns users of typical potential mistakes. We need a similar approach to lexis. Unfortunately, current dictionaries can all too easily mislead; nothing wrong, for example, with the OALD definition of *holier-than-thou* as "thinking that one is morally better than others: *I can't stand his holier-than-thou attitude"*, except can you think of any other noun with which *holier-than-thou* collocates? Because dictionaries are orientated towards de-coding, we do not get information about non-generalisability. For teachers, too, it is a change of mindset, part of the selecting **out** mentioned above. Rather than *You can say ..., and you can also say ...* they need to base their feedback on *Instead of ... I advise you to say ...* . The teacher is an important source of feedback on what is not sanctioned, but as sensitive feedback, not 'correction'.

THE CENTRAL STRATEGY: PEDAGOGICAL CHUNKING

We have seen the ways in which chunking is the basis of spoken fluency, and how it can help listeners and readers, but most importantly from a language learning point of view, the way we chunk the text as we read is the determining factor in the way we 'hear' it in our heads, and so determines the way we de-code the meaning. Usually writers try to guide the reader to correct chunks, by choice of words and punctuation. Here, for humorous effect, a headline writer deliberately misleads the reader:

End of world is nigh
impossible to predict

End of the world is nigh and *nigh impossible* are both lexical items, but the position of the line-break encourages the reader to 'hear' *End of the world is nigh* as a chunk; once you have mis-chunked it in this way, it is impossible to make sense of the headline without consciously re-reading and re-chunking it.

With the central ideas of lexis and noticing in mind, two questions of great pedagogic importance emerge:

1. Are learners aware of the chunks in a text? Do they see chunks when they read, or do they see only a sequence of individual words? If so, the text will be difficult to understand and correspondingly of limited value – input which is unlikely to become intake.

2. Do learners 'hear' a written text in phrase-chunks when they read it? If the mental lexicon is at least partly stored on the basis of sound patterns, text which is unheard or misheard in the learners' heads has no chance of being correctly stored in the phrasal lexicon and its value as potential input is lost. If learners do not hear input correctly chunked, it is less likely to be converted into intake than if it is seen and heard as chunks.

TASK

What classroom activities do you already use which help learners to see or hear text correctly chunked?

Can you think of any activities you currently use which make it more difficult for learners to think in terms of chunks, in other words, activities which may be counter-productive?

Here we need to examine the implications of the central pedagogical principle of the Lexical Approach – the grammar/vocabulary dichotomy is invalid. Contemporary language teaching is diverse; few teachers remain stuck with a strict structural syllabus and vocabulary building based on 'learn these 20 words'; multi-syllabuses, task-based activities and the like are widespread. But old habits die hard, and examination shows even the best modern textbooks retain a strong tendency to focus attention on vocabulary and grammar in the form of individual words and particular sentences. The old dichotomy persists.

TASK

A central task for teachers is to do everything they can to help learners turn input into intake; to help learners get the most out of any language they meet, both inside and outside the classroom. Which of these ways do you think learners use to store language in their brains?

- L1 word = L2 word. What about L2 word = L1 word? Is that the same?
- L1 phrase / expression = L2 phrase / expression. If so, is there a limit to the length of the expressions?
- By individual sounds – for example words beginning /m/ or /str/.
- By similarity of stress profile: *by the way / not at all; on the tip of my tongue / to a certain extent*
- In bits, for novel assembly: *semi-*, hence *semi-detached, semi-conscious, semi-worried(?)*

Research suggests we use all of these storage systems, sometimes storing the same item in more than one place, rather as *my brother John* may be stored as the name of 'a member of my family', a list which comes to mind in certain circumstances, and on 'the list of Johns I know', which comes to mind when someone at work says *John is on the line for you.*

We know it is easier to remember patterns than random lists, tunes rather than arbitrary sequences of notes. We know we can recognise our own language being spoken even when we cannot hear a single word of what is being said, so it must be the sound patterns which we recognise. Most importantly, we recognise wholes to be broken down, not parts to be built up.

The evidence is in favour of much of our language being stored in units larger than individual words. It is certainly not enough that learners are 'learning new words'; an adequate lexicon is also about the quality of the lexicon. It is part of the teacher's task to guide learners towards better learning strategies and make the task more manageable. McCarthy expresses concern that this does not always happen, and the value of phrasal storage is still given insufficient attention:

> Over-concentration on learning single words may hinder the development of the L2 phrasal lexicon and deny the opportunities this gives for rapid retrieval and fluent connected speech in the stressful conditions of speaking and writing.

TASK

What activities, including things you already do, can you suggest which will help learners add to their phrasal mental lexicon?

Some modest changes to classroom procedure will help:

1. Any dialogue which occurs in the coursebook should be **heard** at least once, but better twice, once for content and once when attention is directed to some feature of how it is said, i.e. chunked. If the dialogue is available on tape, use it. If not, read it aloud to the class.

2. Even a prose text is more likely to become intake if it is heard. Read at least a part of it aloud, asking learners to notice some feature of the chunking. This activity only needs 2 or 3 minutes, and needs no elaborate follow-up or checking.

3. Ask learners in small groups to chunk a printed version of something they are going to hear, and then compare their versions, then compare their version with a version you have done on transparency, and finally with what they actually hear. This brief addition to an activity you would use anyway provides a lexical focus and increases the potential acquisitional value of the activity for a minimum of extra time or effort.

4. Ask learners in small groups to identify chunks of different kinds in a printed text: fixed collocations, discourse phrases which organise the text etc. (see page 180). Do the same activity yourself on a copy of the text you have on transparency. Let learners compare between groups, and with your copy. Read a short section, or, with more capable learners, ask one or more of them to do so, taking account of the suggested chunking.

5. Put a short section of text on a word processor and chunk it using line breaks, font changes etc. so learners can see something of how the text sounds. If they have access to the necessary technology, encourage them to do the same – each individual devising a system which helps him or her to see how the text sounds. Mark Powell discusses this more fully in Chapter 8.

6. The first unit of Brazil's highly innovative *Pronunciation for Advanced Learners of English* follows the following pattern (slightly edited):

> Listen to the cassette, paying attention to the meaning of what you hear, rather than the pronunciation.
> Now listen and attend to the short pieces into which it is divided, continue and try to mark the breaks yourself.
> Check by listening again, then try allowing yourself a pause wherever you have marked a break. Be sure that you do not pause anywhere else.

He then explains:

> What you have just done is to break up a stretch of speech into pieces. We shall call these pieces tone units .... you should think of the tone unit as the basic building block of spoken English ....When (English) is spoken it is heard by the ear divided up into tone units. Notice that the sounds that make up a tone unit are usually run together in the way we are accustomed to thinking of the separate sounds of single words being run together.

The next practice then asks learners to:

> Listen to each of these tone units (which are parts of the original extract of used language) and then repeat them, trying to reproduce exactly what you hear, running the sounds together as if you were saying a single word.

> 1. they'd gone   2. it was dark   3. to sit on
> 4. for plants   5. it was winter   6. she was a student
> 7. where market street was

He later asks learners to mark a short extract according to how it is spoken:

i passed some shops bright lights and bargains and fashionable dresses on plastic figures videos and fridges and hundreds of shoes at give-away prices left-over gift wrapping and holly and snowmen.

Finally, he observes: *To speak a tone unit without any breaks in the continuity, you need to have planned it completely before you begin it.*

Brazil's observation ought to be obvious, but language teaching has paid little attention to the planning and processing part of speech production. Pronunciation has tended to concentrate on sounds, while reading aloud has been frowned upon. Any preparation has tended to focus on 'difficult words', but as Brazil clearly demonstrates, it is the chunking of the text which is the main problem in delivering any spoken text, even supposedly unprepared spontaneous speech.

We now have two different kinds of chunks; tone units which are particular to the communicative requirements on each separate occasion in speech, but which also relate to the silent chunking used by effective readers. Secondly, we see that these tone units are rarely built from scratch; many consist of a single prefabricated phrase: *That was hardly my fault, On the other hand;* others are assembled but even then one or more components is likely to be multi-word, typically prepositional phrases and strong collocations: *It looks like the ideal opportunity to make the radical changes in the basic plan that we've all wanted to see in place for a long time.*

The central role of chunking – the ability to discern clearly the component units of any text – becomes clearer and clearer. Unless you chunk a text correctly, it is almost impossible to read with understanding, and unless you speak in appropriate chunks, you place a serious barrier to understanding between yourself and your listeners. Chunking is the key to comprehensibility, hence to making yourself understood in speech, and from a language teaching point of view, to successfully turning input into intake. If you claim to teach in the communicative tradition, helping learners to understand chunks and chunking should have a central place in the classroom. Chunking is central to effective communication, and efficient acquisition.

SUMMARY

Lexis provides the component chunks of language and, if learners are to make best use of the language they meet they need gradually to develop an awareness of chunks of different kinds. Lexis brings together elements of language learning previously usually treated separately – grammar, words and pronunciation; in bringing them together it helps learners turn input into intake. The teacher's job is to encourage good learning strategies and to help learners notice the language they meet more accurately, thereby making it more likely that input will become intake.

In Chapters 6 and 7 we discuss many different sample Exercises and Activities. All, however, have one basic motivation – to encourage learners to notice different kinds of chunk and to ensure that they notice them more perceptively. To slightly misquote David Brazil's neat dictum: It is not a matter of whether language is taught or caught, it is a matter of making the catching process more effective and efficient. In order to do this, we also need to re-evaluate the role of the learners' mother tongue in the classroom. That is the subject of the next chapter.

Chapter 4

The Role of L1 in the Lexical Approach

We have argued that languages do not consist of words but of chunks. Every teacher knows that learners have a tendency to translate word-for-word and, as we saw in the last chapter, we want to encourage identification of chunks, and a recognition that word-for-word equivalence is often impossible. With the idea of pedagogical chunking in mind, we need to reconsider the role the learners' L1 should play in the classroom. The two traditional ideas which rather fell out of favour while the Communicative Approach began to dominate teacher training and classroom practice – translation and interference – turn out to be surprisingly fruitful when seen in the context of a lexical view of language.

TRANSLATION IS INEVITABLE

Perhaps the oldest, and frequently most despised, methodology is grammar-translation, usually dismissed on teacher training courses in a few moments. The dismissal has always been a little too glib, but we certainly do not want to see a return to a methodology which takes long passages of supposedly 'good' but often turgid text into the classroom, to be laboriously translated, and later exploited grammatically or structurally. But learners often ask *How do you say ... in English?* or, as their knowledge of the target language improves, *Can you say ...?* You are more likely to retain something new if you are interested and attentive when you meet the new material. Self-evidently these conditions are likely to prevail if the new material is the answer to a learner's question.

The learners' questions reveal two important points: firstly, rather than 'thinking in English', when you cannot express yourself in the L2, you naturally fall back into L1, and search for a translation from a starting point in L1. Translation is thus an instinctive part of the way the mind approaches learning a second language. Secondly, *Can you say...?* shows learners have an intuitive grasp of lexis – there is a developing awareness that speech communities do not simply make up new ways of saying things all the time; on the contrary, there are often Expressions which the non-native needs to acquire as wholes, either by meeting them naturally, or by them being sanctioned as 'what we really say' by the teacher or book. There is nothing to understand, just items to be remembered so they are available for subsequent use in exactly the same form. Although they often do not act on it, learners have an instinctive understanding that languages have what we shall call equivalents, correct translations which are totally different from manufactured word-for-word 'translations'.

It is worth a brief digression to see quite why translation has had such a bad name for the last 30 years. Two powerful forces have worked against it. Much of the innovation during that period in both materials and methods has come from Britain and the United States. Native speaker teachers (NSTs) and materials perceived as linguistically reliable have had high status, and have been supported by powerful financial interests. The publishers prefer global to country-specific textbooks; NSTs often work in polyglot private schools with multi-lingual classes where translation would be impractical or impossible even if it were desirable. These powerful factors mean translation had to be condemned – but for commercial rather than theoretical or pedagogical reasons. It is a surprise that so many non-native teachers (non-NSTs) have been persuaded so easily to undervalue their own abilities, and discard a classroom technique of great potential value. Let us examine the nature and role of translation more carefully.

LEARNING L2 IS NOT IDENTICAL TO LEARNING L1

The relationship between learning a first language (L1) and a second language (L2) is hotly debated. In *The Lexical Approach* there is an implicit assumption that the two processes are more similar than different, that the human mind handles language in certain non-language-specific ways. There are, however, differences between acquiring L1 and L2. Two important differences may be mentioned, though only the second plays a significant role in the subsequent discussion.

There are two distinct results of the process of acquiring L1: you are able to mediate yourself and your world through language in general, and through a particular language. An L2 allows you to mediate self and world in a wider range of contexts or, with a sufficiently good command of L2, perhaps even in a different way. It is, however, simply a second way of doing something you could already do. There is a second difference, however, between acquiring an L1 and L2, and it is this difference which is of particular interest to us. Acquiring an L2 mirrors acquiring L1 in that you relate L2 words to L2 words, or L2 words to the external world, but you also and inevitably relate L2 words and expressions to L1 language items; in short, you translate.

We recall again the learner's typical questions: *What's this called in (English)? How do you say ... in (English)? Can you say...?* The first, more typical of using the language in a natural context, relates L2 to the external world, but the second question is more typical of the classroom, and it relates L2 to L1, while the third question shows learners are aware that what seems possible to them may not, in fact, be sanctioned in the natural use of L2.

Can a lexical perspective suggest activities which exploit learners' natural tendency to translate? Can we devise principled ways of showing learners helpful relationships between the languages and, at the same time, discouraging the unhelpful word-for-word translation which is the usual first recourse of untrained learners?

TRANSLATION AND LEXIS

Our content focus moves from individual words to Collocations and Expressions. The former are more likely to be prominent in content-bearing written text, Fixed Expressions in spoken language, while different kinds of Semi-fixed Expressions occur in both written and spoken texts, but in clearly different ways for the two modes. Principled re-introduction of translation means taking account of these differences.

We often complain that learners translate word-for-word but rarely suggest a better way. The secret, of course, is to translate chunk-for-chunk. Such a translation will have some rough grammatical edges, but almost certainly successfully conveys the content. But learners cannot translate chunk-for-chunk until they can successfully identify the chunks. The ability to chunk correctly is a necessary, though not sufficient, condition for successful translation. Developing the ability to chunk texts of various kinds is, as we saw in the previous chapter, central to implementing the Lexical Approach. Rather than simply 'teaching them the language', teachers must recognise the real value of developing such skills with their learners.

TASK

Which of the following do you think are easiest to translate and which more difficult? What criteria do you use to decide?

1. The doctor diagnosed a case of acute appendicitis.
2. It never crossed my mind.
3. You're not kidding.
4. Take your time. There's no hurry. It only takes a couple of minutes from here to the station.
5. All urgent orders are dispatched promptly by special courier.

Difficulty of translation is a very different matter from what we usually think of as 'difficult words'. In the examples above *appendicitis* is, most people would agree, the 'most difficult word', but ironically it is the easiest to translate, at least into the languages of cultures with a medical system similar to our own. The higher the information content of a word, the more likely it is that another language will have a direct equivalent and word-for-word translation will work. As we saw in Chapter 2, the rarer a word is, the more likely it is to carry a lot of meaning: contrast *house* and *appendicitis*, or *dog* and *giraffe*. In 1, both *diagnose* and *appendicitis* are high in information content, so 1 is easy to translate accurately.

Examples 2 and 3 exemplify a different kind of language; each is a whole Expression; the pragmatic meaning is socially determined and bears little relation to the meanings of the individual words. Crude "translation" is impossible; it is necessary to find **equivalent expressions** in the other language. Despite consisting of "easy" words, 2 and 3 are difficult to translate accurately.

Example 4 is similar, but less obviously so. It contains uses of the de-lexicalised verb *take* – *take your time, take (a period of time)* – and the polyword *a couple of minutes*. Despite its apparent ordinariness, it is in fact precisely the kind of 'ordinary idiom' discussed in Chapter 2, and requires correspondingly subtle ideas if an appropriate equivalent is to be found.

Example 5 is more similar to 1, although the words do not have quite as much information-content. This will be easy to translate, **providing you start in the right place.**

TRANSLATION AND COLLOCATION

Although Collocations are a type of lexical item, they differ from Words and Fixed Expressions in that we can develop a principled methodology for translating them successfully.

TASK

Which word in example 5 above is the best starting point for constructing an accurate translation? Which is most likely to have a word-for-word equivalent in another language?

For which word class do you think direct word-for-word equivalents most often exist?

The largest word class by far, in which the items usually have high information-content, is the class of nouns. As nouns frequently call the shots in collocations, so the noun is almost always the best starting point for good translation, at least for sentences with real referential rather than phatic social content.

In searching for the correct English translation *tall boy*, the problem is not *boy*, but the correct collocating adjective; similarly in example 5, *order* almost certainly has a direct equivalent; the problem is to find the correct collocations: the adjective, *urgent* (not *important* or *pressing*) and verb *dispatch* (not *convey* or *transmit*); finally the question of appropriate adverb which collocates with *dispatch, promptly* (not *hastily* or *instantly*).

To summarise: a lexical view allows us to see specific areas in which word-for-word translation will be unsatisfactory:

• idioms, both traditional and the Fixed Expressions of the normal spoken language

- Collocations and Expressions using de-lexicalised verbs or other common words which individually carry very little meaning, but which are often elements in multi-word lexical items.

A lexical view also gives us a general strategy and procedure for effective translation of referential language:

- find and translate the key noun
- search for appropriate collocating verbs and/or adjectives
- search for adverbial phrases which collocate with any adjective or verb.

There is a hierarchy of word classes which guarantees that for any referential text the sequence is the same: noun – verb/adjective – adverbial. Once these lexical items are found, they must be correctly grammaticalised, but, as we expect from a lexical perspective, the process involves grammaticalising lexis, not lexicalising grammar.

THE VALUE OF TRANSLATION

There are several excellent reasons for paying increased attention to translation:

1. It is inevitable that language learners use L1 as a resource, and that they make both helpful and unhelpful assumptions on the basis of their experience of L1. Sound pedagogy should exploit rather than try to deny this.

2. I have argued elsewhere *(The English Verb, LTP, 1986)* that English grammatical structures acquire their meaning and use by contrasts within English, and that constantly comparing L2 and L1 is unhelpful for learners seeking to master those contrasts internal to English. It may appear inconsistent to argue the opposite case for lexis, but this is not so. Learners inevitably equate L2 word = L1 word; this is unhelpful and frequently untrue. But it is, as Swan pointed out in a famous article, frequently **very nearly** true, and if the equation becomes L2 lexical item = L1 lexical item it is **very often** true. Correctly identified chunks do have equivalents in other languages, and to ignore this fact is to make the task of learning the L2 unnecessarily burdensome.

3. An important part of the teacher's task is to ensure learners waste as little time as possible in fruitless or mis-directed activity. Listing certain types of words or expressions in L1 word = L2 word vocabulary lists is counter-productive; searching for, discussing, and recording appropriate L1 lexical item = L2 lexical item, is a useful and efficient procedure, but using the technique successfully requires the kind of language awareness which few learners will employ without help from a teacher.

4. I am not recommending translation for its own sake. The argument is that

the techniques and processes made explicitly in consciously searching for equivalents exactly mirror the processes which every student uses when trying to express something for which the necessary language does not come automatically to mind. Translation is a form of consciousness-raising, which is a central technique in the Lexical Approach.

Writers who suggest activities which raise learners' awareness of certain features of the target language suggest it often helps if learners first do the task in L1, so they realise similar features occur in their own language. Joanna Channell, for example, suggests introducing learners to the all-pervasive nature of vague language *(in his thirties, a sort of greenish colour)* by asking them to do simple tasks involving speculating or guessing in L1 before they do them in L2.

INTERFERENCE CAN BE HELPFUL

At any point, learners have a mental picture of the target language; this consists of a mental lexicon and a personal perception of the structure of L2, an intergrammar. This knowledge is built from different sources, most notably exposure to appropriate reading and listening in L2, and by analogy with L1. Most, if not all, of the processes by which this knowledge develops are subconscious; we are reminded again that there is little evidence for assuming the influence of direct teaching on the development of either the learner's mental lexicon or intergrammar. This is not, however, to deny the value of teaching, but to re-focus it on awareness raising, the development of learning strategies, the selection of materials and choice of activities. These are all indirect teaching, aimed at maximising the conversion of input into intake. In this context we ask how best to use the learner's inevitable tendency to assume that features of L1 apply also to L2.

The term 'interference' was used in the days when structure was all-important, to explain the preponderance of certain types of mistake in the learner's L2 output. Many parallels with L1 are untrue, so intermediate learners who rely, consciously or otherwise, on L1 will make mistakes, and the source of those mistakes will be particularly obvious to teachers who speak the learner's L1. This frequently encouraged correction and explanation. We note also that the language used to describe the effect of L1 always carries negative connotations: *interference, false friends*. But this is half a story – many analogies with L1 **do** work, and are a positive aid to L2 acquisition. Many similar-looking words **are** similar in meaning (much more often than the relatively few false friends); many structural features **do** transfer. I much prefer the more neutral term 'transfer' for the effects of L1 on L2 precisely because I recognise that the effects are both helpful and unhelpful, and part of the teacher's task is to raise learners' awareness of the effects, so helping them both to avoid the unhelpful, and to benefit from helpful, parallels.

L1 AWARENESS AS A RESOURCE

We have already argued above that it is unhelpful to teach **structure** by comparing L1 and L2; English grammar expresses meaning by a system of contrast internal to English, and classroom activities should reflect this. Few grammar mistakes, whether the result of interference or not, impede communication and thus do not merit more than occasional correction. In contrast, lexical mistakes do matter and activities aimed at raising awareness of false friends are correspondingly valuable.

Increased learner awareness of certain lexical parallels can be helpful. Some of the difficulties encountered in L2, are based on, or exacerbated by the learners' general linguistic naivety. Most learners will not have thought closely about features of their mother-tongue. It is helpful, therefore, to show learners ways in which their own language and the language they are learning are lexically similar:

* collocation is a feature of all languages
* different genres contain different kinds of collocation
* Fixed Expressions exist in their language as well as in English and have immediately recognisable pragmatic meaning
* Expressions suitable for use to one person may not be suitable if used to a different person; all languages have ways of marking formality.

Learners will have views on the way people use their language as an L2; calm discussion of this can make learners more aware of problems they face in actually using English for real purposes outside the classroom. Activity 25 in Chapter 7 provides sample material to stimulate such discussion.

SUMMARY

Teachers now have much greater access to a wide variety of texts and text-types. Many classes nowadays exchange e-mail with a class in Britain or the US, so it is relatively easy to find texts written for, or even to, your own class; pen-pal letters or textbook dialogues are varied and easily available. New possibilities are opened up by this easy access to 'real' texts. In Chapter 7 we give examples of Activities which make principled use of translation in ways far removed from those of the old reviled grammar/translation methodology. The lexical nature of much language provides a clear justification for a cautious return to translation as a helpful classroom activity.

L1 has been banished or considered rather disreputable for too long, for reasons which do not bear close scrutiny. In the next chapter we turn to the principles which underlie the Exercises and Activities which are appropriate to the Lexical Approach. As we shall see, many involve receptive skills and developing learners' general awareness of language. Encouraging this development should be a **small, but regular** feature of classroom procedure and partly involves comparison of L1 and L2.

Chapter 5

Organising Lexis

The traditional perception is that grammar organises the chaos of the lexicon. If we want lexis to be accessible to learners we must find helpful and accessible ways of organising it.

PRINCIPLES

There is no attempt to find a single organising principle to describe the language; we look for a set of principles which are appropriate to different lexical areas. Encouragingly, the principles are more accessible and closer to the learners' everyday experience than grammar rules which were often abstract and remote from the experience of using the language. We first note three familiar principles which require only brief comments:

1. Topic

Language teaching has always recognised Topic as organisationally useful, most notably as a parameter for designing coursebook units. In the Lexical Approach, however, we must remain constantly aware of the different types of lexical item which may be organised within a Topic framework, otherwise a surfeit of uncollocated nouns may result, as is often the case with vocabulary materials.

The sample materials on pages 68/9 illustrate two topics from general English and from business English. Notice the emphasis on both pages on both Collocations and Expressions. *Food* is not only a matter of referential vocabulary, but also of what we say; not only Words and Collocations, but also many useful Expressions can be predicted. This represents a significant extension of the conventional use of Topic as an organising principle for traditional vocabulary.

2. Situation

If you know where a conversation takes place, you can predict likely lexical areas. Again, we must introduce lexical items of all types: *Where do you keep the (N: sugar)?* is as much part of the lexicon of *In the Kitchen* as *sieve*. However, conversations on particular topics may occur in many different places, while in a given place language may be used which is in no way connected to the place. Used selectively, physical Situation is occasionally the most appropriate way of organising a bit of the lexicon.

Food

A. What nouns form strong word partnerships with *all* the words in each line below? Try to find the partners yourself, then check and see if you have used each of the words at the end of the lists once.

1. salad   chicken   cheese   freshly-made   club
2. rare   medium   well-done   rump   fillet
3. mixed   green   side   fruit   potato
4. delicious   light   heavy   three-course   evening
5. light   full-bodied   robust   fruity   complex
6. dry   medium   sweet   crisp   fruity
7. Indian   fast   plain   spicy   rich
8. traditional   Thai   vegetarian   fish   trendy

food	meal	white wine	red wine
steak	salad	sandwich	restaurant

B. Now complete these so that they are true for you:

1. How would you like your steak?
    > . . . . , please.
2. I (don't) really like . . . wines, (but) I prefer . . . .
3. I don't dislike . . . food, but I'd never choose it. I prefer
    . . . (food).
4. There's a very nice . . . restaurant near my . . . but it is
    rather . . . .
5. At lunchtime I usually have quite a . . . meal, but my evening
    meal is usually quite a lot . . . .

C. You are having a meal at home with a friend. One of you will probably say all these things during the evening. Mark each G = Guest or H = Host. Number them in the most likely order.

No thanks, it's lovely but I'm fine.
Oh, go on then, just a drop.
This looks lovely. Did you do it yourself?
Shall we eat?
Sugar?
Now, what can I get you?
Would you like a bit more (quiche)?
Don't wait for me.
Make yourself at home.
Goodness, is that the time?

Administration

A. Which of these things do you have in your office?

1. printed envelopes
2. letterhead
3. address labels
4. plain paper
5. compliment slips
6. sellotape

B. Make five word partnerships. Match each verb to a partner.

1. book
2. reserve
3. make arrangements for
4. order
5. hire

a. the Annual Conference
b. extra supplies
c. an early flight to Athens
d. the AV equipment
e. a table for six at 8 o'clock

How many different kinds of AV equipment can you name?

C. Which of these words is not usually used with *form*:
application   order   supply   registration   duplicate

Which of these words is not usually used with *memo*:
send   circulate   internal   external   write

Which of these words is not usually used with *file(s)*:
open   save   copy   delete
create   make   merge

Write the initials of someone at your work who deals with these things:
telephone enquiries   complaints
correspondence   day-to-day problems

D. Write the equivalent in your own language for each of these expressions:
I think we'd better send them a reminder.

Can you send them a reminder, please?

Did you get my memo?

Don't worry, it's already been dealt with.

Could you sign this form, please?

Could you fill in this form, please?

In American English you *fill out* a form; in British English you *fill in* a form.

3. Collocation

Collocation forms a central feature of a lexical view of language and noticing collocations is a central pedagogical activity. From an organisational point of view, many strong collocations need to be recorded as individual word-like objects, perhaps with their L1 equivalents, while there are also helpful patterns such as groups of adjectives or verbs which precede a given noun, or contextual opposites which can be recorded in helpful formats (see below).

4. Notion

'Notion' is not used in the loose sense of 'idea', nor in any of the many, frequently contradictory, ways suggested by the notional/functional materials which, in practice, were almost exclusively functional. The term is used here to mean a synoptic description of an event which has psychological unity. Particular words or phrases may be used when comparing, apologising or reassuring; this is familiar functional language. But Notions such as Comparison, Apology, and Reassurance are wider terms which cover whole speech events. All of these Expressions belong under the Notion *Apology*:

I'm sorry. I was miles away.
I'm sorry about yesterday. I was out of order.
I shouldn't have (told her). I'm really sorry.

I brought you a few flowers.
I hope you'll let me pay for the damage.
Don't worry. I've done the same thing myself.
Don't worry. It wasn't your fault.
You couldn't have known.

Only the first set are covered by the function Apologising, but **all** these examples are included in the Notion of Apology as an event. In encouraging learners to organise language into a lexical notebook we may use Functional headings, but in general Notions are more helpful in ensuring good cover of a lexical area.

5. Narration

The Narrative Principle can be very simply stated: in producing speech the human mind follows a simple pattern: nominalise – narrate – explain. When we want to talk about something, it must first be **named.** Only rarely is nominalisation enough: Jack! FIRE EXIT. Typically, we use sequences, tell stories; we **narrate.** Finally, and optionally, we may **explain** the relations between elements within the story.

The idea of a narrative needs to be given a wide interpretation; a comic sketch, a set of instructions, or even a recipe are narrative in the way the term is used here. The human mind likes stories, strings of nominalisations sequenced in time: arrange these partner-verbs to the noun *letter* into a story sequence: *sign, post, receive, reply to, check, address*. Real-world constraints make some sequences impossible or at least very highly unlikely: few of us post a letter before signing it. Some sequences are a combination of the fixed and the more ambiguous; the Narrative Principle provides a powerful organisational tool. The sample material on page 72, taken from *Presenting in English, Mark Powell LTP 1996*, demonstrates the principle.

6. Metaphor

Metaphor is one of the most fruitful of the novel ways of identifying patterns in lexis. Sometimes thought of as a literary device, modern research in both philosophy and linguistics has shown that metaphor pervades **all** language, including everyday speech and writing. More usefully from a pedagogic point of view, much metaphorical lexis is patterned in ways which are both relatively easy to describe, and accessible to learners.

The pioneering work is Lakoff and Johnson's *Metaphors We Live By*, but teachers with imagination, a good dictionary and the idea that metaphor provides a useful lexical patterning principle, can both devise classroom materials and help learners use metaphor as a pattern which aids recording and remembering.

Some non-literal expressions are inexplicable: *He kicked the bucket*. Although fairly transparent because it is so graphic, *He was running round like a headless chicken* does not form part of a system of, for example, farmyard idioms. Systematic patterning involves two semantic areas, where talk of an abstract area is pervaded by words from a corresponding concrete area. Lakoff and Johnson devised the now standard typographical way of stating this kind of metaphorical equivalence: ARGUMENT IS WAR. UP IS GOOD. TIME IS MONEY. *Time is money* is a proverb in English, but this is accidental to our focus of interest; a metaphorical pattern involves the relationship between two semantic fields. Kövecses and Szabo suggest: *Emotional concepts and concepts denoting personal relationships are particularly susceptible to metaphorical understanding*. Some of their examples make this clearer:

Anger is Fire
She was fuming.
They had a blazing row.
Smoke was coming out of his ears.

Enthusiasm is Fire
He was burning with excitement.
Don't be a wet blanket.
Her enthusiasm was ignited by the new teacher.

If a metaphor is identified, it can be the basis for an awareness-raising activity of the kind given on page 127. Teachers will find it helpful to look at

Business Terms 4

> Many processes – price movements, product development etc.
> – describe a more or less fixed sequence of events. Make sure
> you know all the words you need to describe each stage in the
> processes you want to talk about.

TASK

Put the verbs and verb phrases in the word partnerships below into the *most
likely* chronological order. Are there any alternative sequences?

1. THE MARKET   take over target be forced out of re-enter break into

2. NEGOTIATIONS   break off complete conduct resume enter into

3. PRICES   cut set re-think raise receive complaints about

4. THE CONTRACT   draw up breach negotiate terminate renew

5. THE PRODUCT   manufacture distribute launch withdraw develop

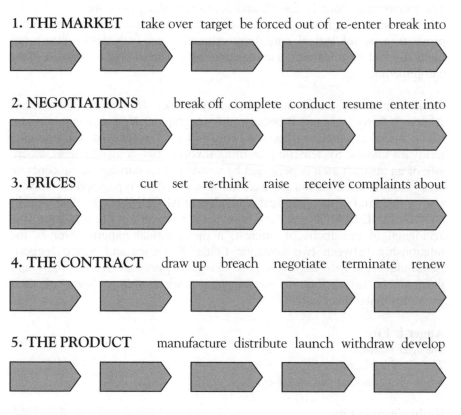

Choose the keywords above which are more relevant to your job and expand
the five stages into a short presentation.

non-literal language use on the assumption that it may be part of a pattern, often one which will not carry over between L1 and L2, so L1/L2 comparison or contrast may be useful.

7. Person

We are used to grammatical paradigms, and many exercises consciously use examples beginning with the different grammatical persons. The Lexical Approach in some ways turns this on its head. Changing the grammatical person of these examples produces some strange sentences:

I'll see you tomorrow.
>You'll see me tomorrow.

I've got something in my shoe.
>You've got something in your shoe.

Hello. I haven't seen you for ages. You're looking well.
> Hello. I haven't seen him for ages. He's looking well.

I'm sure I've met her before.
> They're sure they've met her before.

Though not impossible, the 'transformations' are highly improbable; the different persons are simply not substitutable in many examples of 'used language'. Many common Expressions beginning *I . . .* sound absurd or at least odd if any other person is substituted: *I'm sorry I'm late, I've got a pain in my . . . , I really enjoyed that.* Real-world constraints skew the kind of language we use; I tend to **tell** about me, and **ask** about you.

Learners often say *I can't say what I mean / think / feel*; that is partly because they have not been given enough of the appropriate language used to say how I think, felt, reacted or whatever. Learners' classroom language rarely has the *I*-centric quality of everyday language. Classroom language is at worst formal practice but even at best it is often about the content of a text which does not help learners talk about themselves.

If we claim to be teaching communicatively, and to be helping students **speak** English, we need more emphasis on *I*-statements and, to a lesser extent, *You*-questions. The best source material I know is *NTC's Dictionary of Everyday American English Expressions,* the content of which is skewed in favour of *I*-sentences. A good repertoire of such expressions is of particular importance to ESL learners, or those who are visiting a country where English is the L1.

Awareness that changing the grammatical person does not produce pragmatic equivalents means teachers can consciously look for real equivalents when the person is changed. Instead of *I'm sorry – it wasn't my fault*, it is clear that *Don't worry, it wasn't your fault* is a more useful Expression than the transformation to the implausible *You're sorry – it wasn't your fault.* This is the principle behind the Cascade format, discussed below.

8. Phonological chunking

To many teachers 'pronunciation' suggests learners' difficulties with individual words or even individual sounds. However, much of the mental lexicon is stored in prefabricated chunks, and articulation – the physical production of speech – is planned over varying stretches, almost all longer than a single word. The 'citation form' of a word (the way it is pronounced out of context), is exceptional rather than typical; most words are produced in chunks in the stream of speech. The utterance *By the way, I have to get up at six tomorrow. I have to be at work by half past seven at the latest* is typically spoken chunked as follows (though this is a matter of how the sounds are grouped, rather than real audible pauses):

By the way / I have / to get up at six / tomorrow / I have / to be at work / by / / half past seven / at the latest.

Conventional EFL teaching includes the following: Telling the time: *It's half past seven*; Necessity: *must, have to, need to*; Prepositions: *by six o'clock* etc. Phrasal verbs: *to get up* etc. All the bits of the utterance appear to be taught, but in fact this is not so.

Teaching has often mis-chunked the language. Instead of the 'theoretically possible' sentence *I'm getting up at six tomorrow,* consider the 'real-world utterance' *I'm getting up at six tomorrow.* The difference is startling. Henri Adamchewski has pointed out that the verb in the utterance is not *get up* or *getting up*, but *getting up at six*. What motivated the speaker to produce the utterance? Not the desire to tell someone that he was *getting up*, but precisely that he was *getting up at six,* presumably a change from the normal routine. The chunking is not *I'm getting up / at six*, but rather *I'm / getting up at six*. In the middle of the chunk, you produce *u'pat*. From a pronunciation point of view, *getting up at six* is a single chunk.

The other slots are similar: in place of *half past seven* we can substitute *nine;* in place of *at the latest, to open the place up*. The stress patterns of:

> *I've got to be there by half past seven at the latest.*
> *I need to be there by nine to open the place up.*

are similar, because the chunking is similar. It is easier to remember a tune than a random sequence of notes; chunks which have the same 'tune' are easier to remember if learned together. Phonological chunking, which is discussed further in Chapters 6 and 8, provides another principled way of helping learners see patterns in lexis.

9. Keywords

One of the insights of the Lexical Approach is the importance of the most common words of the language, particularly the de-lexicalised verbs. These words are closer to generative grammar than fixed vocabulary and accordingly enter into a wide range of Expressions and patterns. They have been given scant attention in the past, and learners tend to overlook them, believing they already 'know' the word. Teachers who recognise the importance of these words in many multi-word items can help learners develop their phrasal lexicons by using these words as the basis of classroom activities and to organise part of learners' Notebooks.

10. Grammar

In Chapter 2 we noted that lexis was not enough; the content and role of grammar teaching is modified in the Lexical Approach but it remains an important element of a balanced course.

Far from language being the product of the application of rules, most language is acquired lexically, then 'broken down' or in Martin Bygate's term, syntactisised, after which it becomes available for re-assembly in potentially new combinations. Chapter 2 introduced certain sentences which have a special status in the language. Noticing these, and maximising the chance of turning input into intake, involves drawing special attention to, and encouraging learners to record this special status language in their notebooks, which assume great importance in implementing the Lexical Approach.

NOTEBOOKS

Probably the only learning aid which every learner has is a vocabulary notebook. These vary from disorganised scraps of paper through neat notebooks in which words and perhaps phrases are listed day-by-day as learners meet them, to more thoughtful, alphabetically indexed books, with complete expressions, usage notes and other helpful information. Given the central importance of the learner's lexicon, the role and format of a truly lexical notebook deserves our close attention.

Several principles are self-evident:

• Inclusion of every 'new word' should be discouraged and if such words are recorded learners should be encouraged to use a Miscellaneous section, away from more organised language.

• No item should go into the Notebook unless learners can retrieve it on demand. Computer experts use the slogan *Rubbish in, Rubbish out*; it applies to lexical notebooks too.

• The Notebook must be sectioned and formatted to allow for different kinds of lexical item. Formats should encourage systematic structuring of the language which is recorded.

• Relatively few single words (*L1 word = L2 word*) should get in. The Notebook is a tool to develop learners' awareness of the lexical nature of language. For receptive vocabulary recording, from L2 to L1 may be best, but for productive items the order should be from L1 to L2. Teachers need to introduce learners to this difference.

• New language may be collected in class during a particular lesson, or in a less organised way over a period of time, then class time used to review and organise it to ensure what is recorded is accurate, useful, organised and retrievable.

The purpose of a lexical notebook is to be a fully personalised learning aid so every learner's notebook, although perhaps containing language recorded by everyone in the class, will also include individually chosen items. Using such a book in class over the period of a course should leave learners fully equipped to continue using it on their own. With the increased size of the lexicon suggested by the Lexical Approach it is more important than ever to try to ensure that the items added to the learner's necessarily limited lexicon are maximally useful to each individual.

Content of the Notebook

The Notebook will contain all of the following:

• Words, strong collocations and fully Fixed Expressions, with L1 equivalents
• Collocation patterns with, for example, a noun plus a group of collocating verbs or adjectives
• Semi-fixed Expressions with several similar examples listed together to emphasise a pattern
• Prototypical grammar examples, of the kind mentioned in Chapter 9, often in the form of high frequency Expressions
• Miscellaneous language, chosen by individual learners, in a separate section, away from the more organised language.

The Notebook may include pre-designed photocopiable pages which encourage the recording of particular patterns, or be a conventional exercise book, which learners arrange themselves in sections and into which they organise the language on a more ad hoc basis, as described in Chapter 8 by Heinz Ribisch, all of whose students including beginners keep lexical Notebooks.

For some learners relatively straightforward listing is best, but you can indicate the semi-fixed parts of Expressions by using ( ) for optional elements and [ ] for variable but obligatory elements like this:

I'm afraid that's not (very) convenient (at the moment).
I've got to [pick the children up] [T: at four o'clock].

Organisation of the notebook

An essential skill for teachers is the ability to move systematically from one language item to another so that a lexical Notebook contains selected language, covering the full range of types of lexical item, helpfully organised. The organisation may be based on the principles discussed above and on the most easily retrievable system of all – the alphabet. Lexical understanding provides ways, as demonstrated in the Formats below, of moving systematically from one item to other related lexis.

Teachers should be alert to the opportunity occasionally to re-organise the language already recorded by learners into patterns or pages which may not be apparent to the learners without guidance. The range and sophistication of the headings can be tailored to particular classes. Helpful pages or sections could, for example, emerge with titles such as:

- Expressions with (a Keyword such as *keep, way*)
- Expressions in (a Situation such as *Taking people out for a meal*)
- Greetings, including leaving expressions (*I really must be going.*)
- Sentence adverbials used in writing (*In contrast, In much the same way*)
- Saying what is coming next (*What I think you should do is ...*)
- Misunderstandings (*That's not quite what I meant / said*)
- Checking common ground (*Do you know how to ...?*
  Have you ever used a ...?)
- My feelings (*I didn't know what to say. I was flabbergasted.*)
- Expressions of place (*in the middle of the room, on both sides*)

The importance of the Notebook needs emphasising. In *The Power of Reading* Stephen Krashen observed: *Sometimes a little bit of writing can make a big difference.* As usual, he emphasises the importance of input, explaining that the best way to improve your writing is not to write more, but to read more. But he also values writing because it enables learners to see and manipulate the language on the page, detached from actually using it, which helps awareness. Writing helps you to think; as he puts it *Writing can make you smarter.*

FORMATS

While our mental lexicon clearly contains many individual words (otherwise we would be unable to create any novel combinations), it also contains many multi-word items. My mental lexicon seems to contain all these:

bus   catch   cold
catch the bus   catch a cold
have breakfast   have lunch   have a snack   have supper   have a barbecue

If the information was stored only in paradigms, I could not be certain about items such as *have (a?) snack, catch a/the(?) cold.*

The natural and most efficient way of storing a large part of your mental lexicon is in multi-word chunks. We do this in L1, and anyone who has learned an L2 in an environment where it was the L1 will be aware of having done the same. It is easier to build using prefabricated bits, with comparatively little grammatical processing, than from single words with much more processing.

Earlier we suggested two major changes to the way learners record new language:

• Try to learn whole expressions containing useful words, rather than just the words, even though that seems much more difficult.

• When you record a new lexical pattern in your notebook, consciously try to think of other similar examples to those of the pattern.

If we want to encourage learners to record larger chunks, they need something more than a basic two-column vocabulary book. In a truly lexical Notebook, Formats will encourage the recording of complete Collocations and Expressions. Different formats, designed to promote the most helpful and memorable record and suited to different kinds of lexical patterns, are needed. Experiments with learners suggest that formats with 3 or 5 alternatives are large enough to be useful and small enough to be manageable. Teachers will undoubtedly wish to experiment, but it seems anything larger than those proposed here are confusing rather than helpful.

Collocation

We already know that the headword of most collocations is a noun, and that patterns are found by identifying useful collocating verbs, adjectives or both. Long lists confuse, so a limit of 5 collocates is probably best. The following boxes show the different possibilities:

Five verbs	+ noun
dismiss	
express	
meet	objection
raise	
withdraw	

Five adjectives	+ noun
bleak	
daunting	
dismal	prospect
exciting	
vague	

These may be combined into the **5 – 5 – 1** box:

Five verbs	Five adjectives	+ noun
attract	adverse	
be subject to	blunt	
deserve	constant	criticism
react to	helpful	
provoke	severe	

Sometimes other **5 – 1** or occasionally **1 – 5** formats are useful:

Five nouns	+ noun
export	
management	
labour	costs
transport	
overhead	

Verb   **+ five adverbs**

change	abruptly
	drastically
	for the worse
	significantly
	visibly

The language should be edited before being recorded, first with the teacher's guidance and later by learners themselves. The idea is not to fill the box with **any** words which **could** collocate but to selectively record only those which:

- collocate strongly or frequently
- are new **as partners of the headword**, even though learners perhaps knew the individual words before
- are useful to the individual learner's specific needs or interests.

It is not necessary to fill all the spaces in a box at one time, or indeed ever. Some words may have 5 useful verbs and three adjectives; with others you may initially put in three verbs and three adjectives, leaving the spaces for the learner to complete while doing personal reading. The formats are helpful frameworks, not constraints. Sometimes a very high percentage of all the occurrences of a particular item is covered by a comparatively small number of collocates, so teachers may wish to emphasise this by asking learners to record these items from the start while leaving space for any possible addition(s):

close the door	quietly
	gently
	properly

much	
slightly	
marginally	better
significantly	

	cold
bitterly	disappointed

Contextual opposites

EFL frequently over-simplifies and distorts by setting up crude pairs of supposed opposites: *ugly/beautiful, good/bad, old/new*, which are often unacceptable in natural examples. 'Used' language shows two features of common words such as *good, old*: firstly, they occur in strictly fixed phrases: *an old friend* (who need not be old at all), *an ugly incident, Have a good time*. These fixed items need to be recorded with L1 equivalents.

Secondly, when used in other Expressions, the opposite is contextually determined: *Sunday was a really beautiful (awful) day, This is a good (poor) result, old (young) people*. Learners should record such combinations with the contextual opposite in formats such as:

Opposite	Adjective	Noun
silly	bright	idea
cushy	challenging	job
slight	serious	hindrance

Thought-Speech bubbles

The format on page 83 is used to emphasise for learners that what we say is not the same as what we (first) think. The thought bubbles are filled with 'what you think' in the most straightforward way: *I don't like that, What? He's out*, the speech bubbles are filled with the normal polite Expressions which are the standard lexical items used to express the same ideas.

Story boxes

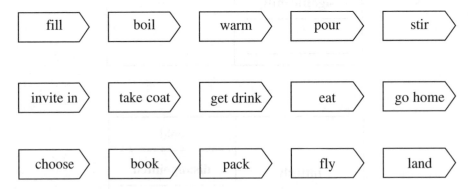

This simple format is used with an everyday situational heading such as *Buying something, Checking someone's address, Making a phone call.* Learners complete the five boxes with five verbs in the correct sequence; later the format is used to revisit the language as discussed in Chapter 3.

Cascades

Here is a type of exercise familiar to many teachers from their school stencil bank:

Give three possible responses to the following:
1. We're having a party on Saturday. Would you like to come?
2. We've run out of coffee.
3. I don't feel very well.

Studies show that the paradigm of brief spoken exchanges is not the 2-part *question-answer*, but the 3-part *initiator-response-acknowledgement:*

Have you got the time please?
> It's twenty past.
So late! I'd better be going then.

This suggests these two simple cascade formats to reflect this pattern. The teacher can direct the learners' attention to different **kinds** of response by using suitable formats. In (1) a systematic set of responses would be:

What you think   **What you say**

+	Oh, thank you. That's very kind of you.
++	Oh, thank you VERY much. That'd be really great.
–	Sorry, I'd love to but I'm (going away this weekend).

The responses are neutral positive (+), warm positive (++) and negative (–). The pragmatic opposite bears little relation to any formal grammatical opposite.

In (2) systematic responses can be developed on the basis of *I* and *you:*

I	Oh, right. I'll get some on my way home from work.
You	Oh, you'd better put it on the shopping list then.

In (3), the responses can be supportive (+) or critical (–):

+	Oh dear. Can I get you an aspirin or a glass of water?
–	Serves you right. You shouldn't have .... last night.

Familiarising learners with simple two- or three-part boxes encourages more systematic building of the lexicon by directing their attention to different **kinds** of response, rather than miscellaneous alternatives.

Collocation cascades

Learners who need an extensive lexicon in a specialised area can build it systematically by moving from collocate to collocate:

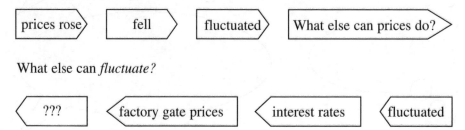

What else can *fluctuate?*

The best sequence is usually *key noun + collocating verb* which gives rise to a string of collocating verbs, each of which can in turn be used to search for nouns which collocate with it. Again, a simple sequence of boxes, either pre-printed formats or drawn by learners, can encourage the systematic development of the lexicon.

Semi-fixed Expressions in 5-formats

It is helpful to emphasise both the generative power and the restrictions of lexis for learners by asking them to record more than one example of a Semi-fixed Expression, choosing those which they record as far as possible to cover the 'frame' to reveal the pattern which underlies here. These two 5-formats give verbs related to the same situation, *Giving a Presentation*, or the notion *Reactions*:

	emphasise	
	point out	
I should	draw your attention to the fact	that ... .
	remind you	
	explain	

	surprised.
	shocked.
I hadn't heard. I'm really	upset by that.
	amazed.
	taken aback.

SUMMARY

Effective implementation of the Lexical Approach places great emphasis on noticing the basic multi-word chunks of language. Accurate noticing means teachers need a set of organising principles so that they can encourage learners to record selected language in carefully designed lexical Notebooks after studying a text, or doing the Exercises and Activities which are the subject of the next two chapters. Some learners find fixed formats helpful, while others prefer a more conventional book as discussed in Chapter 8. The key is that accurate recording – writing – of new lexis aids noticing and maximises the chance of input becoming intake.

Chapter 6

Exercises in the Lexical Approach

The emphasis on input runs through the Lexical Approach, but changes as learners' language level increases. A mature adult L1 lexicon is simply too large to have been acquired by formal vocabulary teaching. In both L1 and L2 a mature lexicon is acquired in very similar ways – firstly by large quantities of listening which is largely comprehensible, and later by similar quantities of comprehensible reading. I therefore advocate learners listening and reading as much as possible, confident that this is the best way to develop their lexicons. This alone is, however, obviously unacceptable. Learners expect to be taught and we ignore this at our peril. With a certain scepticism about the value of some productive practices, I ask what kinds are most likely to aid acquisition and at the same time satisfy the reasonable expectations of learners.

I contrast *Activities*, which are usually best done co–operatively in pairs or groups, and have both non-linguistic and linguistic outcomes, and *Exercises,* which are usually solitary, paper-based and have an exclusively linguistic focus. The Activities of the next chapter are typically for the classroom, while the exercise-types which follow are for reflective class time or homework.

No course should, however, be wholly consistent; while the teaching should be informed by explicit principles, classrooms mean complex social interactions, with many diverse individuals co-operating. Like any similar social setting, that means compromises; the introvert and extrovert, the talkative and the thoughtful, the best and worst students, all have to be accommodated and an important part of the teacher's task is to maintain a balance which accommodates everyone. This is impossible if the teacher takes a doctrinaire approach, whether it be audio-lingual, structural, communicative or lexical. A little well-chosen variety is better than dogmatic adherence to any set of principles.

EXERCISES DESIGNED ON LEXICAL PRINCIPLES

Exercises need to be carefully constructed on lexical principles. The length and sequencing of examples requires more care than is sometimes recognised. Compare these examples:

1a. If things ...., we might be able to afford to go.
1b. We might be able to afford to go, if things ....
2a. When you ...., you have to show both your passport and your

ticket.
2b. You have to show your ticket and your passport when you ....
3a. .... is more important than money.
3b. Money is not as important as ....

The (b) examples are much easier and there are sound linguistic reasons for this. English sentences usually go from known information or 'topic' to new information or 'focus'; the first words of a sentence usually tell you 'what the sentence is about'. Predicting sentence endings is part of our everyday linguistic experience; finding the beginning is usually a perverse exercise in guesswork unless the sentence is a fully Fixed Expression or one of the few exceptions such as question words. If exercises use de-contextualised gapped sentences, it is a good general rule that the gap should not occur in the topic element.

TASK

Choose two grammar points and look at the examples in a grammar practice book which your learners use. Can you imagine learners actually using the sentences they produce in the exercise? If not, can you think of more useful language, suitable for your learners, which would practise the same grammar point?

Do you agree that we have tolerated unlikely and even bizarre examples in grammar books for a long time? If so, why do you think that is so?

Consider these two examples from an exercise:

1. She told me to take a few days to .... his job offer.
        a. think   b. wonder   c. consider   d. decide

2. Call the airline to .... your reservation for the early flight.
        a. affirm   b. confirm   c. contest   d. agree

Such exercises are fairly standard, but they miss an important opportunity. The completed sentences are no more than formal exemplifications of English, rather than utterances we imagine have been used. If such de-contextualised, single-sentence exercises are to be used, it would provide more useful lexical input if modified to:

1. There's no need to decide now. You might need a couple of days to
    .... the offer.

2. Can I just make a quick call, please? I need to .... my return
    flight, just to be on the safe side.

It is the quantity and quality of the input which most influences progress, so it obviously helps if even mechanical exercises are at least based on highly probable, and correspondingly useful, examples. It is depressing that so much practice material is not only directed at comparatively unimportant grammar points, but also that it is often based on correct but highly unlikely language.

TASK

Do these two exercises, both on the topic of a healthy life-style. In each case match a word or phrase from List 1 with a word or phrase from List 2.

Exercise 1

List 1	**List 2**
1. daily	a. a balanced diet
2. short-term	b. your weight
3. regular	c. an exercise programme
4. healthy	d. routine
5. to follow	e. weight-loss
6. to control	f. targets
7. to eat	g. food
8. to set	h. benefits

Exercise 2

List 1	**List 2**
1. to balance	a. fit
2. to keep	b. your weight
3. to lose	c. carefully
4. to watch	d. your diet
5. to eat	e. weight
6. fresh	a. diet
7. daily	b. lifestyle
8. balanced	c. routine
9. healthy	d. exercise
10. regular	e. fruit

Although they look almost identical, the exercises are, in fact, very different. If such exercises are to teach rather than merely test, learners must **recognise** some answers and **deduce** others by a process of elimination, using linguistic clues, the group's shared knowledge, and a small element of plain guesswork. If there are too many examples, too many possible answers, or the items are badly ordered, the exercise is simply a rather perverse activity based mainly on guesswork. There are explicit differences in properly designed exercises such as Exercise 2 above which make them greatly superior to the apparently similar, but defective, Exercise 1:

- The collocations are strong rather than weak.
- The order of the examples has been chosen, roughly from easiest to most likely to be confused, so learners use knowledge rather than guesswork.
- There is much less ambiguity.
- Some pairs are explicitly chosen to highlight differences: *to lose weight/ to watch **your** weight, daily/regular routine/exercise*, but *daily routine* is a very strong collocation.

Teachers who devise their own materials must make principled choices which affect each item, the number and order of items and where they are used in the course. Such exercises are quite different if done after learners have used a text in which the target lexis occurred in context, rather than as arbitrary vocabulary exercises. Properly constructed exercises are designed with careful reference to lexical principles.

BASIC EXERCISE TYPES

The following are basic types of lexical exercise:

1. Identifying chunks

Self-evidently this is the single most fundamental strategy, the basis of lexical teaching and already mentioned in the earlier discussion of pedagogical chunking. Learners need to be weaned away, from the very earliest stage of L2 learning, from the *L1 word=L2 word* assumption which they naturally make. The idea of equivalents needs to be introduced early and then used frequently to discuss examples. Learners who identify chunks correctly can make better use of dictionaries, translate better, and avoid certain kinds of mistake. It encourages accurate recording in their lexical notebooks, and more importantly, storage in chunks in the mental lexicon. Correctly identifying chunks is the fundamental skill which aids both formal learning and acquisition.

2. Matching

This exercise type, familiar from grammar practice, is given a lexical focus by asking learners to match parts of Collocations, Expressions, lines of stereotypic dialogue etc. There are examples in the Sample Exercises below.

3. Completing

The traditional gap-fill is given a lexical focus by ensuring the gaps are partner-words from relatively fixed Collocations, or that gapped Expressions are relatively fixed. The gap-fill idea is extended in the Lexical Approach by a new exercise type, the double-gap, devised by my colleague Mark Powell.

Complete these dialogues by adding the missing pair of words:

   could – got   wouldn't – were   might – let

1. I'm going to leave, unless things improve very soon.
   > I .... do that if I .... you.
2. I don't know how to give him such bad news.
   > No, it .... be better if you .... me do it.
3. Can you manage?
   > Well, as a matter of fact, I ...... do with some help, if you've
   ...... a minute.

(Based on an exercise in *Business Matters, Mark Powell, LTP 1996*)

A full exercise contains more examples, but here we are concerned only with the principle. We noted earlier that *Grammar tends to becomes lexis as the event becomes more probable.* Study of used language shows that certain two-clause utterances are particularly common because certain real-world events are common – I agree but add a condition; see a problem and offer help; ask for help, but provide an 'escape'. Useful lexis, acquired as unanalysed chunks, can form the basis for grammatical generalisation, rather than result from knowledge of grammatical patterns. This means highly probable two-clause double-gapped examples are a small but significant step forward from the similar-looking traditional gap-fills of the grammar book. Full examples of double gap-fills are given as Types 29 and 30 later in this chapter.

Other completions include finishing Fixed Expressions from the first two or three words, and, occasionally, for the reasons mentioned above, providing the first words which precede a given ending of an Expression.

4. Categorising

Much lexis is patterned and the perception of pattern is an aid to memory, so it is helpful to ask learners to sort words or expressions, either according to categories they perceive, or according to some guideline suggested by the teacher. Examples include:

• Verbs or adjectives which partner one or other or both of two given nouns
• Expressions which are elements of two different dialogues
• Expressions which are more formal, or more informal
• Words or Expressions which have positive or negative connotations.

5. Sequencing

The human mind likes stories; some events have a natural, or at least a most likely, order. It may need a 30-line dialogue to contextualise fully five Expressions; this is methodologically impractical – learners do not like to be told 'only this bit matters'. Fortunately, however, Expressions frequently do not need to be fully contextualised. They are of interest precisely because they express a readily accessible pragmatic meaning, something that happens often enough to be an easily recognisable event. Most adult learners, at least those from culturally similar backgrounds, recognise those same **events** but do not know the specific Expressions which express the pragmatic meanings which they recognise are needed. Sequencing takes advantage of the learners' real-world knowledge. They are given (usually 5) Expressions or verbs and asked to put them in the most likely order.

6. Deleting

Learners often over-generalise, often by analogy with L1. Some errors can be prevented by predicting likely problems of this kind and asking learners to delete the Odd One Out. For example, which of the following words do not form a strong word partnership with the word given?

PAY	a debt	a meal	a bill	a ticket	the taxi
STRONG	language	cheese	intelligence	accent	indication

In Chapter 2 I discussed the value of deleting all the content words to reveal a discourse frame and in Chapter 3 the importance of negative evidence. Odd One Out practices are one non-threatening way of providing some of that negative evidence. As so often, light-hearted, game-like activities have an important motivation role. A sample exercise is given as Type 6 below.

Sample exercises

I now give some thirty sample exercises which have a strong lexical focus. Different types are more or less suited to particular levels, or particular kinds of lexical item; this is not intended to be an exhaustive list of suitable types, nor is it in any way implied that other traditional exercises do not also have a part to play. These samples hopefully extend the range of exercise types.

Exercise Type 1:   Polywords 1

Some pairs of words are always used in a particular order; we say *bread and butter*, not **butter and bread*. First make two-word phrases joined by and using these words and then complete the expressions below using each of the phrases once:

hither	fro	wide	low	down	now
thither	here	up	to	high	far

1. I've searched .... but I can't find my wallet anywhere.
2. I've been very busy recently because we've had to go .... to the hospital every day to see my grandmother.
3. Sit down for a moment. There's no point in just running .... , that's not getting you anywhere. Stop and think for a moment.
4. I do go to the cinema ...., but not very often.
5. I'm not waiting any longer. I want the matter sorted out ....
6. People came from .... to help.

Do you know the equivalents of the phrases in your own language? If they are two-word pairs, are they the same as or different from the English phrases? In the same order?

EXERCISE TYPE 2:   Polywords 2

Some fixed expressions are made with more than one word:
>   *by the way, on the other hand.*
Complete each of the phrases in List1 with one word from List 2. Each phrase should have the same meaning as a word in List 3, which is more common in written English.

List 1	**List 2**	**List 3**
1. by and	end	a. immediately (now)
2. every now and	run	b. occasionally
3. once in a blue	then	c. repeatedly
4. in the long	again	d. ultimately
5. in the	away	e. (very) rarely
6. straight	now	f. eventually
7. there and	moon	g. immediately (past)
8. time and	large	h. previously
9. up to	again	i. generally

EXERCISE TYPE 3:   Collocation 1

Choose from these words five which make strong word partnerships in business English with each of the verbs below:

bill	presentation	costs	invoice	discount
debt	lunch	message	expenses	deal
service	calculation	mistake	money	promise

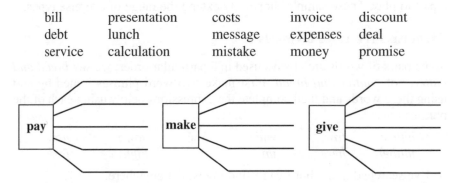

Learners can then use some of the partnerships to say or write something about their own jobs. You may also want them to record selected partnerships in their lexical notebooks in a suitable format or in individually relevant Expressions. Notice the use of the phrase **strong** word partnerships in the instruction. Most partnerships are possible; the exercise is about strong or very likely partnerships.

EXERCISE TYPE 4:   Collocation 2

Fill in column 2 with an adjective which is opposite in meaning to the adjective in Column 1 and also makes a correct collocation with the word in Column 3.

Column 1	Column 2	Column 3
helpful	....	suggestion
efficient	....	system
careful	....	piece of work
safe	....	choice
light	....	green
light	....	suitcase
light	....	rain
light	....	work

The second group in this exercise is deliberately chosen to show learners that the idea of 'opposite' is very dangerous unless confined to contextual or collocational opposites. Too often teaching over-simplifies this idea unhelpfully. After they have done the practice, ask them to find L1 equivalents for the *light* expressions.

EXERCISE TYPE 5:   Collocation 3

Find two words which make strong word partnerships with each of these nouns:

1. weather
2. operation
3. experience

4. sympathy
5. job
6. effort

Use each of these adjectives once:

a. changeable
b. conscious
c. desperate
d. emergency
e. foul
f. heartfelt

g. routine
h. sincere
i. unenviable
j. valuable
k. wide
l. worthwhile

This is a quick test, perhaps from a text read in an earlier lesson. Too many words or using nouns from the same semantic field can turn the quick test into an infuriating puzzle. Remember the warning about the principled construction of exercises: here, notice the nouns are approximately in descending order of information-content; this tends to make the first examples also the strongest collocations.

EXERCISE TYPE 6:   **Collocate deletion**

One word in each group does **not** make a strong word partnership with the word in capitals. Which is the odd one?

1. BRIGHT   idea green smell child day room
2. CLEAR   attitude need instructions alternative day conscience road
3. LIGHT   traffic work day entertainment suitcase rain green lunch
4. NEW   experience job food potatoes baby situation year
5. HIGH   season price opinion spirits house time priority
6. MAIN   point reason effect entrance speed road meal course
7. STRONG   possibility doubt smell influence views coffee language
8. SERIOUS advantage situation relationship illness crime matter

EXERCISE TYPE 7:   **Sentence anagrams**

Rearrange these to make fixed expressions with the verb *(get)*.

1. Things much can't worse get.
2. What we to there are supposed time get?
3. I you the very weren't happy impression got.
4. We've we as as the for can far moment got.
5. We be to don't anywhere seem getting.
6. What you I can get?

Which of these suggests:

flying   offering a drink   frustration   despair

Complete these with a phrase using part of the verb *(get)* and some other words:

7. Oh dear. Is that the time? It's ....
8. I don't .... of the story.
9. I think we .... across the fact that we were disappointed.
10. So what? I don't see what you're ....
11. It helps if you can speak the language, but you can .... without it.
12. I've been working too hard. I need to .... for a while.

Are you the sort of person who likes to get involved in lots of activities?
Do you get on well with other people?
What sort of people do you find it difficult to get along with?

Complete one or more of these with things which are true for you:
I get upset when I hear/think about/see ...
I get very impatient if I ...
I get a lot of pleasure out of ...

EXERCISE TYPE 8:   Fixed Expressions

There is one word wrong in each of these expressions. Correct it. Then write the equivalent of the expression in your own language.

1. It's up with you.
2. Look at it from my line of view.
3. It never touched my mind.
4. Could you hold in a moment, please.
5. Have your time – there's no hurry.
6. Sorry, I didn't take that. Could you repeat it, please?

Learners must notice the exact words of a Fixed Expression. This simple exercise can be used to follow up watching a video or hearing or reading a dialogue. Fixed Expressions are usually only three to seven words long, but even a small mistake can change the meaning or make the expression meaningless. Accuracy matters here, and always for the same reason – a lexical mistake can hinder effective communication, unlike a grammar mistake which rarely does.

EXERCISE TYPE 9:   Sentence heads

The first part of each sentence in List 1 can be completed with *all* the examples in one of the groups of endings given in List 2. Match the first parts with the endings.

List 1	**List 2**
1. I'm wondering	a. to concentrate. to understand it but I can't. to remember where I put them.
2. I'm trying	b. quite pleased with myself. a bit off colour. more confident than I did.
3. I'm feeling	c. what I can about it. nothing yet! the best I can.
4. I'm doing	d. what we can do about it. if it will make any difference. if anyone else knows yet.

Can you think of a situation where you would say each of the twelve sentences? Choose one of them and write a short dialogue so that one of the people in the dialogue says **exactly** the sentence you have chosen.

Can you find L1 equivalents for (some or all) of the examples?

EXERCISE TYPE 10:   Semi-fixed Expressions with intensifiers

Put the word(s) in brackets, which make the expression stronger, in the right place(s), then say the expressions aloud, paying attention to exactly *how* you say them. Make them sound strong.

1. It's obvious something's gone wrong. (quite)
2. There's no chance of me changing my mind. (absolutely)
3. It's too late to do anything about it now. (far)
4. I was disappointed but there was nothing I could do about it. (bitterly, absolutely)
5. I was grateful for their help. (really, all)
6. I was annoyed that he was late. (really, so)

Expressing emotion in L2 is difficult, particularly perhaps in English where it is shown more by how you say things than by the words themselves. Many Expressions contain intensifiers such as *very, really, extremely* and although the sentence is possible without them, the strong version represents the most useful expression. This exercise gives learners a way of extending the emotional range of what they can say.

Notice the examples tend to be Semi-fixed: *I was (really) [annoyed] that [...]*, and that strong collocations such as *bitterly disappointed* are characteristic of these stronger expressions. Encourage learners to record examples with their stress patterns in their lexical notebooks, emphasising their value for showing how you feel.

EXERCISE TYPE 11:   Semi-fixed Expressions with softeners

Follow a similar procedure to the previous exercise but with Expressions which typically contain a word which softens the effect:

1. I still can't believe it. (quite)
2. I was upset when they told me. (a bit)
3. I was upset because I'd expected to do better than that. (rather, a bit).

Everyone tends to talk more about his or her own feelings and experiences, but these are often presented in softened or 'negotiable' form. This exercise deliberately involves many expressions beginning *I ...*, because it exploits lexical rather than grammatical patterning.

EXERCISE TYPE 12:   Softeners

Complete the responses in these dialogues using these words:

   pretend   say   admit   point   things   ways

1. I didn't really enjoy that.
   > It wasn't very exciting, I have to ....
2. It was alright, but I couldn't hear the words.
   > No, the sound wasn't very good, I'm sorry to ....
3. It's very bad news, isn't it?
   > I thought so at first, but I think it might turn out to be for the best in many ....
4. Do you think we'll be there by six o'clock?
   > I doubt it. Not the way .... are going.
5. That was one of the worst meals I've ever had.
   > It was pretty awful, there's no .... in denying it.
6. So the whole thing was a bit of a disaster, then?
   > Well, it didn't turn out as I expected and I can't .... it did.

Now underline the expressions in the responses which help to make the answer softer, and easier for the other person to accept.

The emphasis is on ensuring that the language of the exercise itself forms useful lexical input. Part of that, as in many of the Exercises proposed here, involves a greater emphasis on examples based on situationally evocative spoken language.

EXERCISE TYPE 13:   Related verbs

Complete the following with the appropriate form of *speak, talk, say, tell.*

1. Did you enjoy your trip? You must .... us all about it.
2. If I may .... so, that doesn't sound a very good idea to me.
3. She gets very lonely since her husband died. She has nobody to .... to, you see.
4. I can't .... for anyone else, but I think it's a good idea.
5. If you think it would help, you know you can .... to me about it at any time.
6. It's still a secret, you know. I hope you didn't .... anything to anybody.
7. Could you .... me the time, please.
8. He .... about football all the time. It gets very boring.
9. Is the baby .... yet?
10. Shh. Don't .... We don't want to wake the baby.

The real definition of a word is a combination of its referential meaning and its collocation field. It is the use of similar words in familiar expressions which helps distinguish one from the other(s). Take words with similar meaning, and make a list of Expressions in which one of the words is used. It is on the basis of an internalisation of the contrasts implied by the many Semi-fixed Expressions which native speakers know that they build up a profile of how these apparently similar verbs are used. Learners need a similar experience based on both natural exposure and the guided exposure of the classroom. It may be argued that this type of exercise creates confusion, but the confusion is inevitable, and is better addressed in the classroom rather than leaving learners to develop understanding unaided. Ask learners to complete the expressions, and later record complete Expressions with equivalents in their lexical notebooks.

EXERCISE TYPE 14:   Probable Expressions with slots

Which word in each group means something different from all the others?

1. You look a bit ....
    worried   under pressure   stressed   anxious   off colour
2. I've just had a bit of very .... news.
    exciting   disappointing   good   encouraging   welcome
3. I've .... it, but I haven't had a chance to read it properly yet.
    looked through   examined   glanced at
    flicked through   had a quick look at
4. .... Getting upset isn't going to help.
    Calm down!   Take it easy!
    Keep your hair on!   Pay attention!

The examples are carefully chosen to be probable utterances with useful collocates. Requiring the collocations to fit short contexts is better than simply matching de-contextualised words.

EXERCISE TYPE 15:   Sorting Expressions

Put each of the following into one of these groups:

a. Things which show no special emotion.
b. Things which show you are annoyed or upset.

1. I'm sure I told you last week.
2. I did tell you last week, I'm sure.
3. I don't think that's a very good idea.
4. I do not think that's a very good idea.
5. That was a bit unnecessary, wasn't it?
6. That was so unnecessary.
7. I think you should have told her.
8. I do think you should have told her.

Can you find a pattern which marks the emotion?

This kind of discovery work, in which the learners hypothesise on the basis of carefully chosen, often contrasting, examples, resembles those advocated by Dave and Jane Willis, David Brazil and Jonathan Marks at various points in this book. In the exercise above, there is one stress more in the emotion-carrying examples. All the examples are lexical items.

EXERCISE TYPE 16:   Phonological agreement

Often we agree without saying *I agree*. Here is a useful and common way of agreeing, using the way you say something:

It was a good finish.
>It WAS a good finish.

Agree with these in a similar way:

1. This is good.
2. (S)he's bright.
3. It was expensive.
4. It must be tomorrow.
5. They've earned a rest.

6. This tastes excellent.
7. We knew it was a problem.
8. We deserve our success.
9. We need to hurry.
10. We missed the opportunity.

EXERCISE TYPE 17:   Fixed Expressions with a given stress pattern

How many of the following do you know? Can you give equivalents in your own language? Check any you are not sure about in your dictionary. Say each one using the same pattern.

1. More haste, less speed.
2. First come, first served.
3. Waste not, want not.

4. Easy come, easy go.
5. Nothing ventured, nothing gained.
6. Out of sight, out of mind.

Which would you say in these situations?

a. You put a jar which is very nearly empty back in the fridge.
b. Someone has hurried, but forgotten something so has to go back.
c. You are doing something which might turn out well, but might not.

The expressions are Fixed. Exploiting the similarity of stress pattern makes them easier to recall. Lexis and 'pronunciation' meet to help learners store things more effectively in their phrasal lexicons.

EXERCISE TYPE 18:   Extending a sound pattern

Complete each expression in List 1 with an expression in List 2:

List 1

1. I'll get back to you
2. We'll get there
3. This is top quality, it's
4. The meeting's still on
5. You can stay
6. There's no other explanation, it's

List 2

a. as long as you like.
b. as good as you'll find.
c. as far as I know.
d. as clear as can be.
e. as fast as we can.
f. as soon as I know.

Say the expressions in List 2 using the same stress pattern: as **fast** as I **can.**

Now say these. These have a *similar* pattern, but it is not *exactly* the same:

   7. It's as good as new.
   8. It was as clear as a bell.
   9. I'm as sure as I can be.
10. Try to park as near as you can get.
11. I tried as hard as I know how.
12. They did it as well as they could.
13. Don't worry. I'll let you know as soon as I hear myself.
14. It's beautiful – as fresh as the day it was painted.

The lexical focus comes from choosing only those grammatically similar expressions which carry the same stress pattern, so the chunks share lexical, grammatical **and** phonological features. When learners have mastered the basic stress pattern, it is helpful to vary it slightly.

These slight variations are similar to the variations we find in good poetry, rather than doggerel. Following a pattern rigidly constrains; using a basic pattern, and following it flexibly, is the basis of any effective, fluent language use. Lexis is neither totally random nor rigidly structured; it is organised. Here the pattern which is initially fixed is the **basis** for later creative use.

The following four exercise types were contributed by Jonathan Marks and make more concrete some of the ways he is using the Lexical Approach in his classes and which he discusses in detail in Chapter 8.

EXERCISE TYPE 19:   Discriminating listening

Your teacher will read some of these. Write the numbers of the ones you hear.

   1. I had no idea they'd gone.
   2. I had no idea, they'd gone.
   3. I don't know.
   4. I don't, no.
   5. I don't know John.
   6. I don't know, John.
   7. Don't leave it.
   8. Don't, leave it.
   9. I'm afraid I can't.
10. I'm afraid, I can't.
11. No, she was sitting by the fire, apparently asleep.
12. No, she was sitting by the fire, apparently, asleep.
13. Why is she here?
14. Why, is she here?
15. I'm sorry I can't come.
16. I'm sorry, I can't come.

From the above list, choose the best answer for each of the following:

   a. But surely you knew they'd gone?
   b. You don't know this area, do you?
   c. Why don't you ask John?
   d. I'll take this into the kitchen for you.
   e. Can you tell me when it'll be ready?
   f. Did you see her?
   g. You can ask her yourself.
   h. We're looking forward to seeing you next week.

Make two-line dialogues, using as second lines the sentences you haven't already used.

The examples clearly demonstrate the way in which lexical and phonological chunking are important to meaning, and to how we hear and store chunks.

EXERCISE TYPE 20:   Similar stress patterns

Match each phrase from List 1 with a phrase from List 2 with the same stress pattern.

List 1

1. how do you do
2. by the way
3. let's face it
4. nice to meet you
5. on the tip of my tongue
6. you ought to have been there

List 2

a. not at all
b. I wanted to tell you
c. did you really?
d. to a certain extent
e. don't know it
f. out of the blue

EXERCISE TYPE 21:   The sound shape of a chunk

Match each of these phrases with its stress pattern:

1. away from it all
2. at the crack of dawn
3. there was nothing for it
4. an absolute nightmare
5. it seemed to take forever
6. in the first place

a. oOooOo
b. oOooo
c. oOoooOo
d. ooOoOo
e. ooOo
f. ooOoO

EXERCISE TYPE 22:   Matching chunks

Make sentences by adding an item from List 2 with a low rising intonation to an item from List 1.

List 1	List 2
1. I don't suppose you've finished that article,	a. I'm pleased to say.
2. Yes, everything's OK,	b. most nights.
3. I'm home by half seven	c. can you?
4. I have,	d. as a matter of fact.
5. You often have to work late,	e. have you?
6. Well I can't see it,	f. according to the map.
7. Have you heard from the hospital	g. recently?
8. It should be here,	h. don't you?

Put your sentences together to make four two-line dialogues.

Commenting on the above exercises and on the importance of supra-segmental pronunciation in general, Jonathan comments: *Every lesson is a pronunciation lesson. Whatever the focus of the exercise, pay attention not just to **what** is said, but also to **how** it is said.* As our understanding of lexis develops, one great bonus is the way pronunciation is integrated into teaching in a way which focuses on natural language use and the creation of meaning.

EXERCISE TYPE 23:   Grammaticalisation

Make full tactful questions which you could ask to establish contact with someone you hope to do business with, using the following:

1. What / your areas / responsibility?
2. Happy / offer?
3. Best way / contact you?
4. How soon / make a decision?

Language consists of grammaticalised lexis. Lexis is recalled, prefabricated from memory; grammar requires processing. Very often the quickest way to help low-level ESP learners is to give them certain key words, and let them concentrate on grammaticalising. We saw earlier in this chapter that research suggests that, instead of doing a new exercise the next day, you should repeat the same one; learners improve by repeating the task because they have more processing capacity available the second time.

EXERCISE TYPE 24:   Modalisation 1

General statements about the world are often made using this pattern:

Older people tend to think everything is getting worse.
Young people tend to have a lot more money than I had when I was young.

(A kind of) people tend to .... (in this situation).

Even quite a strong opinion sounds more open, and so more friendly, if you use this pattern.

Say what you think about:

1. Children and television
2. Teenagers and mopeds
3. People who have just learned to drive *(New drivers...)*
4. Politicians

Use a similar pattern to talk without being too definite about yourself. Say something about:

5. Your typical Sunday
6. What you eat
7. What you like to wear
8. Yourself (*I tend to be a fairly ... sort of person*)

EXERCISE TYPE 25:   Modalisation 2

Use some of these to make the opinions less definite, certain or general.

might	perhaps	could be
tend to	look(s) as if	

1. People take their holidays in July and August. (Not completely true)
   People tend to take their holidays in July and August.
2. That's the best plan. (I estimate)
3. You're right. (I guess)
4. It's going to rain. (By the appearance of the sky)
5. They won't mind.
6. I agree. (With some slight reservations)
7. I'll be there. (Well, I haven't actually decided yet)
8. They must be stuck in a traffic jam.
   (That's the best explanation I can think of)

Notice another use of *tend to* in this useful response:
It looks to me as if things are getting worse.
> I tend to agree, but ...

The necessity of practising this kind of language is taken up again later (see page 178). Language is a powerful means of self-expression, a way of showing yourself to the world. Few adults are content to ask questions and state facts, without the ability to show more of what they think, how they feel and who they are.

EXERCISE TYPE 26: Topicalisation

The first words of most sentences tell you 'what the sentence is about'. Sometimes to make the message clearer, the speaker highlights or stresses some information by putting it at the end of the sentence:

Everyone was dressed in a very amusing way.
What amused me was the way everyone was dressed.

Do the same with these:

1. The price surprised me.
2. The acting impressed me.
3. Their lack of consideration annoyed me.
4. The fantastic sports facilities interested me.
5. The way they treated the children shocked me.
6. Nobody apologised, which was disappointing.
7. The thought they had given to the present was pleasing.
8. The way everybody seemed to agree was fascinating.

You can make those stronger like this:
What was most surprising was the price.

Questions can be given greater focus in a similar way:

How much did it cost?
What I want to know is how much it cost.
How long was it going to take?
What I was interested in was how long it was going to take.

EXERCISE TYPE 27: De-lexicalised word

Complete each of these with *point, a point, the point, points.*

1. I don't see .... of waiting any longer.
2. I'm sorry but you've completely missed .... of what I was saying.
3. Can you make .... of checking the date with her, please?
4. You've got............... there. I didn't think of that.
5. Let me give an example to illustrate ....
7. OK, it's expensive but that is beside.............. – we need a new one.
8. Spelling is not my strong ....
9. We're nearing .... where it will be too late to call it off.
10. Up to ...., I agree with you. But there are several important .... which I think you are overlooking.
11. The course is getting more difficult. I'm on .... of giving up.
12. It was an awful experience. At one ...., I thought I was going to die.

What, for you, is the main point in learning English? What are the strongest and weakest points about your English?

EXERCISE TYPE 28:   De-lexicalised verb

One of the best ways to make your spoken English more natural is to learn some of the expressions made with *the verb (get)*. This can be more useful than learning unusual new words. Complete each of the following with an expression containing *get*. Take care to use the correct form of the verb.

1. I woke up at 2 o'clock last night and I just couldn't ....
2. I needed to earn some money, so I had to .... during the summer holidays.
3. It's Jane's birthday on Friday. Don't you think we ought to .... for her?
4. He doesn't look at all well. We'd better ....
5. Right – let's .... We don't want this to take all day.
6. I really .... when I think how little the government does to help.
7. Get the number 8 bus, and .... at Churchill Square.
8. I hate getting up early, but during this course I have to. I suppose it won't be so bad once I ....

Which word does not form a strong partnership with **get**?

frustrated	annoyed	amused	better	tired	married
asleep	well-paid	lazy	anxious	upset	pregnant

Which of the correct word partnerships sound strange if you add *very?*

Complete each of these with the correct part of the verb *get*. Then underline all the expressions that contain *get*. Make sure you underline complete expressions.

1. When I .... my exam results, they weren't very good and I .... quite upset, and my father .... annoyed because he thought I hadn't done enough work. My mother just said, "Well, you'll soon .... over it. You'll just have to .... a job." At least I .... a chance to earn some money before I'm 23! If I'd .... to university, I might have .... better qualifications but I'm not sure I'd have .... through the course. I've .... lots of interests, but studying hard isn't one of them!

2. Do you think you could .... me an aspirin please? I think I've .... a cold coming on. I've certainly .... a terrible headache. I think I'd better .... home and .... to bed as quickly as possible.

3. We've ...... a lot to do at the meeting tomorrow, so we'd better .... the early train and then .... a taxi straight to the office. If we .... there by nine we can .... started by ten past, and really .... something done.

EXERCISE TYPE 29: Double-gapping – modals

Complete the examples with one of these pairs of words:

shouldn't + can't	can't + should	wouldn't + were
won't + might	can + don't	don't + won't

1. I'm just going to go straight in and say what I think.
   > I . . . do that, if I . . . you.
2. It looks as though they are in a very difficult situation.
   > Yes, but we . . . do anything to help even if we . . . .
3. It's very difficult to know what to do next.
   > Well, if we . . . do something, we . . . make any progress at all.
4. It's not really anything to do with us.
   > Perhaps not, but if we . . . help, why . . .we?
5. So when will you let me know?
   > Well, I . . . see you tomorrow, but I . . . ring you.
6. I . . . really tell you this, but I just . . . keep it to myself.

The only two-clause utterances regularly taught in EFL are conditionals, but many situations where the language is highly lexicalised involve two ideas such as *offer + condition, rule + qualification* etc. Double-gapping allows much more of the situationally evocative language which is so important as input. It is common with modal auxiliaries, as here, and other common verbs as in the next example.

EXERCISE TYPE 30: Double-gapping – modal and common verbs

Complete these dialogues with one of these pairs of words:

might + promise	*might + let*	*might + doubt*
should + do	*should + need*	*should + knew*

1. Do you think it will do any good?
   > It . . . help, but I . . . it.
2. I just don't know how to tell him.
   > It . . . be better if you . . . me do it.
3. I'll see you there tomorrow, then.
   > I . . . be there, but I can't . . . .
4. Why didn't you tell me as soon as you knew?
   > I . . . have told you, but I . . . you'd be upset.
5. Do you think it's all right to take pictures here?
   > I . . . think so, but you . . . to ask.
6. Do you think we need to ask first?
   > I suppose we . . . , but we never . . . .

SUMMARY

It is perhaps necessary to repeat that I am not claiming that many of the exercises in this chapter are original, nor that the list is more than a small number of possible lexical exercise types. On the contrary, many of those listed will certainly be familiar to readers already, but similar-**looking** exercises may not have the carefully selected lexical focus which is the hallmark of the Exercises discussed here. It is the consistent application of lexical, rather than the still dominant norm of structural principles, which is the novelty. Similar considerations apply to the Activities discussed in the next chapter.

Chapter 7

Adapting Activities in the Lexical Approach

ADAPTING ACTIVITIES TO PROVIDE A LEXICAL FOCUS

The Lexical Approach does not represent a revolution. It provides principles for re-thinking many familiar activities and techniques, and a new way of looking at the content of courses. As Henry Widdowson has observed, if you claim your teaching is eclectic, and you cannot state the principles of your eclecticism, you are not eclectic, merely confused. Many of the Activities in this chapter will be well-known to teachers already; what may be new is the consistent attention to ensuring each Activity has a carefully selected lexical focus. Many other techniques and activities can easily be similarly adapted to give them a lexical focus. Jigsaw reading, where a text is chopped into pieces and the students' task is to re-construct it, is a simple example: what the Lexical Approach provides is a principled way of deciding where the breaks should be made. Similarly, a lexical perspective provides a principled way of:

• gapping a text
• stopping in pause reading
• selecting lines for deletion/translation in dialogue.

The fundamental principle is that Activities should be designed to encourage noticing of chunks. This will often be coupled with encouraging learners to record new language in their lexical notebooks in ways which emphasise Collocation, Fixed Expressions, patterned Expressions with slots, all of which, in their turn, help learners build their phrasal lexicons.

SAMPLE ACTIVITIES

ACTIVITY 1:   Text Search 1

Ask learners to underline chunks they can find in a text. It helps to give them different kinds of chunks to look for, such as:
• Completely Fixed Expressions
• *Adjective + Noun* Collocations
• Expressions with the verb (*call*)
• Expressions which show the discoursal meaning of the next sentence/paragraph.

They could mark different kinds of chunk in different colours. The choice of target chunks, and the language you use to direct the learners' attention to that kind of chunk depends on their level, the type of text and the language you think most useful for those particular learners. Do not try to squeeze the text dry; an important feature of the Lexical Approach is teachers and learners getting used to using texts, some of which may be 'too difficult' for them to read fully. This means teachers and learners feeling comfortable with the idea of **using** a text to take something useful from it without worrying about parts of the text which they do not understand.

As they complete the task, alone or in small groups, mark a copy yourself on an overhead transparency of the text. When learners have marked their own texts, let them compare their texts with other groups, and then with your copy.

Lexical Focus One focus is self-evident, but note that this activity is also intended to help **you** to see what the learners think are chunks. If they are looking at the text in unhelpful ways, their 'mistakes' provide you with essential feedback. The task should be presented in this light – as a way of exploring the text together – not as 'you do an exercise and I'll show you the correct answer'.

ACTIVITY 2:   Text Search 2

Distribute copies of the sheet on page 110 having completed it with verbs or headword nouns in collocations taken from the text. Put the word in the appropriate column to indicate the type of collocation the learners are looking for. Try to include at least these different types: adjective-noun (*strong possibility*), noun-noun (*portrait painting*), verb-noun (*take the opportunity to*), verb-adjective-noun (*embrace the latest technology*), verb-noun-noun (*raise your blood pressure*), verb-adverb (*fail miserably*).

Lexical Focus Learners understand Collocations (and the fact that certain sentences of English have a special status as mentioned in Chapter 2) if they are actively taught these ideas early in their course.

ACTIVITY 3:   Find the noun, find the collocate

Learners read or look through a text quickly, with a time limit which ensures that they **know** they cannot even try to read the text word-for-word. As they read, they underline every noun they notice. They then look through the text again without time pressure, actively searching for each noun which has a collocating verb in front of it, though perhaps not immediately next to the noun. They underline these partner verbs in a different colour.

Learners call out *verb + noun* partnerships, which, if correct, you record on a transparency. With books closed, the whole class or small groups use the collocations as a basis to try to recall and summarise the main content of the text. At the end of the lesson, do Activity 10, and ask learners to record some of the most useful collocations in their lexical notebooks. Revisit the language a few days later as suggested in Chapter 3.

Lexical Focus The whole activity reminds learners of the importance of

The following business words appear in the text / broadcast in the order in which they are listed. How many of their word partners can you find in just . . . . minutes?

1.		
2.		
3.		
4.		
5.		
6.		
7.		
8.		
9.		
10.		
11.		
12.		
13.		
14.		
15.		
16.		
17.		
18.		

Now work with a partner. Cover up some of the boxes above. Your partner should try to complete the phrase.

seeing, noticing and recording words together with the other words with which they occur. *Verb + noun* partnerships are among the most useful in the lexicon.

ACTIVITY 4:   **Green Cross Code**

An extension to the above is suggested in an article by Philip Brown in *Modern English Teacher (November 1994).* He advocates a formula similar to that used to teach road safety to children in Britain called The Green Cross Code:
When you see a word, even a word with which you are familiar, STOP, LOOK LEFT, LOOK RIGHT, LOOK LEFT AGAIN, AND, WHEN SATISFIED, PROCEED.

Lexical Focus Encourages learners to look actively at the language environment in which they have met a new or interesting word, but also a familiar word where they may only be familiar with some of its collocates. This helps them to make maximum use of language they meet.

ACTIVITY 5:   **Pronoun search**

Pronouns usually replace previously mentioned nouns or noun phrases ('usually' because there are also dummy pronouns: *It's going to rain*, or pronouns which stand for a very long stretch of text). This means texts usually contain large numbers of concealed collocations which are not obvious to learners. Ask learners to look again through a text you have already used in your usual way and identify the antecedent noun for each pronoun in all, or a section, of the text. Encourage learners to record useful collocations in their lexical notebooks.

Here are two examples of how a collocation may be concealed:

Did you remember to bring my book back?
> Sorry, I haven't quite finished it [your book] yet. I promise I'll bring it [your book] in tomorrow.

The Government is considering an overhaul of the rules for the payment of allowances to single mothers. "They [the rules] need to be tightened, and brought into line with other similar benefits," said a government spokesman.

Worth recording: *to finish a book, to tighten rules, to bring into line with*

Lexical Focus Firstly learners develop greater awareness of (hidden) collocation which will help them with reading generally and help turn input into intake. Secondly, the teacher has an important role in developing learners' sensitivity to what is, and is not, worth recording. In the above example you can *bring [almost anything] in*, so that is not worth recording.

ACTIVITY 6:   **Collocate search**

Use small extracts of text, such as one of the Concordances published by Cobuild, to explore the possible environments of a word more fully. George Woolard has found samples of the Cobuild data (free on the internet at the moment of writing this) useful. In a few moments, for example, one of his classes gathered the following collocates of the key word *criticism: attracted, take, come in for, face, draw, been the subject of, repeated, sharp, harsh.*

Providing you use the text by actively searching rather than browsing, I have been surprised at the usefulness of articles in the *Encarta Encyclopaedia,* which arrived as part of the 'free' software with my computer; simply search for the word (usually noun) for which you want to know the collocates by using the 'Find' and 'Word Search' instructions.

Lexical Focus You have to learn to ignore a lot of what comes up on screen and search for specific information, such as *What other collocates of ... can I find?* Reference texts are often lexically, and therefore collocationally, rich.

ACTIVITY 7:   **Examine a word**

This is a more comprehensive version of the previous activities. When a word is selected by the teacher as worthy of special attention, its grammar is examined carefully. Learners do some or all of the following:

• Look at its collocates in the original text.

• Compare the text use with the example sentences in one or more English/English dictionaries. This may produce examples which are similar or different, or with some words, mean learners find new meanings or patterns for the word.

• Examine some concordance lines from a printed concordance, similar material available by internet, or prepared by the teacher using a mini-concordance program.

In each of these cases, it is important not to overwhelm learners with too much data. Teachers who have experimented find 8 concordance lines enough for lower intermediate learners, and a maximum of about 20/30 enough for even university students. In the case of the latter, the teacher may need to choose the most revealing lines from the larger set available directly from a concordance program.

For readers unfamiliar with concordances, my colleague Heinz Ribisch used the material below, which he had selected from many more lines available from his concordance program, to explore the words *measures* and *extent* with his students.

Record carefully chosen examples in lexical notebooks.

```
view that, whatever broader measures were taken to deal
he past decade for concrete measures to protect the rec
t to 'legal" discriminatory measures _ for the most par
ts and threatened draconian measures to root out corrup
y in support of the economy measures so that they could
as come when even emergency measures may be necessary i
i co-operate 'to adopt firm measures to prevent such re
ed at the emphasis on legal measures and discouragement
 a consensus on a series of measures that two years agc
take economic and political measures to achieve their i
ic environmental protection measures _ is the best the
 wide variety of responsive measures, emanating from bc
i that only normal security measures had been taken. <p
tly as a result of 'serious measures" by the authoritie
jovernment will take severe measures against those resp
parliament approved special measures allowing the milit
nsport officials that stern measures would be taken if
first time Peking has taken measures to express its dis
```

```
selves to it, but the actual extent of the immunity is
ternational practice". To an extent, the anger is to be
he possessor. The nature and extent of the control and
t that there was an enormous extent of subterranean wrc
leaders well before the full extent of the damage was i
 probably to an even greater extent _ Hitler's image wa
he case before, to a growing extent of the person of ti
bing" _ escalated rapidly in extent and ferocity. A toi
urbance so as to clarify its extent and its limitations
es were, however, to a large extent already introduced
 patient throughout. To some extent this is frustratinc
 assault or battery. To that extent there may be said i
acts of violence. So to what extent is juvenile violenc
```

Lexical Focus Teachers need confidence to recognise that time spent on a single word like this is not wasted, providing the words given this extended treatment have been carefully selected. The example sentences of modern dictionaries constitute excellent input, and encouraging learners to observe carefully, hypothesise, discuss and record lies at the heart of a discriminating expansion of learners' lexicons.

ACTIVITY 8:   Word Choice

Choose two confusable words such as *say/tell, lend/borrow* and print half a dozen concordance lines for each word mixed up, with the word itself omitted (concordance programs usually do this at a single keystroke). Use the mixed lines for discussion of the difference in the way the two words are used.

Lexical Focus The definition of a word is partly determined by its collocational field. This activity highlights possible confusion, particularly for false friends.

ACTIVITY 9:   **Paragraph headings**

Learners are given a text of 6-10 paragraphs together with a set of possible paragraph headings. They skim the text quickly, and then match the headings to the paragraphs.

Lexical Focus If learners only experience word-by-word reading in class, they soon regard that as the only way to 'read'. They need to be actively taught other, more global and purposive ways of using text. Paragraph headings are typically three- or four-word summaries of the content. In other words, they are lexically dense.

ACTIVITY 10:   **Phrase matching**

After reading a text learners are given a set of incomplete phrases taken from the text and asked to complete them, either by scanning the text again, or by matching from a list of alternatives. Here is an example:

> *Recently we decided to spend a few days away from it all in a cottage in the country. We set off at the crack of dawn to avoid getting stuck in a traffic jam on the motorway. Everything was going smoothly, and we were making excellent progress until I suddenly realised I had left the keys of the cottage at home. There was nothing for it but to turn round and collect them. The return trip was an absolute nightmare. We crawled along at a snail's pace; it seemed to take forever, and all because I hadn't checked everything properly in the first place. I was very cross with myself. Then there was an accident – a lorry had skidded right across all three lanes. That was the last thing we needed – more delay. Instead of getting away from it all, we were stuck in the middle of it all.*

to go	to check	to make
the crack	the return	the last
away from it	at a snail's	in the first

1. .... place   4. .... thing we needed   7. .... progress
2. .... all   5. .... of dawn   8. .... pace
3. .... smoothly   6. .... trip   9. .... properly

Lexical Focus Expressions like these can rarely be translated word-for-word, so it is often appropriate to direct learners' attention to L1 equivalents for some of them.

The next eight Activities focus on one of the key types of lexical item. Often collocation is highlighted rather than the individual words or grammatical patterns which are often the focus in the familiar versions of similar activities.

ACTIVITY 11:   Spaghetti matching

Collocations are arranged randomly on the page, and the partner-words joined by spaghetti thus:

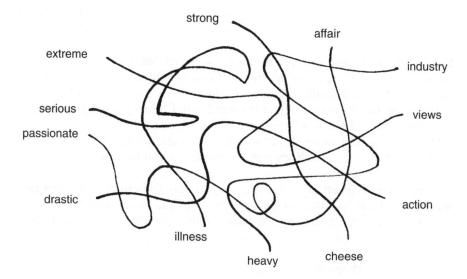

Learners find the pairs. This is basically a very simple matching exercise, but self-correcting and visually more interesting. Learners could make their own puzzles.

Lexical Focus It is a simple matter of highlighting collocation rather than, for example, L1/L2 translations, or synonymy, as has been the standard use of such puzzles.

ACTIVITY 12:   Collocation transparencies

During the lesson write useful partnerships as they occur in a clear two-column format on a transparency. At the end of the lesson show the transparency with one or other column covered and ask learners to recall, and perhaps record in their Notebooks, the whole collocation. We earlier discussed the value of revisiting new lexis; in later lessons use one or other column of the transparency for a couple of minutes to revise.

Lexical Focus Constant emphasis with very short activities on the fact that the individual word is not the basic unit of language.

ACTIVITY 13:   Word dominoes 1

Prepare an A4 blank sheet with about 20 domino shapes. Keep copies of the sheet on your desk. Use a smaller number of dominoes, perhaps 10/12 for a lower level class, and the full set for more advanced classes. The first domino has a blank left-hand half and the last has a blank right-hand half.

| First | Most | Last |

These two should be used even if you use less than the full set, as they help the activity by making clear the first and last dominoes. Write collocations such as *verb + noun* on the dominoes, putting the verb on the right-hand half and the noun partner on a different left-hand half. Collect partnerships as they occur in class, perhaps from the text which is being studied.
Later, cut up one or more sets of the dominoes and let learners working in small groups revisit the collocations by building a domino chain.

Lexical Focus The activity is lexical, but you may want to extend it to a full realisation of the fact that language consists of grammaticalised lexis, not lexicalised grammar, by asking groups to use the collocation chain to produce a summary of the text.

ACTIVITY 14:   Word dominoes 2

Lexical dominoes can also be played with *adjective + noun* cards. The words may be chosen from a field such as the language for a particular job, or a more linguistically generative game by using a number of de-lexicalised words, mostly verbs.

ACTIVITY 15:   Collocation Dictation 1

Prepare a sheet with between 12 and 20 verbs generously spaced in two columns:

to make a	to start a .....
to join	to lose...
to take	to arrange a ...

Distribute a copy of the sheet to learners, working individually or in small groups. Read a sequence of nouns, one by one with pauses long enough for learners to write down the noun beside a verb with which they think it forms a strong partnership. In the whole class, compare answers and ensure learners keep a correct record or transfer useful partnerships to their Notebooks.

Alternatively, follow the procedure above, but instead of individual nouns dictate full sentences, each of which contains a fully-contextualised example of one of the collocations. Learners complete the sheets as before. In the whole class, ask learners to recall the whole expressions, using the partnerships they have recorded as clues.

Lexical Focus Choose strong collocations which are part of useful Expressions.

ACTIVITY 16:   Explore a de-lexicalised word

Prepare a sheet similar to that on page 118, taking examples from an up-to-date corpus-based dictionary.

Lexical Focus It makes no sense to ask if a word like *just* (or *way, point, thing*) is known. Learners need to return to such words regularly until they have built a phrasal lexicon of Expressions containing the word. Often there are sub-patterns to which learners' attention can usefully be drawn.

ACTIVITY 17:   Common words

Explain the importance of the de-lexicalised verbs and common words. Use the excellent examples of a good dictionary to write short contextualised examples of a particular word, then use the text for key-word dictation where learners write down only the key verb/word expression.

You could give 2/3 examples of, for example, *have, put* or *take* in each of a series of lessons. When learners have a number of expressions on their sheet, distribute blank copies of the formats discussed in Chapter 3, and use some class time to ask learners to re-organise and re-record the examples so that patterns begin to emerge.

ACTIVITY 18:   Happy Families

Prepare several sets of cards: a set with a useful adjective on each card; a set with a useful verb on each card; a larger set with a noun on each card. The verb and adjective sets should contain relatively de-lexicalised words with large collocational ranges. These cards can be regularly re-used. Sets to copy are on pages 119/120.

Although you may want to use a 'standard' set of noun cards, it is better to prepare a set containing recently acquired words, perhaps as a follow-up to a text studied in a recent lesson. Learners take turns to ask: *Have you got a (verb) that goes with (accident)? / Have you got a noun that follows (play)?* They collect matched pairs (collocations) and play till the cards are exhausted or no more matches can be made.

Lexical Focus This activity increases the value learners get from language

Keyword: just

Match these remarks and responses:

1. Would you like a cup of coffee?
2. Are you ready? It's time we were off.
3. It looks as if the train is going to be late.
4. Were you late last night?
5. Everybody is worried about the situation.
6. They've changed their mind again.
7. It's almost 9 o'clock. It's time we got started.
8. Have you got Helen's phone number there?

a. That's just what we don't need.
b. Oh, it's not just me, then.
c. No, we got there just in time.
d. I think so. Just a moment – I'll have a look.
e. Not just now, thanks.
f. Don't worry. I think everything is just about ready.
g. That's just what I expected.
h. Right, I'll just get my coat.

Notice all the responses include the word *just*. It is very difficult to translate *just*, but it is used in a lot of fixed expressions. Can you think of a similar word in your own language? Learn the responses so you can use them yourself. Make sure you know the equivalents in your language.
Sometimes *just* is used to make a problem or mistake seem less important or serious:

It just slipped my mind.
I just couldn't get there any earlier.
I'm just not going to get upset about it.

Notice how *just* changes its meaning with different parts of the verb:

Pres Perfect: *I've just passed my exam.*   (*just* = very recently)
Pres Cont.:   *I'm just making some tea.*   (*just* = emphasising exactly now)
was going to: *I was just going to ring you.*   (*just* = very soon after now)

Can I just ask/tell you/say that ...   (If you know an interruption will be quick)
I was talking to her just now.   (*just now* = a short time ago)
I couldn't tell you just then.   (*just then* = at that particular time)

© L a n g u a g e   T e a c h i n g   P u b l i c a t i o n s

Common Verbs
Copy this page and cut up into cards for Activity 18.

break	change
find	give
have	let
lose	make
meet	miss
produce	provide
put	send
see	show
start	supply
take	use

Common Adjectives
Copy this page and cut up into cards for Activity 18.

actual	basic
broad	chief
clear	different
good	great
important	key
large	little
modern	new
obvious	quick
real	simple
serious	strong

they already know, by helping to overcome the problem we discussed earlier where learners are often unaware of possible collocations of words they regard as already fully known.

ACTIVITY 19:   Expressions with a keyword

Discuss in what situations someone might say these, which contain the word *head:*

1. I can't make head nor tail of this.
2. On your own head be it!
3. Two heads are better than one.
4. Off the top of my head, I'd say about 200.
5. If I were you, I'd give her/him her/his head.
6. I think things will come to a head very soon.
7. I think we're heading for trouble.
8. Heads or tails?

Lexical Focus Shows learners that there is much more to knowing the language than knowing words, and that often you can improve your fluency by learning new uses for words you already know. This kind of language is often closely connected to metaphor and idiom, and often patterns can be found.

ACTIVITY 20:   Multi-word prepositions

Use a diagram similar to the one below and ask learners alone or in groups to identify the places marked.

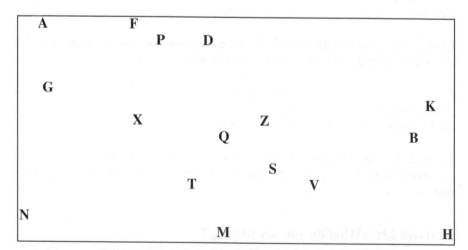

Lexical Focus In many EFL materials designed to practise prepositions of place, objects are conveniently placed under, on or peeping out from behind another object. Actual language used to talk about place is more complicated and includes phrases such as *in the corner, on the table*, and more complex multi-word adverbial expressions such as *on the right just near the church,*

immediately opposite the door. Some references are explicit (*about half-way down*), some relative and some purely deictic (*over there*: the meaning is clear on a particular occasion in context). This wider range of lexical items for describing position rarely receives the attention in the classroom that it deserves.

ACTIVITY 21:   **Prepositional expressions and Kim's Game**

Play Kim's Game; show a number of objects for a short time, remove and ask learners, alone or in teams, to recall as many as possible. It is better and more convenient to use an overhead transparency, particularly if you repeat the activity, but this time ask learners to remember not only the object, but also where it is, perhaps in relation to the other things in the picture.

Lexical Focus Use real pictures or photographs where the locations do not fit the standard prepositions of place neatly. Encourage use of multi-word and deictic adverbials: *on either side of, just to the right of the ...., in the far corner, near the .... .*

ACTIVITY 22:   **Multi-word adverbial phrases**

Give learners a set of multi-word adverbials and ask them to sort them into two or more groups, for example, phrases which answer different questions such as *When? Where? Why?* Here is a sample set:

At the side of the road	*By the end of the week*
On the way to work	*For a change*
Over the next few days	*For some time*
For fun	*In the 60s*

Groups can write questions which have each phrase as a possible answer. In this set the Expressions are either literal or metaphorical:

In two minds	*In his fifties*
In deep water	*In a good mood*
In the wrong direction	*In a tight corner*

Lexical Focus Multi-word adverbials have been largely ignored in conventional materials, but they contribute greatly to fluency in both speech and writing.

ACTIVITY 23:   **What do you say when ...?**

Give learners individually, or (better) in small groups, cards describing different stereotypic situations such as:

You visit a friend on their birthday.
You feel unwell at work.

A friend who lives in another town phones because they are unexpectedly in town.

Ask each learner/group to write five things which they are sure will be said by one of the speakers during the conversation. They can write the five sentences in any order.
Exchange sentences with another learner/group who then:
a. puts the five sentences into the correct order
b. describes the situation in which they think they were used
c. writes (all or part) of the dialogue which contains the expressions
d. acts out the scene

Discuss (some of) the situations and expressions with the whole class.

Lexical Focus Make sure the lesson ends with learners recording a few expressions word-for-word with L1 equivalents in their Notebooks.

ACTIVITY 24:   Discussing Fixed Expressions

Give students a group of correct Expressions such as the following:

How are you?
How's things?
How's tricks?
What have you been up to recently?
What's new with you?
How's life been treating you?

I don't agree.
I'm afraid I don't agree.
Rubbish. That's just not true.
I'm not sure that's really quite what's happening.
Yes, I suppose so, but...

Discuss the expressions briefly in the whole group, then ask learners to work in pairs or small groups and decide:
a. which expressions they feel completely comfortable using themselves
b. which they think they will never use
c. why they like or dislike certain expressions
d. the factors they think make an expression suitable or unsuitable for them to use

Ask for their choices and reasons; avoid the temptation to explain that they 'should' feel comfortable with more or different examples than those they chose. Everyone knows and understands a lot of English they would never use for reasons of age, politics, personality etc. Simple vocabulary teaching is relatively uncontentious; Expressions raise difficult questions about which are appropriate for people of different ages, for both men and women, quieter or more forceful personalities, or even whether some language is unsuitable for intermediate learners because its successful use is so dependent on nuances of intonation. Teachers need to be sensitive and to use a few activities to encourage learner awareness of the factors which influence the effect they create by using particular expressions. Teachers must advise, not dictate; ultimately the language learners acquire is deeply personal, an important way of showing who they are in English. The choice of what is or is not suitable is finally a matter for the individual.

ACTIVITY 25:   My personality, my language

Ask learners to complete the questionnaire on page 125 or, if you have a group of learners with the same L1, make a similar one using L1 examples.

Ask learners to compare their answers, and follow up by discussing the issues referred to in Activity 24 in the whole class. This activity can usefully be done at least twice at different points in a course.

Lexical Focus Correctly used Expressions are a powerful aid to fluency, but small mistakes can lead to misunderstanding. The Lexical Approach encourages great tolerance of small grammatical errors, but emphasises the importance of getting some language exactly right. Teachers need to build learners' awareness of this important distinction, which can at first seem like a rather confusing contradiction.

ACTIVITY 26:   Fixed Expressions

Give learners these questions:

For each of these Expressions, can you guess:
who said it – a man, a woman, a child, someone with a special job?
where it was said? **why** it was said?
what had **just happened** or been said immediately before the expression?
what was **the response** – the next thing someone else said or did?

Sometimes it is easy to guess, for example, **where** the expression is usually used, at other times **who** said it. How do you guess? Are you certain, fairly sure or **just** guessing?

Give learners a list of perhaps 20 Expressions such as these to discuss in groups:

Don't worry – I'll pick you up.
It's the sort of thing you think can never happen to you.
Can I give you a hand?
*Do we **have** to ask your mother?*
Not tonight, I've got a headache.

Language and Personality

1.If someone offered you a cup of coffee in your own language, what *exact* words would you use if you did not want one? Write how you would answer:

a. someone older than you, whom you did not know very well
b. a good friend
c. a good friend, but you are upset or annoyed because of something they have just said or done

How are the three answers different? Will your friend know you are upset from **what** you say, or **how** you say it?

2.Translate these dialogues into your own language:

a) Would you like to come to a party next Saturday?
      > Oh, yes. Thank you.
b) What has happened to this glass?
      > Oh, I'm sorry, I broke it.

Now change the answer in a) so:

i.   it is much more enthusiastic and positive
ii. you seem to say *Yes,* but show you mean *No.*

Change the answer in b) so:

i.   the apology is stronger and more sincere
ii. it suggests *Don't be stupid – you can see what's happened. It's broken.*

How did you change the answers – did you change the words, or how you said them? Did the answers get longer or shorter? Do you think you always mean exactly what you say in your own language, or do you sometimes say one thing, but you are sure the other person will 'read between the lines' and understand a different meaning?

3.Which of these words do you think your friends use to describe you?

friendly	enthusiastic	excitable
irritable	reliable	optimistic
calm	dull	quiet

Do your friends have this picture of you because of the way you speak your own language? How do you show your personality through your language?

4.Does your language have a lot of swear-words, which many people never use?

If so, do you ever use those words? Can you think of some words or expressions in your own language (Don't write them down!) which you would never use? If so, say why.

Do you think you can do the same things when you use English? Do you think you show your personality when you speak English? If not, would you like to be able to? What improvements in your English would help you to do that?

Lexical Focus The activity is a serious contribution to sensitising learners to the appropriacy of language to people of different ages, backgrounds, etc. but works best if some expressions have humorous possibilities, and if the whole activity is not taken too seriously. We noted earlier the special status of certain examples, particularly Expressions, which immediately suggest a whole situation or event.

ACTIVITY 27: Metaphor Patterns

Learners use a worksheet like that on page 127, devised by George Woolard, based on a passage in *The Lexical Approach* which was itself based on the language of news reports at the time of the destruction of the Berlin Wall.

Lexical focus Meaning is often best understood differentially, *trickle* by contrast with *flow, flood, stream* etc, so it helps to exploit a group of words from the same semantic field. As we saw earlier, what makes metaphorical language useful is the existence of **systematic** patterning between two semantic fields, one literal and one metaphorical.

Other areas which could be exploited in this way are emotions, love, enthusiasm, argument, buildings, journeys. The best source of ideas, listed in the bibliography, is Lakoff and Johnson's *Metaphors We Live By,* but careful listening or reading will reveal metaphorical language which may permeate the special interest or field of study of your students; George has noted academic texts full of words like *rising, plummeting, soaring* etc. which are given scant attention in most general English classes.

ACTIVITY 28: Pause Reading

The teacher reads a text aloud; this may be either the first reading of an unknown text or a text which is read and then re-read with pauses to which learners respond with RVR (Random Volunteered Responses). The technique can (usefully) be given a grammatical orientation by pausing in mid-structure:
It was a difficult situation and something needed . . . to be done.
Nobody can predict . . . what will happen . . . .

These pauses draw learners' attention to particular grammatical features. If the pauses are random a potentially useful language teaching activity is converted into a frustrating guessing game:
I'd like to begin by . . . talking about . . . the impact on the environment of . . . factories which . . . were designed before our modern concern with environmental . . . issues.

The last pause is clearly much more helpfully chosen than the earlier ones in the same paragraph. In this case the focus is explicitly lexical; the pause is deliberately placed in the middle of a useful collocation: *environmental issues.*

Metaphor Patterns

1. Complete the text by putting an appropriate word in each space.

When the Berlin Wall was breached, at first a . . . . of people came through. Later on the gap widened and people began to . . . . through. There was a constant . . . . of people anxious to visit friends, or restore family contacts. Once the initial excitement wore off, the . . . . of people **dried up.**

- -

2. Now think of a metaphor for the way crowds of people move. The phrase *dried up* in the text may help you.

Do any of the words you chose relate to this metaphor?

Try to complete the text with words based only on this metaphor.

- -

3. The original words removed from the text were:

> *flood   flow   stream   trickle*

Now put them back into the text.

Can you think of other words for the way water moves that may also be used in place of these particular selections?

- -

4. Use the text and metaphor to write a short text describing the fluctuations in the movement of people in different contexts: e.g.

- the number of tourists visiting a particular country
- the number of people in a store at various times of day
- the number of students studying English at your school or college

© Language Teaching Publications

Lexical focus Pause reading acquires its lexical focus only if the teacher is lexically aware, and so able to chunk text lexically while actually doing the activity in class. Balance means using this activity with some grammatically and some lexically placed pauses. It is precisely this linguistic sensitivity which is the hallmark of competent, principled teaching.

ACTIVITY 29:   Correction reading

Read a short prose text or dialogue, having asked learners to listen carefully to the exact words that are used. Tell the class that you are going to read the same text again, but this time you will change some of the details; when they notice a change, they have to correct you by calling out (RVR) **the exact words** used in the original version.

Lexical focus If you change a single word, the correction will be a single word and thus, even though surrounded by other language, the individual word will actually be used by learners in an artificial, de-contextualised way. If you change a phrase or Expression learners will often volunteer the original phrase or complete Expression – their attention is focused on a unit larger than the individual word.

ACTIVITY 30:   Lexical chants

Carolyn Graham has shown the enormous value of rhythmic speech, which can be motivating, lively, but most importantly, memorable. Many of her jazz chants are not directly applicable to the Lexical Approach as they are often based on amusing, innovative, and therefore relatively uncommon language. This is, however, by no means always the case. The Lexical Approach suggests using Semi-fixed Expressions which represent a generative group. A useful source of ideas is NTC's *Everyday American English Expressions,* though you will need to use it selectively, imaginatively and may, in a few cases, need to adapt the language slightly if you are a user of British or another variety of English. Here are extracts of the list of Expressions given under *Stating that you understand and Making the best of a bad situation.* Note that, as we observed earlier, many useful Expressions involve statements with *I.*

I hear you.	*That's life.*
I hear what you're saying.	*That's the way it goes.*
I see what you're saying.	*That's the way the cookie crumbles.*
I see what you mean.	*That's the way the ball bounces.*
I know what you mean.	*It's not as bad as all that.*
I follow you.	*Make the best of it.*
I'm with you.	*Things could be worse.*
I'm there with you.	*Look on the bright side.*
Read you loud and clear.	*It's all for the best.*

Choose some similar lines for the verses and a strongly stressed, contrasting line as the 'chorus' and it is easy to devise your own chants. There are two examples on page 130.

Lexical focus Phonological patterning is one of the ways we store items in our mental lexicon; it is easier to remember a tune than a sequence of notes. Many Expressions have slots which are filled from a restricted range of items. Devising chants – several similarly patterned lines and a contrapuntal last line – on the basis of similar expressions listed in the dictionary, or simply using intuition – is lexis made memorable and fun.

ACTIVITY 31:   Lexical Drills

At the end of a class ask learners to give an expression which contains the verb *have: have a drink, have breakfast, have sex, have a train to catch* etc. Use RVR or go round the class at a brisk pace. If a learner cannot or does not answer, move on. No correction, no explanations, no fuss. All over in a minute.

Alternatively, call out a common verb; learners offer RVR collocations:

T: *Take*
Ss: (Simultaneously) *take your coat off, take your time, take too long.*

Or apply a similar technique to Expressions by calling out a conversational remark which can be answered with a fairly Fixed Expression. Learners call out possible answers.

Lexical focus The choice of language item is collocation- or Expression-based. The whole activity reminds learners of chunks in a very short light-hearted moment at the end of an activity or at the end of a lesson. Useful for changing the pace of a lesson. Absolutely not the traditional drill.

Drills which practise single de-contextualised sentences have long been taboo. They are condemned as mechanistic and uncommunicative. This does not, however, mean that **all** drilling can be dismissed in the blanket way which tends to be current. Many multi-word items need to be noticed **and remembered** so as to be available for production as the prefabricated chunks which they are. The usefulness of lexical drills is explicitly **not** that they teach the language of the drill, but that they increase awareness of the real structure of the target language. Such drilling has a value, but only if it is used briefly, in a light-hearted way, with no pressure on individual learners to 'get the right answer'; the target is absolutely not stimulus/response formal learning.

The lexical focus of the next two activities, which use a good English/English dictionary, comes from the fact that they direct attention to the multi-word, phrasal part of the lexicon.

Two Lexical Chants

You should have come.

You'd love it.
You'd have loved it. You should have come.

You'd like him.
You'd have liked him. You should have come.

You'd enjoy it.
You'd have enjoyed it. You should have come.

You'd get a lot out of it.
You'd have got a lot out of it. You should have come.

Why don't you come?
Why didn't you come? You should have come.

Now it's too late.
You've missed your chance. You should have come.

Wrong Again

I might've, but I didn't.
Perhaps I could've, but I didn't.
Perhaps I should've, but I didn't.
Perhaps **you** would've, but **I** didn't.
Perhaps I would've, if I could've, but I didn't.
Somebody should've, you probably would've, but I didn't.
I thought about it, but I didn't do it.
Wrong again.

ACTIVITY 32:   Common words 1

Have learners look at the entry for *have*.
Can you find 5 words which are used with *have* in a way which resembles
to have lunch?
And 5 like *to have a walk.*
And 5 which will complete *Shall we have ....?*

Encourage learners to record useful patterns and examples in their lexical
Notebooks.

ACTIVITY 33:   Common words 2

Have learners look at the end of the entry for *take* and find a good example
for each of these:

3 idiomatic expressions they already know
3 new idiomatic expressions they would like to learn
1 idiomatic expression which is completely different in their own language

Remind them of the importance of organising such language in their lexical
notebooks.

Teachers will find it helpful to consult the dictionary-skills books which
accompany most of the modern EFL dictionaries. They suggest many
activities which have, or are easily adapted to give them, a multi-word lexical
focus.

Why, in a world of multi-media, do learners pay for expensive language
classes, rather than using technology for top quality natural input? The
answer is other people; the teacher and other learners who provide a human
element which sustains motivation. Part of the challenge for teachers in
implementing the Lexical Approach is to help learners maintain interest and
motivation when faced with the task of mastering an adequate lexicon.
Activities are needed which, while remaining useful and carefully based on
explicit theoretical principles, are also light-hearted, humorous and human.
No language activity used to excess can be effective; for these activities, as
for those which are more obviously serious, it is the occasional use, as part
of the teacher's repertoire, which maintains their value.

ACTIVITY 34:   Pass the Note

Each learner writes a Fixed Expression in English on a slip of paper. The
expressions may be from a recently studied dialogue or may be language
individual learners are sure they know precisely.

They write the equivalent expression in L1 on the other side of the paper. It
is essential to go from L2 to L1 so learners can choose L2 Expressions which
they are confident are correct (though, of course, this may not be so). The

purpose is to check and challenge learners at their own level, so any temptation to encourage them to produce tricky expressions, or to go from L1 to L2, must be resisted.

Pairs of students exchange papers; the papers must be passed so the L1 expression is uppermost. Learners translate the expression they receive into English, then turn over the paper and compare their translation with the original expression.

Discuss in the whole class any expressions where the two versions are different. Ensure learners record the correct version verbatim.

Lexical Focus The important point is that the expressions should be (semi-) fixed, and that you conduct the activity in a positive relaxed way, examining alternatives, errors etc, but end the session with a realistic (small) number of Expressions which learners really understand, see as useful, and record exactly in their lexical notebooks.

ACTIVITY 35:   Feelings

As long ago as 1978, in *Caring and Sharing in the Foreign Language Class*, Gertrude Moskowitz suggested that: *curricular materials don't include much vocabulary for communicating how we really do feel . . . expand the possibilities . . . then students can tell you how they actually **do** feel. This is useful vocabulary in any language.* She suggested that humanistic strategies should inform all you normally do in the same way this book suggests for lexis. She emphasises the value of being able to say how you feel, and the limited lexicon available to most learners for this purpose.

Prepare a large card divided into squares each containing a word or Expression saying how you feel *(I'm tired, I feel a bit run-down, I'm really .... today)*. Put it on the wall. Give each learner a flag, made with a pin and a small square of paper on which learners write their names. At the start of class ask learners each to put their flag in an appropriate square. Let learners circulate for 2/3 minutes after looking at the chart; encourage short private conversations about how and why people feel as they do.

Lexical Focus As Moskowitz wrote, this is useful vocabulary in any language. Some learners will answer honestly, some dully *(I'm OK)*, some facetiously *(I'm a bit sexy today)* and some perhaps revealing a real problem *(I'm a bit depressed today)*. Allow the humour but be very careful to avoid any form of intrusion into an individual learner's privacy.

ACTIVITY 36:   Ice-breakers

Many teachers will be familiar with ice-breaker activities in which students search for a partner using either a series of questions or information given on a card. Many of these activities are content-based – *find someone who has two sisters, someone who likes tea with lemon in it etc*. The activity is a more involving form of a typical matching exercise; it is correspondingly easy to adapt to the Lexical Approach.

Lexical Focus Individuals are each given a card which has on it a verb, adjective or noun. Students mingle and find their collocational partners. The activity can be based on, for example, verb/noun, or adjective/noun pairs, or on students forming groups where several verbs or adjectives form partnerships with a particular noun. It can be done with partnerships from a text previously studied, by using groups of phrases such as those which partner a pair of verbs such as *bring/take, do/make, have/take* etc.

Similar activities can be done with Expressions by asking students to find a question/answer, initiator/response pair, or by asking them to find the matching half of Fixed Expressions which you have copied, cut into strips and cut in half. Dividing the Expressions in principled ways turns a party game into serious language teaching.

ACTIVITY 37:   Lexical Crosswords 1

The clues are lexical items, most typically utterances. The answers to the crossword are found by completing the lexical items.

Lexical Focus Although appearing like an ordinary crossword, the important input is the complete utterance which is the clue. By gapping it, attention is drawn to the exact words. A sample is given on page 134.

ACTIVITY 38:   Lexical Crosswords 2

Use a crossword frame where the answer words are as far as possible common de-lexicalised words. Complete the half-grids with the answers. An example is on page 135. Divide the class into pairs, or an even number of groups of 2/3 learners. Give Grid A to one learner/group and Grid B to the other. They have to help each other complete the grid by giving clues. Each clue should be a sentence which contains the answer replaced by the word *blank*, for example *The blank we enjoyed most was the pool*.

Lexical Focus Most crossword answers are fairly unusual words because these are easier to give definition-type clues for, and crosswords are usually intended to be puzzles. We want to use them for light-hearted but serious language practice. Using common words means the answers belong in many Expressions, and the pedagogical value is for learners to produce good lexical item clues in a relaxed, game-playing atmosphere.

Crossword

ACROSS
  3. Just a minute, I've got some sticky .... on my hands. (5)
  6. Let me think it .... I'll tell you tomorrow. (4)
  7. He's an .... reader – he gets through several books a week. (4)
  8. I think you're leading me up the .... path! (6)
11. I know London .... out – I'm there several times a week. (6)
14. A double room, with .... beds, please. (4)
15. Don't worry – the pain will soon .... off. (4)
16. After all the problems, it's time to make a .... start. (5)

DOWN
  1. I'm sure everything will be all right in the .... run. (4)
  2. Hush! I can't .... myself think! (4)
  4. I'd like to propose a vote of .... (6)
  5. A .... in need is a .... indeed. (6)
  9. Running away isn't the .... to your problems. (6)
10. Why don't you come round for .... tomorrow evening? (6)
12. I don't think that's a very good .... (4)
13. If you want respect, you have to .... it. (4)

Find expressions in the clues which suggest these situations:
a. You are telling a friend to think again about a problem.
b. You think what someone is telling you is not true.
c. You are thanking someone formally, at the end of a talk.
d. You are trying to cheer up someone who has hurt themselves.

Many of the clues are Expressions which you can learn and use. What partner-words can you find in the clues for these words:

an .... reader	to .... respect
the .... to a problem	a .... start

Crossword

Give Frame A to one student / group and Frame B to the other. They try to complete the crossword without looking at each other's frames by giving each other clues. The clues should be in the form of an Expression which contains the 'answer' word replaced by the word BLANK, for example:
3 Across: You wouldn't BLANK me doing a thing like that!
1 Down: The party went like a BLANK.

Frame A
Take it in turns to give clues to the other student or group by using the word *BLANK* instead of the answer, like this:
1 Down: The party went like a BLANK.

Frame B
Take it in turns to give clues to the other student or group by using the word *BLANK* instead of the answer, like this:
2 Down: I'm not quite sure what you BLANK.

ACTIVITY 39:   **Jigsaw Dialogues**

The lines of a dialogue are copied onto strips of paper so that students can physically re-arrange them on the table or walk around the room sorting themselves into the correct order. Learners then re-arrange the dialogue, then read it aloud one or more times until it sounds natural.

Lexical focus The dialogue should contain some unusual or amusing language or event for interest, but must also contain several turns which are or contain useful Fixed Expressions which can be recorded in learners' Notebooks.

ACTIVITY 40:   **Listening**

Prepare the script of a short talk. Gap the text and give a copy to each learner. Have them complete their copies by listening one or more times to the talk, either on tape or by giving it yourself.

Lexical focus Unlike Cloze texts, the gaps are anything but random; remove a word from multi-word items such as strong Collocations *(common sense)* or Fixed Expressions *(Better safe than sorry)*.

ACTIVITY 41:   **Write a reply**

Present a short text with questions, comments or reactions written round it, as in the example below. Ask learners to explain orally or write a short letter, paragraph etc. based on the text and surrounding reactions.

Get more details from this advert.

Write a letter of complaint after your disastrous weekend.

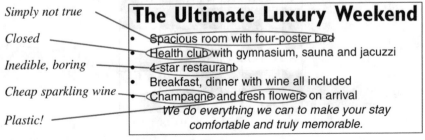

Lexical focus *Language consists of grammaticalised lexis, not lexicalised grammar* is the fundamental principle of the Lexical Approach. Notice the texts chosen here are short and relatively ungrammaticalised; they are lexically dense with the emphasis on content. Adverts, classified ads, very short news items, or summaries are suitable. The surrounding comments give suggested lexical content, leaving learners to grammaticalise.

ACTIVITY 42 Use a Soap

Ask learners to watch (part of) an episode of a real TV soap, chosen as far as possible to suit their age and background. Ideally, get them to follow the soap for a sustained period, either in their free time or by recording it yourself and using valuable class time to show it, perhaps with a pre-listening sheet directing their attention to useful Expressions contained in the episode. Even occasional use of a short extract provides excellent Expression-rich input.

Lexical focus Soap-operas are often decried because they use stereotype characters in stereotypic situations, but this means they are full of stereotypic language, which is almost a synonym for Fixed and Semi-fixed Expressions. The visual, fully contextualised presentation is a great help to understanding the pragmatic meaning of the Expressions, and because real actors speak the lines, you have a concrete starting point to help learners with questions of appropriacy – age, sex, relation of characters etc.

Elsewhere we note that the language most useful to learners *(If I see her, I'll tell her)* is not the most interesting *(If I win the lottery, I'll buy a Harley-Davidson)*. The very banality of soap-operas turns out to be a great strength for teachers keen to implement the Lexical Approach.

ACTIVITY 43 Soap follow-up

Show (part of) an episode learners have seen a day or two earlier. Pause it before important Expressions and ask learners to recall **exactly** what was said. Alternatively, prepare a gapped transcript of part of the script and ask learners to complete it, using the exact Expressions used in the original script. In a later lesson, ask learners:
a. to summarise the story of the episode
b. to act out a short scene based on the language they remember.

Lexical focus Choose the target scene or language carefully, on lexical principles. Don't set your expectation of accuracy too high, but remember the importance of reporting verbs (see page 181) and re-doing the same activity after an interval of a few days (see page 51).

Most of the activities in this chapter are simple variants on old favourites, given a somewhat sharper lexical focus. Most important of all, however, is the change in the teacher's mindset. This is exemplified in two final activities in which George Woolard (Activity 44) describes how a heightened awareness of lexis made a lesson develop in a new way and changed his understanding of how to get the best from a text, and Mark Powell (Activity 45) explains an important change of emphasis in the way we follow up reading a text.

ACTIVITY 44:   Supplementing the coursebook with chunks

Once you have the ideas of collocation and sentence frames in mind, you are encouraged to take a different approach to exploiting texts in class. Ensuring that frames and institutionalised sentences are highlighted, and attention drawn to the way the chunks are spoken, produced a marked improvement in my students' pronunciation, which they are aware of themselves.

Raising awareness of efficient ways of learning and recording lexical items was instructive to both my students and myself. I found myself staying longer with single vocabulary items than I usually would, armed with the mindset that exploring collocates and co-text would increase my students' generative power.

The Lexical Approach suggested that: *vocabulary teaching is almost exclusively directed to naming more and more objects, rather than encouraging the ability to talk about things.* In my experience, chunking stimulates more natural use and genuinely helps students talk about things.

For example, an enquiry in an intermediate class about the word *criticism* was handled first through paraphrase, contextualised example and exemplification. I followed this by drawing attention to the immediate co-text, in particular the collocation *to receive a lot of criticism*; this led the class to extract the frame: *........ has received a lot of criticism for ......-ing* from which I encouraged them to produce their own examples relating to current events:

France has received a lot of criticism for exploding nuclear bombs in the Pacific.
Princess Diana has received a lot of criticism for talking about her marriage.

Interestingly, one student disagreed so much with this that she elicited the word *praise* from me and promptly produced: *Princess Diana has received a lot of praise for talking about her marriage.* The urge to say what she wanted rather than produce a purely formulaic response meant the class discovered the frame was only semi-fixed!

Further decisions face the teacher. Should other variants be introduced? For example: John Major has *come in for* a lot of criticism *for the way he has* handled the economy.

Before this lesson I probably would not have considered the above pattern to be part of my idea of a sentence frame, so I would not have drawn attention to it. I am beginning to appreciate the sheer number of patterns in ordinary texts. Coursebooks tend to highlight traditional grammatical patterns, but this now seems a thin diet. I begin to understand the power of Cowie's observation that competent language users rely on a vast store of prefabricated units to enable them to achieve fluency. This is a strong argument for building more prefabricated units into coursebook materials and until then, for teachers to consciously seek to supplement the coursebook with such language.

ACTIVITY 45:   Responding to a text

Traditionally texts have been followed by comprehension questions, often aimed at checking understanding of the detailed content. In real life we do not use text in this way; we either read to find a particular piece of information or, more frequently, we respond to what we read, using language like this:

	surprising	
	shocking	
What I found (most)	interesting	was ...
	annoying	
	amusing	

I already know ... but I was surprised that ...
I know it says ... but I don't really believe that. I think it's more likely that ...

	ridiculous.	
	shocking.	
Parts of this are	outrageous.	For example, it says ...
	unbelievable.	
	just not true.	

Once learners have been introduced to this language they can be asked to produce real, honest responses to texts they study. A slight modification of the activity allows groups of learners to ask questions about the response of other groups:

Prepare a set of questions about the text. Exchange your questions with another group, and answer the questions you receive.

1. What did you think was the most ... thing about the text?
2. Was there anything in the article that really ... you?
3. According to the article, what ...?
4. What reasons does it give for ...?
5. In what way would ...?
6. Do you agree with the suggestion that ...?

Once again the shift is to more holistic, and more humanistic use of language, a change brought about by a recognition of the lexical nature of the language we use to respond in this way.

SUMMARY

For the moment, coursebooks are unlikely to change significantly and it is on the many Activities and Exercise types described in Chapters 6 and 7, together with the kind of changes George and Mark describe, that we must rely for practical implementation. As we see, the methodological shifts are small but significant.

This chapter has listed sample activities, with background explanation and, in some cases, extended samples. Part of the purpose, however, is to demonstrate the great diversity of activities which are, each in a modest way, implementing the Lexical Approach. There is a wealth of excellent resource books which help broaden teachers' repertoire of activities, such as Moskewich's *Caring and Sharing in the Language Class,* Morgan and Rinvolucri's *Vocabulary,* or Peter Wilberg's superb *One to One,* which, despite its title, contains many suggestions which can easily be adapted to larger classes. There are also many other books of games and other resources for language teaching. Many of the activities described in such books require little modification if they are to have a lexical focus. Experienced teachers with a clear understanding of lexis, and a commitment to raising their learners' awareness of the basic chunks of the language will have no difficulty in adding to the Activities described in this chapter. Here are a few suggestions:

- Contextual opposites for a topic: *book/cancel a holiday, a smooth/ bumpy flight*
- Group expressions by **where** they were likely to have been heard
- Arrange a group of expressions in the **most likely sequence**
- Match the (unvarnished) thought to the appropriate Expression (see page 82)
- Insert discourse language (see page 180) into a script
- 'Discussion language' (see page 142) which learners can use in any class discussion

It is worth returning to a comment of Henry Widdowson's quoted earlier: *If you say you are eclectic but cannot state the principles of your eclecticism, you are not eclectic, merely confused.* This book is concerned to discuss the implications for content and methods of the lexical nature of language, but it cannot be emphasised too strongly that the nature of language is only one, albeit central, principle for determining the overall design of courses. There is absolutely nothing wrong with principled eclecticism, indeed conversely there are considerable dangers in any attempt to introduce a right answer – a one-principle dogmatic methodology – to the complex social reality which is the language classroom. It is easy to identify factors which must be taken into account: the nature of learning, motivation, 'the system', learner and perhaps parent expectations. While theoretical insights are essential, other factors are more to do with the social expectations brought to particular learning contexts. In private schools, the students must come back next week; in the official system, demands may be made which teachers are only too aware conflict directly with the teachers' own understanding of best practice. Although such factors may be a source of irritation, teachers can only ignore the everyday social requirements of their job at their peril.

Implementing the Lexical Approach does not mean ignoring everything we have done before; it emphatically does not mean a doctrinaire new way of doing things; it will not, at least in my belief, be helpful if introduced in a purist, dogmatic way. It does, however, provide powerful linguistic insights, which in turn provide explicit principles, and thus a practical tool which should be one important element in an overall strategy based on principled eclecticism.

In the next chapter six classroom teachers explain how they, again in very different ways, have successfully taken lexical principles into their classrooms.

Fixed Expressions: discussing

These expressions help you to show your reaction in discussions. Make sure you know the equivalents in your own language. Match the Expressions with the situations:

1. It's difficult to say.
2. We're not getting anywhere.
3. Yes, but it depends what you mean by ....
4. I don't see what you're getting at.
5. You can say that again.
6. Perhaps we'd better agree to differ about that.
7. No way!
8. Stick to the point!

a. Avoiding a digression
b. Avoiding a disagreement
c. Avoiding saying what you think
d. Showing doubt or suspicion
e. Showing frustration – try to speed up the discussion
f. Showing strong disagreement
g. Agreeing strongly
h. Focusing on a possible disagreement

These Fixed Expressions show disagreements of different kinds. Match each Expression in List 1 with a meaning in List 2.

List 1

1. That's not the point.
2. That's not what I said at all.
3. That's hardly my fault.
4. That's nothing to do with me.
5. That's a ridiculous suggestion.
6. That's not quite what I meant.
7. That's not my problem.
8. That's taking things too far.

List 2

a. You have slightly misunderstood what I suggested.
b. I refuse to accept responsibility for that.
c. Don't blame me!
d. Don't introduce irrelevant arguments.
e. You are over-reacting or exaggerating.
f. I am annoyed because you are misrepresenting my ideas.
g. Don't argue with me about something I am not responsible for.
h. I am so annoyed I can't think of a reasonable response, so I just reject what you say.

All of the expressions can be used with *It's* instead of *That's*. If you use *That's*, *That's* is strongly stressed, so the expressions sound much firmer, even a little aggressive.

Chapter 8

Classroom Reports

Experienced teachers will exploit the Lexical Approach in different ways depending on their own areas of interest or expertise and their learners' level, needs and interests. Many already use activities which are fully consistent with the approach. Many others have modified their teaching to introduce a more lexical focus and have been kind enough to write explaining what they are doing, and how and why they are doing it. Those who have written are happy that the new activities and emphases they describe represent real improvements. This chapter records the very different ways in which six colleagues have modified their teaching in ways they attribute to lexical ideas and which they report as in some way more successful than their previous practice.

1. Cherry Gough describes a way of introducing collocation to a class.
2. Ron Martínez describes an activity based on the de-lexicalised verb *(get)*.
3. Mark Powell describes sound scripting, which integrates lexis and phonology.
4. Jonathan Marks reviews the whole area of 'pronunciation'.
5. George Woolard describes imaginative, literature-based group-writing activities.
6. Heinz Ribisch describes how he has extended his learners' Notebooks.

CLASSROOM REPORT 1:   CHERRY GOUGH

Cherry Gough teaches advanced learners in Poland. Here she describes an activity which provides an extended introduction to collocation which she first described in an article in *Modern English Teacher*. This is an edited version of her original article which appeared in Volume 5, Number 1, January 1996.

Introducing collocation to a class

I noticed collocation problems particularly in my students' written work, but I was convinced it could not be taught through one-off exercises, but needed a sequence of learner-centred activities, aimed at helping learners help themselves outside the classroom. This is the procedure I adopted to raise my (upper-intermediate Polish) students' awareness of collocation and simultaneously develop a strategy for reading and mining authentic text for collocations.

Step 1   Prepare a list of lexical errors based on learners' written work. These are (slightly edited) errors from my students' work which I used:

1. For many ages, the competition to reach all the top positions at work ...
2. The statement that all people are equal sounds lofty, however ...
3. Every nation which intends to take an activity in the cultural and economic life ...
4. The building was not renewed and it had not been used ever since.
5. accidental sex
6. It has some weeping willows that are now coming into leaves.

They identified these collocation errors:
for many ages   *the building was not renewed*
the statement sounds lofty   *accidental sex*
to take an activity in   *coming into leaves*

Step 2   Ask students to decide on the *type* of error in each case. It is important to stress you do not want the source of the error (usually interference) but the type. To help, I elicited the following types: context, collocation, meaning. Typically, lexical errors are not about individual words, but about the combination of words.

Step 3   Ask students to make suggestions for corrections. As you go, discuss how fixed the 'correct' collocation is. Fixed collocations, in my experience, tend to be:

• set idiomatic phrases: *a new broom, a tower of strength*
• expressions *(I see what you mean, once and for all)*
• connectors *(for example, as a result).*

More flexible collocations are more likely with:

• phrasal verbs *(stick/pin/put up a notice)*
• separated collocations** *(neither ... nor ... , not only ... but also ...)*
• sense collocations such as verb + noun *(redecorate a house/room)*, verb + adverb *(work hard/steadily)*, adjective + noun *(romantic/ modern/detective fiction).*

To avoid the confusion which may result from using more precise terminology such as the taxonomies proposed by Lewis or Nattinger and DeCarrico I stick to the relatively straightforward terms 'fixed' and 'flexible'.

My group decided *casual sex* was fairly fixed, while *redecorate a building* was looser, as it was easier to think of near synonyms for the verb such as *do up*.

**What in this book I have called semi-fixed frames.

Step 4   Authentic texts are introduced, chosen by either the teacher or learners. Allowing learners to choose texts encourages personal interest and shows learners that collocation is a feature of all texts. The task is unfamiliar, so it is better if the texts themselves do not present learners with difficulties which detract from the main task.

The teacher chooses two texts (Text 1 and Text 2) and prepares the following task:

Give a short pre-reading and reading activities based on Text 1 to ensure learners are confident about their grasp of its general meaning. Prepare a collocation task for the same text by finding both fixed and flexible collocations and re-writing the text, omitting one word from the collocations you wish to bring to learners' attention but leaving a whole line of space like this (using a brief passage from above):

To avoid the

....

which may result from using more precise

....

such as the taxonomies proposed by Lewis or Nattinger and DeCarrico I stick to the relatively

....

terms 'fixed' and 'flexible'.

You need enough copies of Text 1 in both original and gapped versions, and Text 2, in original form only.

Step 5   Do the pre-reading and reading tasks using the original version of Text 1, then collect these and distribute the gapped version. Let learners in small groups add suggestions to fill the gaps. Tell them one word has been removed each time, but they can suggest single or multi-word items, provided the meaning of the text is (almost) unaltered. Emphasise that this is neither a test, nor a conventional gap-fill exercise.

Step 6   Return the original version. Ask students to decide how 'fixed' the original collocations are. Go round groups answering questions, as learners compare their suggestions with the original and perhaps with suggestions from a modern corpus-based reference book. Return to whole-class format and discuss the results, without providing too much input yourself – the purpose is to let learners explore the idea of collocation themselves.

Step 7   The most important stage is to distribute copies of Text 2 and let learners suggest gaps for a similar practice. Among my group's suggestions were:

any real encouragement
not that difficult
away from home
to share a house
It's not the end of the world.

The main reasons they gave, which are at least as important as the actual choices, were:
• probably useful when they spoke, or more likely, wrote English
• related to useful topics
• different from Polish, and therefore potential errors.

Step 8 Ask learners in groups to suggest ways of learning collocations. My group suggested:

• Read more
• Look at words in groups, not alone, when trying to work out meaning.
• Keep a notebook for words in context. Avoid noting down individual words.
• Categorise items as useful for ... writing essays, discussions etc.
• Remember bilingual dictionaries do not always help with collocations.

Did it work?

When I asked the same group of learners a month or so later what they had learned on the course about vocabulary, these were some of their comments:

• Learn words from their context, as only then do they have real meaning.
• Always look not just at the word itself, but at the words around it.
• You should learn words not on their own, but together with other words.

Commentary on Report 1

Notice how many of the ideas advocated earlier: the importance of looking at and recording words in groups rather than individually, the value of a lexical notebook, organised for re-accessibility, the deficiencies of bilingual dictionaries, have all been discovered by learners themselves. In addition, they have been actively taught that collocations are of different kinds, and that collocation is a matter of more or less likely, and more or less flexible. The activity is an excellent example of implementing the Approach – it is planned, learner-centred, reflective. It sets out in a principled way to develop learners' language awareness in ways which will be helpful throughout their language learning careers; its pay-off is consciously medium-term.

CLASSROOM REPORT 2:   RON MARTÍNEZ

Ron Martínez is an American teaching at a private language school in California. He was trained in a grammatical tradition but is adapting his teaching as he sees the unsatisfactory nature of some published material and the generative power of some kinds of lexis. Here he describes a sequence of activities based round a patterned use of the de-lexicalised verb *(get)*.

Introducing a helpful pattern of the verb *(get)*

I devised this task-based lexical activity after I saw the following note in my students' coursebooks:

"The *get*-passive is used colloquially in place of *became*. It is used particularly in *get married/divorced*."

Gee, that's helpful, isn't it? If what that book says is in fact true, then the following should be perfectly acceptable:

Hurry up and become dressed!
If you become too close to the fire you'll become burned.
You'll become in trouble if you become pregnant.
I become drunk on the weekends.
Don't become mad – become even.

I became pregnant may be possible, but it isn't probable; in a corpus of 2.5 million words produced by hundreds of native speakers, no one actually did use it, so maybe nobody actually does. (Editor's note: CIDE lists two examples from their corpus, so we see again the dangers of saying collocations are impossible.) At the same time I would never say *He got born in December* nor *At first we were winning but then the score got even*. The use of *get* in this case is collocational; it cannot simply be dismissed as some 'alternative' form. It boggles the mind that all coursebooks give this highly generative *get*-pattern such little attention. So I decided to change that. This is the procedure I used.

Step 1   This step is optional but useful for lower levels. (Mine were low intermediate.) Put together a narrative-builder with a sequence of pictures like the one shown on page 148 which I title *My Friend John's Bad Day*. The students suggest sentences similar to the following:

1. It was a sunny day.
2. It got cloudy.
3. It got dark.
4. It started to rain.
5. He didn't have an umbrella.
6. So he got wet.
7. He got sick.
8. He called in sick and his boss got mad.
9. He got fired.

I drill each sentence in sequence until the story is complete, and concept-

My friend John's bad day

Scott's Terrible Life

Photocopy this page, preferably enlarged, then cut into cards. Give each group a selection of cards and ask them to arrange them in a sequence which describes Scott's Terrible Life.

got worse	got divorced	got angry
got depressed	got fired	got nervous
got into trouble	got killed	got sleepy
got arrested	got into an accident	got shot
got drunk	got desperate	got away with ...
got fat	got too confident	got behind at work
got careless	got involved in crime	got old
got sick	got pregnant	got into debt
got lonely	got stressed out	got evicted
got bored	got caught	got addicted to drugs

Happy Have

The verb (have) occurs in lots of expressions. Quite a lot of them about good news or good luck. Arrange these in any order you like, then use the expressions to tell a story with a happy ending.

had a holiday in ...	had a good time
had nothing/a lot to do	had a good job
had a bit of good/bad luck	had no alternative but to ...
had no difficulty ... *ing*	had a meal/a few drinks
had a friend who ...	had a chance to ...
had a nasty shock when ...	had no way of avoiding ...
had an accident	had no doubt that
had a talk to ...	had a think and decided to ...
had no hesitation in ... *ing*	had a feeling that
(S)he had an idea!	It had no effect.

check by asking: *So, why did he get wet? And why did he get fired? Why did his boss get mad?* etc. Finally, I remove the pictures and, in pairs, students write the story they have just put together as a class. This stage can last as long as you think necessary.

Step 2 Give students, in small groups of 2 or 3, sets of pre-selected *get*-phrases cut up, individually on cards or pieces of paper. There is a set you can photocopy on page 149. To reduce your own workload, try having the students do this for you. I give them about 30 different phrases, then I tell students:

Well, John had a bad day, but that's nothing compared to my friend Scott. Scott had a bad life. On those bits of paper are some of the bad things that happened in Scott's life. In groups, put them in the order you think they happened.

No group's sequence is ever the same.

Step 3 After all groups have decided on what happened in Scott's life and vocabulary questions have been cleared up, students work on writing down a cohesive version of the story. Tell students to choose one person from their group to be the writer, but each member of the group helps put the whole story together. Below is a sample that one group (Brazilian, Japanese and Swiss) wrote with the target phrases highlighted:

One day he found that his girlfriend **got pregnant**. His wife discovered this and then they **got divorced**. He **got lonely**. His girlfriend also left him, so he **got stressed out**. He **got nervous**, so one day he decided to drink. He **got drunk** and on the way back to his house he **got sleepy** so he **got careless** and **got into a car accident**. He tried to **get away** but there was a witness who saw the car accident and then he **got fired**. So he **got poor** and **got into debt.** He **got behind on his rent** and then he **got evicted**. So he **got depressed**, and because of this depression, he **got addicted to drugs**. He wanted drugs so he **got in trouble** to get drugs. He **got involved in crime**, but he was able to **get away**. After that he committed crimes many times but he was able to **get away** every time. So he **got too confident**. He spent a few years in this life of crime. So he **got old** and **got sick**. Nobody didn't care about him. He **got hungry**. Everything **got worse**. He **got desperate**. One day his friend Ron insulted him saying: "Oh no! How did you **get so fat**?" He **got very angry**. They **got into a fight**, he **got caught**, **got shot** and **got killed.**

Sure, it's not going to win the Nobel Prize in Literature, but students certainly have fun doing it. What's more important, they gain an awareness of a very useful lexical pattern in English. Notice the goal is not to master a rule, but to acquire tools for real communication.

When students have completed the written part and I have checked for any major mistakes, they can then read their stories to each other or trade the stories with other groups.

Step 4   Finally the students get to play a game. A set of the *get*-phrases are written up on the board and one half of the class has to try to get a member from their team whose back is to the board to guess all the phrases within one minute. The students give cues like: *He was in the rain so he...; He never came to work so he...; He didn't have any friends so he...* , and so on. That team gets one point for each correct guess and five bonus points for guessing all of them in the allotted time. Then it's the other team's turn and a team-mate who has been waiting outside sits with her back to the board and the process is repeated.

The last thing I have the students do is start a new section in their notebooks, which have different lexically-based sections, dedicated to these get-phrases. Every time another example comes up in class they add it to that special section. From time to time I have them share any new ones they have acquired with the class.

It all makes for fun, useful and challenging learning. Students really appreciate leaving the lesson feeling that they have learned something they can use right away and not have to think about lexicalising some grammatical structure at some point in the future. The language is easily tested, reviewed and built on. It is an example of how a lexical approach can make lessons more valuable and language-enriching experiences.

Commentary on Report 2

This activity resembles a traditional picture-based grammar practice but the target language has changed. This is only a small change in procedure but it moves the emphasis from traditional grammar to a more lexical focus. A similar example for *(have)* in British English is given on page 150. Again we see that many small changes, rather than any radical paradigm shift, is the implementation of the Lexical Approach.

CLASSROOM REPORT 3:   MARK POWELL

Mark Powell has extensive experience teaching business English. He has written a highly successful course *(Business Matters, LTP, 1996)* based on a lexical approach to texts, and *Presenting in English, LTP, 1996*, an innovative course which trains learners in the linguistic and rhetorical skills needed for effective oral delivery. Here, he describes a technique from *Presenting in English* where the learner uses lexical chunking and a word processor to prepare a 'sound script' which integrates phonology and lexis and provides real practical help for learners. Although the example is business-orientated, the technique applies to any text which is to be spoken aloud.

Sound scripting

Several years ago, I was teaching a leading French biochemist. He had to present a paper at an international symposium, and although the presentation was only scheduled to last fifteen minutes, his English was good and he arguably knew more about his subject than anyone else on earth, the prospect terrified him.

As an experienced ESP teacher, I was confident I knew what to do. We spent several lessons practising sequencing and structuring language to help him give shape to his talk. He practised describing charts and diagrams and presenting facts and figures, and pronunciation of technical and scientific terms. All this detailed work, I told myself, would pay off in the end. When I felt he was ready, he made a first attempt at giving the full presentation which I filmed.

The result was depressing. Long periods of monotonous delivery were suddenly interrupted by an alarming crescendo that seemed to come out of nowhere. Key content words were mumbled and swallowed whilst prepositions, articles, and conjunctions were sometimes delivered with startling gusto. Carefully prepared phrases and expressions were dismembered and so rendered meaningless. With great insight into his own difficulties he explained: *It ... is easy for ... you. ... When you begin a ... sentence ... you, of course, know where ... it will ... finish, but I ... never really ... know how I am going ... to stop ... until I am ... arrive at the ... end.*

He was absolutely right. In speech, if you have not thought ahead to the end of each chunk, you **cannot** get your stress or intonation right. This ability to speak in comprehensible chunks, 'sound chunks', is essential. If you don't get that right, nothing else you do will make any difference. What my learner needed was a system for sound chunking, for somehow superimposing the English sound system onto the text of his presentation so that he could **see** how to **say** it.

More recently, before writing *Presenting in English*, I listened to a great many presentations. What impressed me most about the good ones was not the 'structuring language' beloved of EFL materials; it was the speakers' ability to chunk, pause and pace their speech to make the message clear and effective. This is a skill all presenters need.

Indeed, the skill applies even to spontaneous unscripted speech, where it may, in practice, be easier to achieve.

This procedure evolved from the lesson designed to help the biochemist improve his delivery, but you can use it to help anyone who has to give a talk in English to think and speak in chunks rather than individual words.

Step 1 Give your learners a short text to work on. (With an individual who is going to give a presentation, let the learner prepare a passage which (s)he actually needs and will use.) Make sure the text is neither too conversational nor too textual. The sentences should be fairly short. The example below is suitable for a class of learners of either general or business English.

> The world's most popular drink is water. You probably knew that already. After all, it's a basic requirement of life on earth. But did you know that the world's second most popular drink is coke? And that the human race drinks six hundred million cokes a day? Now, let's just put that into some kind of perspective. It means that every week of every year people drink enough coke to fill the World Trade Center.

Ask learners to decide in pairs where they would pause if they were giving this presentation. There will probably be some disagreement. Go through the first three sentences in class and demonstrate how the different chunks they have suggested actually sound. Try to establish that pausing after important content words (often nouns: *drink, water, requirement, life, earth;* or verbs: *know, drink*) usually works. Ask pairs to finish the chunking task.

If you have access to computers, put the text onto PCs and ask learners to press RETURN where they would pause. Some will favour relatively large chunks and end up with something like this:

> The world's most popular drink is water.
> You probably knew that already.
> After all, it's a basic requirement of life on earth.
> But did you know
> that the world's second most popular drink is coke?
> And that the human race
> drinks six hundred million cokes a day?
> etc.

Others may prefer smaller chunks and produce a script something like this:

> The world's most popular drink
> is water.
> You probably knew that
> already.
> After all,
> it's a basic requirement
> of life on earth.
> But did you know
> that the world's second most popular drink
> is coke? etc.

By presenting the two versions yourself, you can show learners that, although the first version sounds more fluent, the second creates more impact. Frequent pauses in the right place, of course, are helpful. This encourages lower level learners. Your English can be **too** fluent and rapid, and you actually make your message clearer by slowing down and pausing more, **providing** the pauses are in the right places.

Step 2 Ask learners to look again at their texts and highlight the stressed words. Then ask them to underline the words which are stressed the most. If they are working on PC, they can use bold, underline, etc. They may come up with something like this:

> The **world's** most popular **drink**
> is **water.**
> You **probably knew** that **already.**
> After **all,**
> it's a basic **requirement** of **life** on **earth.**
> But **did** you **know**
> that the world's **second** most **popular drink**
> is **coke?**
> And that the **human race**
> drinks **six hundred million** cokes a **day?**

Learners will soon see that strongly stressed words tend to occur at the end of each chunk or to be used contrastively (as in *second most popular drink*). Encourage learners to vary the system they use to suit themselves; some may find too much marking distracting, while others find it helps. The important thing is that the chunking they use actually helps them to deliver the chunks more effectively.

Step 3 Now ask learners to space out the words they want to deliver more slowly. If they don't have access to computers, get them to highlight them in colour instead. They may produce something like this:

> The **world's** most popular **drink**
> is **water.**
> You probably knew that **already.**
> After **all,**
> it's a basic requirement   of life   on **earth.**
> But **did** you **know**
> that the world's **second**   most **popular**   drink
> is **coke?**
> And that the **human race**
> drinks **six**   hundred   million   cokes   a **day?**

If you are using PCs, photocopy a printout of the final script onto an overhead transparency so that it can be projected on a wall. Then ask learners to deliver the text by reading from the wall. Looking up, rather than down at a piece of paper will help them to deliver better. Point out that as a general rule they should keep their voice up in the middle of chunks and let it drop at the end.

Step 4 For homework, ask learners to prepare a short text of their own choice in the same way. In a subsequent lesson get each to give a mini-presentation.

Getting learners to consciously sound-chunk instead of speaking disjointedly takes a little time. They need to get in step with a new rhythm in order to stop themselves getting stranded in the middle of chunks. They need to realise that fluent monologue is not about speaking swiftly but about speaking smoothly in measured phrases. Pausing in the wrong places may frustrate listeners, but pausing in the right places gives the listener time to process the message. In short, help learners to understand that clear speech and easy listening both rely on effective lexical chunking.

Commentary on Report 3

Although the report refers to preparing a relatively formal presentation, the technique is useful for the many school students who have to give mini-presentations to their class and find it stressful, particularly if they have not had adequate preparation. It is helpful for most classes in simply making learners more aware of the importance of the tone units, referred to in discussing David Brazil's work in Chapter 3, and taken up again in the next report.

CLASSROOM REPORT 4: JONATHAN MARKS

Jonathan Marks is an experienced freelance teacher trainer. He has written extensively on pronunciation. In this more theoretical review, he describes how he increasingly sees grammar and suprasegmental pronunciation as linked by lexical ideas, of the kind discussed in Chapter 3.

Integrating pronunciation, grammar and lexis

Three elements of oral proficiency in a foreign language have often been thought of and treated as independent of each other: knowing the language, fluency and pronunciation.

'Knowing the language' still tends to mean knowing grammar and vocabulary. Fluency has a variety of interpretations; for teachers, the term often means the ability to express yourself adequately, and communicate successfully, even if your speech contains mistakes, approximations, reformulations and so on. For many learners, fluency means speaking at length, at speed, smoothly, without needing to pause or hesitate – like a river, not like a dripping tap.

Such continuous speech is impossible, and would not be useful even if it was possible. Only speakers, such as tour guides, who are reproducing rehearsed material, approach this kind of delivery, but even they have to take a breath now and then. We also need to pause to gather our thoughts and to plan what to say next; we stop to gauge listeners' reactions, slow down to emphasise some phrases while reducing others to a mutter, and sometimes we get momentarily lost for words or change our minds part way through a stretch of speech we have already started. Most of the time we don't realise these things are happening, but problematic instances can draw our attention to them. In a meeting recently I wanted to express something like *We should abide by these regulations* but I started in the passive: *These are regulations that should be . . .* and I stopped, with no idea how to continue, because I didn't know the past participle of *abide: abided, abidden, abode* all seemed equally possible but equally unlikely. So much for the fluent speaker.

From the listener's point of view, fast speech with these performance factors smoothed out would soon become impossible to listen to with much understanding. As listeners, we rely on a certain amount of packaging of the message into bits, and at least a minimal amount of time to process what we have just heard, and perhaps to respond, if only with a "mhm". So factors that might at first seem imperfections are actually essential to both speakers and listeners in the process of successful communication.

Pronunciation has often been seen as an add-on element of syllabuses, appearing as a 5-minute pronunciation slot in lessons or brief pronunciation exercises in coursebooks. Most typically, the focus has been on the accurate use of 40-odd phonemes – the ability to make *sit/seat*, or *hard/heart* sound different – or on accurate word stress – the ability to say COMfortable, rather than comFORTable. Often the implicit, and surprisingly ambitious aim espoused by many learners has been the hope of speaking 'Queen's' or 'BBC' English.

In classrooms where attention is paid to pronunciation, it is normally the teacher who decides whether learners' performance is adequate, what to correct, and how to correct it. But elsewhere, context determines what is or is not adequate, in sometimes unpredictable ways. It has been remarked that in Singapore, anything sounding approximately like *ship* or *sheep* is likely to be interpreted as *ship,* since there are plenty of ships there, but no sheep. On the other hand, I was once walking along the cliffs in Sussex with some visitors, green fields on our right, the main shipping lanes of the Channel on our left; one of the visitors exclaimed: *Look at that big sh*p !* and until I turned to look, I didn't know whether she had said *ship* or *sheep.* I was confused, but such confusion is the exception; such occasions are extremely rare, and easily sorted out when they do happen.

Wrong word stress is said to be more likely to impede comprehension; *comFORTable* might be easily understood in isolation, but perhaps not in the stream of speech, especially if accompanied by other similar mispronunciations. So word stress is certainly worthy of attention. There are, however, possible complications; if a learner says *INTernational,* a teacher might correct it to *interNATional,* but this does not take account of the likely stress in a phrase such as *INTernational reLATions*. This suggests a need to work at the level of phrases rather than words.

Interpretations of the communicative approach have tended not to give a high priority to pronunciation. Native-like pronunciation is certainly neither realistic nor necessary for most learners. But at the other end of the spectrum of achievement, poor pronunciation can cause real problems, no matter how 'good' the English the learner is trying to articulate. The notion of 'comfortable intelligibility' has gained wide currency as a reasonable goal, and although the concept is by no means unproblematic, depending as it does on so many contextual factors, including the disposition of the listener towards the speaker, it does seem to make sense in an approach that values success over accuracy.

Recently pronunciation teaching has encouraged greater attention to suprasegmental features – stress, rhythm, intonation – at the expense of individual phonemes. Among teachers there is still a widespread feeling that segmental phonology is easier to teach. But the evidence of learners who, after years of trying, still can't pronounce 'th', or distinguish between /l/ and /r/, might suggest that segmental phonology is not easy to learn, even if it is easy to teach. On the other hand, the teaching and learning of suprasegmental phonology is made difficult if it is abstracted from work on knowing the language and speaking skills.

Adopting a lexical approach opens up the prospect of integrating knowledge of the language, fluency and pronunciation in ways which are mutually-reinforcing.

Pronunciation and the Lexical Approach

The study of lexis and discourse shows clearly that the traditional focus on grammar plus vocabulary does not adequately describe how language is organised, constructed and processed. Nor does it hint at the scope of the differences between spoken and written language. Most learners are interested – whatever else they might want – in **speaking** the language. You cannot speak without pronouncing, and speech is increasingly seen to be constructed from multi-word units, or "chunks" of various kinds. This strongly suggests that it will be useful to examine the pronunciation features of such units. In this way, pronunciation becomes part of knowing the language, with the focus not primarily on distinctions like *sit/seat,* but rather on larger-scale features, which have greater communicative value, and are more learnable.

Sensitivity to chunking in spoken discourse helps learners in many ways: identifying units for learning, relating vocabulary to grammar, processing language they are listening to, planning and producing language fluently themselves. It also helps with pronunciation in a number of ways:

1. Some lexical units will be heard as separate chunks, thus forming a natural unit for noticing and practising pronunciation features: *I don't know about you but I've had just about enough of this* is typically said as two chunks, divided in one of these two ways:

I don't know about you / but I've had just about enough of this

I don't know about you but / I've had just about enough of this

The unstressed *but* can be attached to either chunk. There may be an audible pause between the two chunks; even if there isn't, there tends to be a lull, or relaxation in delivery.

2. Some conventional lexical units have a characteristic stress and intonation pattern, or at least a limited number of typical patterns. It makes sense to teach such phrases with their patterns, and to draw learners' attention to the patterns; *I don't know about you (but) . .* is one such example, with stresses on *don't* and *you,* and a typical intonation.

Some further examples:
by the way, you see, let's face it, you can say that again, not that I know of

3. Some of these lexical/phonological patterns are generative. You can build on the above pattern to produce:

I don't know about the rest of you but . . .
I don't know what you think but . .
I don't know what the others'll say but . . .

and so on, typically following the same stress and intonation pattern.

Some further examples:

as far as I know/can tell/can see
it's just a question/matter/etc. of
whatever you like, whichever you want, whenever I see her, etc.
down on the beach, onto the bridge, up to the top, on the TV, on the way back,
all the way there, etc.
out of the blue, out on a limb, up to my neck, etc.

Research into the structure of the mental lexicon suggests that words are stored, among other ways, by reference to their stress patterns. It seems equally likely that lexical phrases are stored by phonological shape. This suggests that a phrase will be retained better if the learner gives attention to its pronunciation (in this broader meaning of the term), and that it might be beneficial to teach phrases with the same phonological shape together. Learning the phonology while learning the words will enhance learners' confidence as they know how to say whole lexical phrases. It will also improve their fluency, encouraging pausing in appropriate places, and relatively smooth, connected production between those pauses.

Relevance to the written language

What I have said so far suggests a focus on speaking and listening but, perhaps surprisingly, phonological chunking has considerable relevance also to the written language and to both reading and writing. This is illustrated by my own recent reading, where I made the following mistakes: I read *In science eponyms . . .* , taking the whole phrase as the subject of a sentence about 'eponyms which are used in science'; but I then read on: *In science eponyms abound, and . . . .* In order to interpret this correctly, I needed to hear *In science eponyms* as two units: *in science / eponyms.* It seems to be the case that we do indeed 'hear' our reading.

I read: *Case studies also show strategies beginning* and chunked it so that it predicted something like: *Case studies also show strategies beginning to do something* or *Case studies also show strategies beginning + a time phrase.* What I actually then read was: '*Case studies also show strategies beginning learners use when . . .*' In other words, *beginning* goes with *learners,* not with *strategies.*

These predictions, misreadings and repairs were over in a fraction of a second, but they did disorientate me. Learners are much more handicapped by mischunking and might not even realise that listening to alternative versions – either in the head or by reading aloud – may solve some reading problems.

Clearly this is relevant to writers, too. As I write this, much of the time I proceed by formulating a succession of phrases. Some of them, like *as I write this* or *much of the time*, come prefabricated; others I have to construct, and this forces me sometimes to switch to a word-by-word procedure. As I proceed I hear a kind of inner echo of the text, including the chunking and intonation. Similarly, as I revise and edit what I've written, I repeat chunks to myself to test if they sound right. Sometimes I can help to make my intended chunking clear through my use of punctuation, and sometimes through making grammatical relations explicit (*the problem that children have* rather than *the problem children have*), but in other cases I cannot be sure that my readers will hear the text as I wrote it. If they do not, they will, in a very real sense, read a different text from the one I wrote.

The layout of poetry predisposes readers to chunk it, and so to hear it, in a certain way. The following does not look like poetry: *When we climbed the slopes of the cutting we were eye-level with the white cups of the telegraph poles and the sizzling wires.*

But this does:

When we climbed the slopes of the cutting
We were eye-level with the white cups
Of the telegraph poles and the sizzling wires.

The words are from Seamus Heaney's poem *The Railway Children*. There's nothing obviously "poetic" about the choice of language here; rather the poetry is suggested by the explicit chunking.

In prose, chunking can to some extent be suggested by punctuation. The authors of *In science eponyms* above could have added a comma, and this would have predisposed me to hear it correctly. Commas are often used in English, as they are in this sentence you are now reading, for example, to represent phonological chunking – rather than clause divisions, as is the case in some languages. (In the sentence beginning *Commas . . .*, some languages would require *in this sentence, you are now reading*). But the role of punctuation is limited. Reading continuous text with understanding is clearly not just reading a horizontal list of words. Since the organisation of those words into meaningful units is frequently not explicitly marked, it is clear that we must read with our ears as well as our eyes.

Descriptions of English pronunciation make use of an element called a tone-unit. (There are also various alternative names.) This is a short stretch of speech containing a major intonation movement on a stressed syllable. *I'm sorry, I can't* is two tone units. The alternative *I'm afraid I can't* is only one tone unit. If said as two tone units *I'm afraid, I can't'*, it means something completely different: *I'm frightened, so I can't*. This raises the question of the relationship between tone units and phonological chunks.

Intuitively, *I'm sorry, I can't* seems to belong together, and is generally, though not always, spoken as a continuous unit. For teaching purposes it seems to make sense to treat it as one unit or chunk, as long as its rhythm and stress pattern are preserved. So, although an analysis in terms of tone units would distinguish between *I'm sorry, I can't* and *I'm afraid I can't*, this might not be necessary for teachers or learners.

Here are some general strategies based on the above considerations which teachers may find useful.

1. When you model the pronunciation of a word encountered in a text, don't only say the word itself – though this will certainly be useful sometimes – but give a model of the chunk of which it is a part.

2. When you meet a new word teach it in one or more typical collocations which are likely to be useful to learners, and include any typical stress and intonation patterns. Get the learners to practise these orally and record them in their notebooks.

3. Make use of reading and listening material (including transcripts) to work on identifying, practising and developing chunked language together with relevant features of pronunciation. For example, at an early stage, when you are going to use a written text for a reading activity, instead of using the text as it is printed, prepare a version with divisions between chunks marked.

Make copies of this for the learners to use. If you have access to a computer you can easily produce a version with the chunks physically separated from each other.

Once they are used to this form of presentation, you can ask them to mark a text in a similar way themselves. (Pencils are useful, in case of changes of mind!) They can work individually and then compare with others. Often, of course, there may be more than one possible solution. In discussing alternatives, learners will quite naturally start reading bits of text aloud, and this can serve as an introduction to more deliberate work on reading aloud. Here again, it is useful to start by marking a text yourself, and providing a model, unless you are confident learners will make a good job of it. The next step is to entrust them with the task of preparing a text for reading aloud. It is helpful to use texts for reading aloud which learners are already familiar with to the extent of knowing what the text is about, and understanding most of the vocabulary. It also helps if they can already pronounce most of the individual words reasonably well.

Reading aloud has been a much-maligned activity and was frequently a painful ritual but, correctly used, it has great potential. A lexical view of language encourages a natural progression towards its use in a principled way. Teachers sometimes claim that reading aloud practises pronunciation, but all too often it practises poor pronunciation. Here it is seen as one opportunity of many to work on some of the skills of identifying, learning and producing language at phrasal level, by taking seriously the lexical chunks of which the language is composed.

Commentary on Report 4

Jonathan endorses many of the ideas expressed earlier: learning new words in useful collocations as phonological units, the ability to 'hear' chunks when reading (even in silent reading), and perhaps most importantly the intimate relationship between aspects of the language previously seen as quite separate from each other. Like Mark Powell, he has found lexis brings pronunciation and grammar together, a theme taken up again, more obliquely, in George Woolard's report below. What initially looked rather destructive – destroying the grammar/vocabulary dichotomy, turns out to have powerful unifying consequences, a point taken up again in Chapter 11.

CLASSROOM REPORT 5:   GEORGE WOOLARD

George Woolard works in Edinburgh with a wide range of multi-lingual classes. Some critics of *The Lexical Approach,* reflecting a concern expressed in the book itself, saw it as behaviourist and potentially boring in the classroom with lots of rote learning. While learning Expressions is part of the whole, another part, as George describes here, shows literature and lexical frameworks can combine to fire the imagination. Lexical frameworks can be a vehicle for original and personal expression.

Using Poems and Songs in a lexical framework

Reading *The Lexical Approach* I was struck by the reminder that a primary purpose of language is to allow people to express their personalities and ultimately themselves. The book suggests that the sequencing inherent in most language syllabuses can have the effect of restricting what the student can express intellectually and emotionally:

> In the early stages students are taught to communicate factual information, later opinion, and only at comparatively advanced stages, attitude. This can be intensely frustrating for mature adults studying an L2. Such people are used to conveying information, opinions, attitudes and most importantly, self, through L1.
>
> Syllabuses are directed towards language teaching, but ultimately it is not languages which are being taught, but people. People want and need to express emotion and attitude. It is a challenge to language teachers to ensure that they provide even elementary students with at least limited linguistic resources to express these important parts of life.
> *(The Lexical Approach, p39)*

Teachers, then, must encourage students to explore and value language as a personal skill and resource and not to see learning as simply a process of gradually accumulating bits of some external system. A focus on literature is one way of achieving this, switching the focus from the language being learned to the learners themselves. Literature is a rich source of opinion, attitude and emotion, and literary texts can be exploited in different ways to encourage learners to express their own opinions, attitudes and emotions. I used the following activities with this in mind.

Activity 1: This is just to say ...

This activity, based on the William Carlos Williams' poem, *This is just to say...* aims to sensitise students to one way in which the meaning of a chunk of language can be affected by the form in which it is presented, and secondly to encourage individual students to experiment with, and exploit this strategy for their own purposes. The poem is used to raise awareness and to provide a model for the students' own production. The preparation stage follows a similar course to that laid down by McRae & Pantaleoni in *Chapter & Verse* (OUP, 1990). I am indebted to them for the idea.

Preparation: Prepare a work sheet similar to the one on page 164 and give the **top half** to students and ask them to answer the questions.

Some students will recognise the situation. Get the students to put themselves in the position of the writer of the message and ask them whether they would write exactly the same words. Discussion should fall on the sensual words,

Worksheet for George Woolard's Report 5

Who wrote this?

This is just to say I have eaten the plums that were in the icebox and which you were probably saving for breakfast. Forgive me, they were delicious, so sweet and so cold.

Why did they write it?

What do you think the relationship between sender and receiver is?

THIS IS JUST TO SAY

I have eaten
the plums
that were in
the icebox
and which
you were probably
saving
for breakfast

Forgive me
they were delicious
so sweet
and so cold

William Carlos Williams

© Language Teaching Publications

so sweet and so cold which some students will feel are not essential. Explore this: Does it say something about the relationship between sender and receiver? Does it change the basic message?

Ask students if they think the text is a poem. Most will probably reject the idea, although some will feel that the final five words are poetic.

Give the students the bottom half of the worksheet with the poem and discuss. Most will now accept it as a poem. Get the students to explore how the form of the text makes a difference to their perception and reading of it. Get them to read the text aloud, first as a message, then as a poem, and to note the difference in delivery and effect.

Production: Ask students to think of messages they might want to send and to consider how they might use poetic form to some strategic effect. Suggest negative situations like *Excuses* and positive ones like *Thanking someone.* Ask them first to write their message in the usual way, then to revise the text in a similar way to *This is just to say ...* . Allow students to read each other's poems; this leads to useful discussion and editing. A selection produced by my students is given on page 166.

Activity 2: Happiness is ...

A similar procedure can be followed using W. H Davies' poem *Leisure* as the starting point. It leads naturally onto discussion of the type of lives we think we should lead and to what part happiness plays in them.

LEISURE

What is this life if, full of care,
We have no time to stand and stare.

No time to stand beneath the boughs
And stare as long as sheep or cows.

No time to see, when woods we pass,
Where squirrels hide their nuts in grass.

No time to see, in broad daylight,
Streams full of stars like skies at night.

No time to turn at Beauty's glance,
And watch her feet, how they can dance.

No time to wait till her mouth can
Enrich that smile her eyes began.

A poor life this if, full of care,
We have no time to stand and stare.

This Is Just to Say

It was a pleasure for me
to share that beautiful moment
seeing you so happy
and proud of yourself
I will never forget that garden
with all those roses
and I will never forget that time
You will stay in my heart

This Is Just to Say

How tired I feel
this morning
I've got pains
in my legs
because of
how far I walked
I've got a frozen body
because of
the cold outside
Better delay
today's meeting
Sorry.

This Is Just to Say

I have been waiting
for you
two and a half hours
anxiously first
desperate later
but now I leave
because I'm bored
This is just to say
goodbye

This Is Just to Say

I can't live
without your briefs
without your lips
without your hands
without you
This is just to say
I live for you

This Is Just to Say

I bought
that book
of poetry
Guess
the title
of the first
This Is Just to Say

This Is Just to Say

that today I'm mean
that today I'm cruel
that today is no good
that today ought to be cut out
that tomorrow I'll be good
that tomorrow I'll be happy
Please forget today
and be mine tomorrow

This Is Just to Say

I feel sorry
for leaving you
with
your own
bored person
while
I
am trying
my own way
far away
now.

This Is Just to Say

that
although I'm mean
although I'm slow
although I sometimes
will be far away
The thought of you
always makes
my heart jump
at once

The poem, together with a few questions, encourages students to explore their ideas of what happiness is. The group will almost certainly generate a large number of different ideas of happiness, but, as with other emotional categories, no overall definition. It is through such responses that we explore and express individuality which is what we wish to encourage in learners.

Production: Ask each student to write up to five sentences beginning with the sentence head *Happiness is ...* . These are then gathered together and arranged by the teacher or the group of students into a poem which expresses the many senses of happiness within the group. An extract from a longer example produced by an advanced class is given on page 169.

Notice that the students' responses reflect a range of language ability, creativity and sophistication. To truly reflect the group nature of the activity it is important that both weak and strong responses are included.

Activity 3: Love is . . .

Love receives much attention in poetry and is easily explored in similar fashion. Two poems by Adrian Henri provide ideal sentence heads. Below is a verse from his poem *Love is,* and a few lines from another poem with the sentence head *Without you:*

> Love is feeling cold in the back of vans
> Love is a fanclub with only two fans
> Love is walking holding painstained hands
> Love is.
>
> Without you indifferent colonels would shrug their shoulders
> and press the button
> Without you they'd stop changing the flowers in Piccadilly Gardens,
> Without you Clark Kent would forget how to become Superman,

These simple introductions prompted the following responses from students:

> Love is the meeting of fingers through hot, golden sand.
> Love is the drop which fills my soul.
> Love is buying a pint and expecting one back.
> Love is playing tennis mentally.
> Love is like a leaf which drifts away.
> Love is a long story.
> Love is life.
>
> Without you I would walk around like a mechanical toy.
> Without you the rainbow would lose its colours.
> Without you I wouldn't stop in the corners of dark alleys.
> Without you everything would be as simple, as clear as logarithms.
> Without you the Black Sea would lift its enormous cloud and go.
> Without you I would feel homeless.

The following lines from *A red red Rose* by Robert Burns:

> I will love thee still, my Dear,
> Till a' the seas gang dry.

can be used to focus on the proclamation of love for life, providing a more fully grammaticalised sentence head *I will love you until* . . . . . . In response a group of intermediate students produced this poem:

TRUE LOVE

> I will love you till the sun stops rising.
> I will love you till the stars stop shining.
> I will love you till the flowers stop blooming.
> I will love you till the birds stop chirping.
> I will love you till the children stop smiling.
> I will love you even if the darkness drinks up the sunshine.
> I will love you till the colours leave the earth.
> I will love you as long as I can follow your shadow.
> I will love you as long as I can see myself in your eyes.
> I will love you as long as I can hear the words your eyes speak.
> I will love you till the end of the end.

Activity 4: If . . . , then the world would be a better place.

This uses part or all of Kipling's poem *If* to stimulate a group of students to use conditional structures as a vehicle for their ideas, beliefs and opinions on how we could improve the world in which we live, and secondly, to present the collective ideas, beliefs and opinions of the group in a persuasive form. The poem, incidentally voted Britain's favourite poem in a radio survey in 1995, introduces the theme and provides a model for the students' own production. Here are a few lines; the whole poem is easily available in many anthologies.

> If you can talk with crowds and keep your virtue,
> Or walk with Kings – nor lose the common touch;
> If neither foes nor loving friends can hurt you,
> If all men count with you, but none too much;
> If you can fill the unforgiving minute
> With sixty seconds' worth of distance run,
> Yours is the Earth and everything that's in it,
> And – which is more – you'll be a Man, my son!

Preparation: Tell students they are going to read a poem entitled *If*. Ask them to predict the content of the poem.

Let them read the poem and discuss the theme, who is speaking and to whom. Explore students' knowledge of the world at the time in which the poem is

HAPPINESS IS . . . .
Happiness is when you realise a dream
Happiness is when you let a silly smile escape
Happiness is when you are free to do what you want
Happiness is when I can really be with myself
Happiness is homemade strawberry jam in mother's kitchen
Happiness is when you are in love
Happiness is a huge red lollipop to a child
Happiness is when you are at home alone and you hear the door bang
Happiness is spotting your beloved through the window of an arriving train
Happiness is when you look in his eyes, and it's love
Happiness is to find love when all is lost
Happiness is the thing you feel when you wake up on Saturday, wipe the sleep from your eyes and realise that you have the whole weekend in front of you
Happiness is to be content with yourself
Happiness is to unexpectedly receive a token of love
Happiness is feeling a surge of joy within me
Happiness is when everything appears to be bad, and suddenly everything is fine
Happiness is to be self-sufficient
Happiness is walking through the meadows at sunset
Happiness is response
Happiness is very rare.

IF
If sunshine would find its way into the human heart
If the greed in our minds would lie calm
If everyone had a sense of humour
If there were no borders with bloody barbed wire
If our species had another way of communicating with each other
If nobody in the world had to die of hunger
If we silenced the thunder of armed fears
If you could see yourself with a stranger's eye and still be proud of what you do and are
If the wind could sweep away our sorrows
If the hand of man was never a fist and remained a palm
If we spent more time with each other
If we were not Spanish, French, British . . . . but Pepe, Pierre, Peter . . . .
If there were a God who loves us
If Medical Science could cure all illnesses
If we cultivated loving whispers and quashed hateful cries
If you could live a life without lies and be happy when you are not the star
If there were neither Good nor Bad
If we could speak their language
If the 'Mighty' wouldn't suppress the 'Weak'
If we always protested loudly when someone dies unfairly
If there were no violence in the world
If we listened more attentively to each other
If rain would only fall in times of drought
If mist would appear when outlines need to be softened and snow would gently fall to soothe the painful harshness of the landscape
If our rulers were the voices of roses and the tongues of our young
If we thought more about consequences before making decisions
If we said less 'It's mine' and more 'It's ours'
If there were no difference between the two sexes
If nations loved each other and lived together in peace
If we listened to the starving tears of children
If you and I could always be together and believe that love lasts for ever
. . . . **then the world would be a better place.**

set. It was written at the height of the British Empire when Britain was the world's greatest imperial power. *If* contains a long list of pieces of advice given to a young man by his father before he sets out on his career as a colonial official. It outlines the qualities the British considered necessary at that time for such a career.

Look at the text more closely and discuss new vocabulary in the process. Focus on the long list of *if*-clauses which give the father's advice and the main clauses in the last two lines which they are the conditions for. Discuss with the students whether this type of advice is appropriate in today's world. Encourage discussion of the differences between the problems of the 1890s and 1990s and the solutions needed.

Production: Ask students to re-write the poem for young people today. The main clause of the poem will be *then the world would be a better place.*
Ask each student to write up to five *if*-clauses to express their ideas, beliefs and opinions on how to make the world a better place. Gather these together and arrange (or let the group arrange them) into a poem similar to the original. An example produced by an advanced class is given on page 169.

Activity 5: The richness behind a word

This activity encourages rich use of vocabulary which may remain largely ungrammaticalised – more likely in a poem than in prose writing – and encourages students to work as a group and to move from the abstract definition of a word to the rich variety of individual types that are covered by the word. The poem *Horse* by George Mackay Brown is used to introduce the activity and to provide a model for the students' own production.

Preparation: Ask students in groups to define a horse. Discuss, then get them to classify horses into different types, e.g. race-horses, the horse pulling the plough etc. Then present them with the poem. Focus on the simple structure; the first line defines a particular type of horse, the second line fills this out with a burst of rich images. Draw the students' attention to the almost total absence of verbs.

HORSE

The horse at the shore
Casks of red apples, skull, a barrel of rum

The horse in the field
Plough, ploughman, gulls, a furrow, a cornstalk

The horse in the peat-bog
Twelve baskets of dark fire

The horse at the pier
Letters, bread, paraffin, one passenger, papers

The horse at the show
Ribbons, raffia, high bright hooves

The horse in the meadow
A stallion, a red wind, between the hills

The horse at the burn
Quenching a long flame in the throat

George Mackay Brown

Production: Ask the students in groups to choose a creature or creatures and try to reflect their diversity in the same way as the poem does. Get the group to discuss and explore the range of types of creature, then individual students try to write a few lines or a verse which captures one of these types. The group then re-convenes, edits and arranges the individual contributions into a poem, then presents this to the class. Encourage the students to move onto other concepts. An advanced class produced this text in response.

The Bird over the sea
The stable glide, the chirping sound.

The Bird over the land
The meadow, a brown sparrow, beetles and berries.

The Bird in the forest
Trees, nuts and branch nests.

The Bird in the city
Chimneys, parks, cats and dogs.

The Bird in the mountain
The imposing eagle, wind, snow, the prey.

(My thanks to Susan Gellaitry for this example.)

Activity 6: Songs

Strong sentence heads are frequent in songs as well as in poetry and are equally suitable for exploitation. Commonly held facts, beliefs, opinions are often expressed through structures like *It is generally known / agreed that ....,* *Most people know / agree that . . . or* as in the Leonard Cohen song *Everybody knows.* The song provides a rich text in terms of ideas and images, and is a great song to listen to. Here are a few lines, which are enough to use, though you may prefer to use the whole, which is, of course, much longer:

EVERYBODY KNOWS.

Everybody knows the dice are loaded.
Everybody rolls with their fingers crossed.
Everybody knows the war is over.
Everybody knows the good guys lost.
Everybody knows the fight was fixed:
the poor stay poor, the rich get rich.
That's how it goes. Everybody knows.

After exploring the text, students can be encouraged to use the sentence head *Everybody knows . . .* to hang their own perceptions upon. Whether they then want to sing it is a choice worth offering.

Commentary on report 5

In each activity a poem or song is used to stimulate ideas on a theme which is personal and emotional, rather than factual. Individuals are encouraged to offer personal contributions, which are edited and arranged by the whole group into a co-operatively produced final poem. The emphasis is on saying what you want to say, using (often ungrammaticalised) vocabulary and sentence heads. In many cases, the samples George's learners produced were arranged by them, consciously or not, with obvious sensitivity to the rhythmic patterns of different lines. Once again, lexis, grammar and phonology are combined.

CLASSROOM REPORT 6:   HEINZ RIBISCH

Heinz Ribisch teaches in a secondary school in Vienna. He also works at Vienna University and is extensively involved in teacher training in Austria. Here he describes the way lexical principles have influenced the Notebooks of his young learners.

Lexical Notebooks

My teaching situation is a particularly favourable one. I teach at a gymnasium in Vienna, and this short report is based on my work with a first-year class (26 boys and girls, 10- and 11-year-olds) and a second-year class (14 boys and girls, 11- and 12-year-olds). I am also especially lucky in the sense that the children in both classes are bright to very bright and highly motivated. Their motivation, it seems to me, is partly due to the fact that since September 1995 I have been experimenting with and developing my own personal variety of the Lexical Approach.

Introducing language lexically for elementary pupils

Maybe I should start by saying that adopting the LA did not mean that I had to turn my teaching upside down. I had already been doing quite a few things which advocated in the LA. Over the years, I had considerably changed my idea as to what "grammar is all about" and the way in which I presented it in class; I had always insisted that the pupils' personal vocabulary lists had to be words in context, and I had always tried to confront my pupils with a lot of language rather than giving them "explanations". But now, for the first time, I also had the theoretical basis for my classroom practices. I felt encouraged and went a long way beyond what I had dared do before.

Thus, in this year's first year I used structures like: *Do you live in Vienna?* from the very beginning, long before they are introduced by the official coursebook that we also use. Needless to say, I did not 'explain' the 'grammar' of this question.

About two months into the course I had already introduced some common past tense forms (*was, were, did* and *got*), which has made it possible for us to express a whole new range of things in class – and this at minimal intellectual effort. (*Did you ....?, Yes, I did*, etc.) Towards the end of November a serious accident which happened outside the school led to the sentence, introduced as a single lexical item: *Last week two girls were run over by a car*. Two weeks later, at a written test, 24 out of the 26 pupils in the first year were able to reproduce this sentence without a single mistake. I shall now allow this phrase to sink to the bottom of their English-language-learning cauldron, where it may stew for a while, until, in a few weeks' time, I shall come up with a similar structure, reviving the first and linking it to the new one.

I should perhaps also mention that I am extremely careful in doing all this, and while I try to push my classes to their limits, I make sure I do not overtax or unduly confuse them. As for testing and grading, I mainly reduce my requirements to the language and the structures covered in the coursebook, which they find very easy. To them this is "peanuts", they get good marks, which makes them (and me) happy and permits us to work in a stress-free atmosphere.

Learners' Notebooks

I have always regarded the pupils' vocabulary books, which we now call "Words & Phrases", as important and powerful tools in the process of language acquisition. Even when vocabulary books went out of fashion and you were frowned upon if you used them with your classes, I continued to use them. I have to admit, however, that I had problems with regard to organising the different items. I felt I ought to do something about it, but once I started, the whole thing became so complicated that in the end the disadvantages always seemed to outweigh the advantages. After years of thinking about this question I, for my part, have now made the conscious decision that a high level of organisation is not my first priority.

This has to do with the fact that vocabulary in a classroom situation reflects real life and, for this very reason, is often arbitrary and incoherent, but also exciting and relevant at that moment. In this sense our "Words and Phrases" is no dictionary, it is the result of the work we do in class and if it is not organised to the last detail it only reflects the fact that the process of learning a foreign language cannot be organised in every detail.

In addition to this, a pupil's personal vocabulary book is, intrinsically, of a temporary nature. Six months from now, the 1st year pupils will no longer have any need to look up what we write down today. With beginners, more than half of the 10 or so new lexical items of a particular lesson will, through constant use, have been fully integrated into their active vocabulary three weeks later anyway. So why should they want to look them up? As for the remaining items, I do not mind if, after a certain period, they are allowed to sink to the depths, from where they can be retrieved fairly easily at a later stage. Teachers who insist on every detail of their teaching being well-organised will not like this element of chaos, an element, however, that I would not want to sacrifice, as without it my lessons would be bloodless and stale. After all, to me, "chaos" seems to be the pre-condition of creativity.

However, and most importantly, by adopting the Lexical Approach I have also become much more strongly aware of the necessity to do something to counterbalance this arbitrariness in the recording of vocabulary, and I try to do this in two ways:

1. Wherever a lexical item that comes up in class seems to have special generative power with regard to the structure that is incorporated in it or wherever it seems of interest to pursue a whole set of possible collocates of a particular word, we spend some class time on that and often make a whole list of items, which we then put in a box and which the pupils are encouraged to highlight according to their own artistic abilities.

These are the items also that we will be returning to again and again in the following weeks to ensure that they leave the desired traces in the pupils' memories.

2. I try to encourage the use of a dictionary, not with real beginners but already at a relatively early stage in the learning process.

Maybe I should also mention that as far as I am concerned it is entirely left to the pupils whether they write down the German equivalent of a phrase. The recommendation I give them is not to do so when the meaning is 100 percent clear to them anyway. But I do not mind if they do. And wherever possible I draw funny pictures on the board instead of giving translations.

Teachers are sometimes afraid of going beyond the limits set by their coursebooks or curricula. This is something that each of us has to decide on a personal basis. But I have found that with success on your side, there is no need to be afraid of complaints. However, as I said at the beginning, my teaching situation is a particularly favourable one.

I cannot believe, however, that any parents or colleagues are going to complain if you encourage learners to keep lexical notebooks, and if these include multiple examples and collocation groups. Both will, however, make the notebooks a more powerful aid for your learners.

Commentary on report 6

Heinz emphasises the importance of small but consistent changes motivated by a lexical perspective. He shows that changes can be introduced from the beginning, for elementary learners and young children. Interestingly, the classroom teacher argues strongly for a **partially** organised Notebook, rather than the more rigid formats proposed in Chapter 5. I see his point, and would only suggest a middle way: some formats, some 'chaos' as mentioned by Heinz, but surely a section at the back of the Notebook for some of the truly miscellaneous language which arises spontaneously in class.

Some examples from his learners' notebooks are given on page 176, and show a clear exploitation of Collocation, and both fixed and semi-fixed Expressions.

SUMMARY

The enormous variety of ideas discussed in Chapters 6 and 7, together with the suggestions provided in this chapter by classroom teachers who have taken lexical ideas into their classrooms, serves to emphasise yet again the fundamental fact that implementing the Approach involves a big change in your perception of the building-blocks of language perception, which results in many diverse and modest, but principled changes in procedure.

Chapters 6-8 provide the major examples of ways in which teachers can take the Lexical Approach into their classes. Two major issues remain, of concern mostly to anyone involved in teacher training: the changes in the language content of EFL courses and materials implicit in the Lexical Approach, and any consequent changes of emphasis which may be necessary for teacher training courses. These are the subjects of the following two chapters.

Extracts from learners' lexical notebooks

I know where you live.
I know what you think.
I know what you did.
I know what you like to read.
I know what you like to eat.
I know what you like to watch

Raphaela Mayer, first year.

I get three hundred shillings.
  one thousand
I save | most of my money.
 spend | all my pocket money.
I buy presents | With | the rest
            | my pocket money
I spend all my money ON cinema tickets.
My parents buy | all (that) I need / for school/
 mum buys | ..... alles, was ich brauche

Gloria Warmuth, second year.

a zebra crossing	Zebrastreifen
a pedestrian crossing	Fußgängerübergang
a block of flats	Miethaus
an apartment building	Miethaus
once a month	1x im Monat
twice a month =	2x im Monat
once a fortnight =	1x in 14 Tagen
every second week	jede 2. Woche

Alexandra Stehno, second year.

Chapter 9

Language Content

Although this book is predominantly about ways of adapting Exercises and Activities, a lexical perspective has considerable implications for the language content of courses. This concerns both specific areas which the lexical perspective shows to be under-represented in most contemporary materials, and broader issues concerning the theoretical basis for deciding on suitable target language, and consequently the choice of content for teaching materials. There are a number of language areas which deserve more attention than they have traditionally received.

LANGUAGE AREAS DESERVING MORE ATTENTION

Increasing learners' communicative power depends on expanding the learner's lexicon by adding lexical items of all kinds. Positive steps must be taken to avoid simply adding an unhelpfully large repertoire of uncollocated nouns. We can identify a number of areas which are usually under-represented in contemporary materials.

TASK

Chunk the following, then identify any items which are useful but which are unlikely to receive attention in current materials:

1. Older people tend to find it more difficult to come to terms with change.
2. He must be getting on for 50, but I haven't seen him for two or three years.
3. To put it simply, I think it's very expensive for what it is.
4. There's a door on either side of the main gate.
5. The main cause of the problem is too much traffic.
6. The information content of written text is usually higher than that of spoken text.
7. I would if I could but I'm afraid I can't next week.
8. Anyway, we got there before we ran out of petrol, after all.
   > That must have been a relief.
9. The earlier we set off, the quicker we'll get there.

In practice, none of the following are likely to receive the attention they deserve in current materials:

Tend to... – modal expression which makes statements non-factual

Getting on for 50, two or three years – deliberately vague language
To put it simply – multi-word sentence adverbs
on either side of – prepositional phrases
The main cause of the problem is ... – discourse organising sentence heads
The information content of written text... – complex noun phrases
I would if I could but I'm afraid I can't – two clause frames
That must have been a relief. – discoursal responses
The ...er, the ...er – lexical patterns

Each of these areas is worth looking at in a little more detail.

1. Modality

There is much more to 'saying what you mean' than simply stating the facts
of the situation. Halliday has shown that spoken discourse has three
independent components:
• ideational language, concerned with the **content** of what is said
• interpersonal or 'modal' language, which shows the speaker's **attitude** to
  what is said
• textual language, which shows the **development of the discourse.**

The first has always featured in courses, but the others deserve more
attention.

Speakers and writers mark how they intend the listener to interpret the factual
content, so factual (ideational) content such as *These results show a
connection,* may be reported as *These results tend to/may show a connection.*
Carter and McCarthy report their surprise at the frequency of *tend to* in their
corpus of spoken English. Observation of used language shows that modality,
in this technical sense of how the speaker wants the content to be interpreted,
is widespread, important and often lexical. It is certainly not confined to the
modal auxiliaries, usually the only treatment of modality in standard EFL.
The ability to say things other than bald factual statements is an important
social use of language.

TASK

**Rewrite the following using a form of *(tend) to*. Sometimes changing
some of the other words might make the example more natural.**

1. Families with children take their holidays in July and August.
2. Men study science and women study arts subjects.
3. The Japanese education system is very strict.
4. More and more people get their view of the world from TV, not from
   newspapers or books.
5. The winters have been a bit warmer in the last few years.
6. Years ago, there was no TV and people made their own entertainment.

Notice how using *(tend) to* makes a general statement less direct, and more open, so the other person can more easily comment, or even disagree. Do you tend to agree or disagree with the comments made in the exercise? Learners could do the above task which could then be extended using Exercises 24 and 25 in Chapter 6.

Many other lexical ways of expressing modality also deserve a place in class:

There's a chance that ....
I'm not sure whether I'll ... but I might.
I'm not really sure.
I have my doubts.

In speech there are a lot of Fixed Expressions beginning with *I*. Modality in writing tends to be realised lexically:

There is some speculation that (interest rates may have to rise).
The prospects of an early election seem to increase every day.

2. Vague language

Education has taught most of us to 'say what we mean' and that imprecision is a bad thing. Like all such generalisations, it is only partly true. What matters is the appropriacy or otherwise of any vagueness. Sometimes, as in these cases, simply stating the facts sounds odd, even if the examples sound suspiciously like standard EFL:

Do you like coffee?
> Yes, I do.
How often do you go to the cinema?
>Often / Regularly / Seldom.
What do you have for breakfast?
> I have cereal and coffee.

Conversation depends on the participants co-operating and telling the truth as they know it, which includes, as we have just seen, indicating tentativeness, approximating and so on.

Joanna Channell has described many strategies for deliberate vagueness *(Vague Language, OUP, 1994)* without which language can seem brusque, aggressive or immodest. Because of its importance in projecting your personality and attitudes learners need some of this language from the very earliest stages: *I (don't) think so* and *It depends* as well as *Yes* and *No*.

Some learners may need to be convinced, perhaps by asking them about L1, that such language is universal, all-pervasive and in no sense sloppy or uneducated. Joanna Channell suggests letting learners listen to an audio recording of native speakers doing a task in which vague language naturally arises, so they fully realise that such language is in no sense sub-standard.

Much of this language consists of strongly patterned Semi-fixed Expressions which are strictly constrained by non-obvious criteria: *between about (25) and (30), in his (fifties)* express age, *in the low sixties* expresses temperature, *greenish, fairish, sixish* but not **intelligentish*. Such language clearly deserves a place in an Approach which values lexical patterns, and which is based on helping learners convey meaning in a wider sense than the stating of bald facts.

3. Polyword phrases

These can be divided into three basic sub-categories:

a. discoursal phrases – expressions which tell the listener the function of the next bit of the speaker's contribution; this is Halliday's 'textual' language, referred to above:

To put it bluntly, On the other hand, If I could just interrupt for a moment, I can only repeat what I said earlier when I said...

David Brazil neatly called these talk-about-talk; they tell you that the next bit is to count as an aside, a piece of negative news, an acknowledgement etc.

b. prepositional phrases:

on either side of, just to the left of, half way up

c. social phrases – an extension of traditional 'politeness phrases'

That's very kind of you,   I know just how you feel.

4. Discourse-organising language

Choosing particular lexical expressions allows the speaker to focus attention on a particular part of what is said. These expressions have a similar function to the talk-about-talk. Dave Willis has pointed out that there is an important group of nouns which are often followed by *that...* and that these play an important role in highlighting ideas in discourse varying from informal conversation to formal academic papers:

The fact/problem/suggestion/danger that .... .

As we saw in Chapter 7 Activity 45, we react to texts. This directs attention to frames such as: *What surprised / interested / amused / me most was ...; It says here that..., but I don't believe that. I think it's much more likely that ...*

5. Complex noun phrases

Speech consists largely of a string of unprocessed prefabricated phrases, but written text has usually been heavily processed. This makes an important difference to its lexical content.

TASK

You give a short talk on a particular subject and write a short article on the same subject. How do you think the two texts – a transcript of the talk and the article – differ? Which do you think is shorter?

Almost certainly, the article is significantly shorter than the transcript and this economy is achieved largely by the use of complex noun phrase subjects in the written text.

> *When we are saying something we tend to use more words than when we are writing. When you are writing, of course, you have more chance to review and revise and even to completely re-draft ideas so that you can express them more concisely. We know if we pack too much information into a written sentence, the reader can easily pause to think, go back and re-read anything they don't understand on a first reading.*

> *The information content of written text is usually higher than that of spoken text. The conditions under which text is typically read allow the reader to reflect, revise, and even re-read. Competent writers, aware of this and with time to revise a first draft, generate complex noun phrases which increase the density of information.*

The second paragraph contains 54 words, but the first has 75. The 'written text' contains about 25% fewer words. The 'difficult constructions' in the first sentence of the written text are of the subject and complement, while the grammar of the verb is trivial, the simplest available in English. Complex noun phrases, and simple verb phrases; but EFL grammar has always concentrated on the verb phrase to the almost complete exclusion of the noun phrase. These lexically dense phrases need more attention. Ability to construct such noun phrases is a necessity for any learner who needs to write English for professional or academic purposes; they also greatly improve the perceived quality of writing for learners writing exam essays.

It is worth noting here how much processing is required in the production of good written text. The significance of this and the marked contrast with much spoken language is taken up again later.

5. Event-reporting verbs

EFL has always paid great attention to the grammatical construction called reported speech, but observation of used language shows it to be very rare and of little use to learners. At the same time the observations reveal an important defect in contemporary syllabuses.

Task

How do you think you would report each of these to someone else a day or two later?

1. Be careful – don't touch this, it's very hot.
2. I'd take a taxi from the airport – it's much easier, and it's not very expensive.
3. Yes, that's fine. I'm quite happy with this.
4. Unless this noise stops immediately, I'll call the police.
5. Right, listen everybody. Good news – they've agreed. We've got the job.
6. They might agree, but I don't have any great hopes.

You probably produced something like these:

1. ... warned me.
2. ... said it was best to take a taxi.
3. ... (S)he agreed straightaway.
4. ... threatened to call the police.
5. ... announced that we'd got it.
6. ... said he was very doubtful whether or not they would agree.

Notice the report is of the whole event, not simply of the words that were said. A short phrase may report a long sentence or even a whole dialogue. Notice, too, the similarity with Willis's suggestion above of the importance of nouns like *fact, problem*. Once again, the speaker helps the listener by making explicit what is being reported – a recommendation, warning etc. Our ability to help our listeners is based on rich lexical rather than grammatical resources. Learners need lexis (*recommended, threatened to ... , announced that ...*) not the convoluted grammar of 'reported speech'.

6. Events described in double-clause sentences

EFL has tended, with the exception of conditionals, to concentrate on the verb phrase in single clause sentences. Many typical real-world events, however, are expressed in two-clause utterances:

Promise with condition: *I will if I can.*
Request and escape: *Can you give me a hand, if you have a moment?*
Uncertainty and likely outcome: *I might not, but I probably will.*
Temptation and fall: *I shouldn't really, but I will.*

These two-clause utterances can be developed into the double-gapped exercises like Exercises 29 and 30 on page 106.

Samantha Couzin, writing to the TESL-L group on the internet, responded to a request for suggestions on good ways to teach the modals by suggesting writing on the board: *I would if I could, but I can't so I won't* and asking learners to write similar sentences. One student's suggestion is particularly worth recording: *He would if she would, but she won't so he can't*. These two sentences summarise very neatly the change of emphasis implicit in the Lexical Approach; the interesting and amusing sentence is novel; the Semi-fixed Expression is less interesting, less amusing but more useful. It is in the nature of stereotyped lexis that it is associated with stereotyped, and therefore relatively uninteresting, situations. But here teacher and learners have conspired successfully to gain maximum benefit; the input was maximally useful, and provided the basis for novelty and imaginative use.

7. Responding and initiating

EFL, particularly under its functional label, has regularly over-simplified the reasons for which we use language. The practical simplicity and superficial attractiveness of relatively controlled pairwork mean many two-part interchanges have often been structurally linked:

Do you like...?
> Yes, I do. / No, I don't.

Would you like to ...?
> Oh, thank you, that'd be wonderful. / I'd love to, but I'm afraid I can't.

There is nothing wrong with such practices, as far as they go, but they do not go very far. Natural conversation rarely resembles a question and answer session; typically control of the topic or direction of the interchange is up for grabs at almost every turn-change. The ability to take the initiative is an important linguistic skill. If you can (discreetly) change the subject, you can maximise the chance of compromise, avoid embarrassment for yourself or the other person. Rather than asking and answering, competent language users respond and initiate. Many conversational responses are Fixed Expressions, or Frames:

That's not the point.
That's not my fault.
That must have been really awful / exciting / gratifying.

There was an example from the Cobuild course on page 39 and a sample activity on page 142 which practised this language, but note again that the Expressions consist of the most common words of English. It is more efficient to learn these as Expressions, then break them into parts, rather than the reverse.

Initiative-taking is more difficult, usually involving a response **and** a development which changes the direction of the conversation:

I agree with you up to a point, but I wonder if....
It's funny you should mention that, I was talking to.... / reading ... / watching a programme the other day and they were saying ... (new topic).

This extended frame could be introduced as part of the structural practice of the past continuous. It is this interface between lexis, grammar and phonology (try reading the frame aloud; the lexical chunks also form phonological units) which makes Expressions so central to the Lexical Approach.

8. Lexical patterns

McCarthy has noted that in his spoken data, agreement is more likely to be lexical than overtly grammatical:

Beautiful day, isn't it.
> *Wonderful.* A big improvement on *the weekend.*
> You're not joking ... *Sunday* was dreadful, wasn't it.

Did you say two hundred pounds? That was pretty *expensive.*
> Too right. It was a *rip-off.* I told them what they could do with it!

Expressions like *The sooner, the better* represent prototypical examples of important patterns which can be extended very slightly or increasingly freely until they merge with the novelty we think of as the product of grammatical possibility rather than lexical probability:

The stronger, the better.
The stronger the dose, the better you'll sleep.
The more powerful a dictator becomes, the less attention he pays to the people.

Lexical awareness constantly reminds us that we are less creative in our language use than we like to think. In almost any text – essay, weather forecast, anecdote, sermon, conversation or whatever, there are patterns which it may be helpful to draw to learners' attention. In Activity 44 in Chapter 7, George Woolard described how awareness that a frame may be present in a text influenced his teaching in a helpful and easy-to-introduce way.

REAL ENGLISH AND THE CLASSROOM

Certain features of EFL are relatively standard, but are not necessarily reflected by observation of real native-speaker English. With the ever-expanding electronic media, the 'real thing' is increasingly available to teachers but this is not necessarily an unqualified benefit. The suitability of language for classroom use depends on a number of factors, and we now briefly consider some of these and the changes to content which they imply.

Possible and Probable English

Language teachers often concern themselves with the **possible** sentences of the language. When students ask *Can you say ...?* teachers, subconsciously at least, ask themselves *Is that **possible?*** Unfortunately, almost anything is possible; the more helpful question is *Is that **probable?*** Again, however, we must be careful; what is maximally useful is certainly not restricted to the most common sentences of the language. Many grammarians are interested in possibility, although many are now turning their attention to what David Brazil has called 'used language', language which has already 'happened'; lexicographers are concerned primarily with typicality – the most frequent patterns of the language. Neither possibility nor typicality are, however, quite what language teaching is looking for. Several factors need to be considered so no single parameter will reveal the language which is most useful to learners at a particular stage of their study.

Models and Targets

It is helpful to keep the distinction between the **model** – language to which the learners are exposed as 'good' samples – and the **target** – what they themselves are expected to produce – in mind. Targets can change during a learner's learning career, during a particular course, or even from activity to activity. The differences discussed between EFL and native-speaker use above influence our choice of model language, most notably in suggesting language which, although it is 'what we really say', is not appropriate to the classroom for anything other than receptive purposes, but teachers must constantly remind themselves that native-speaker-like productive ability is rarely the target. The setting of unattainable targets, particularly concerning accuracy, is likely to be counter-productive.

Is there a core lexicon?

Most contemporary research on real English is based on language produced by, and between, native speakers. At one time it was at least tacitly assumed that learners' ultimate objective was native-like ability but it is increasingly clear that vast numbers of learners will remain intermediate throughout their lives, and that they are both happy with this and derive enormous benefits from their, albeit partial, mastery of English. Native-like ability is now recognised as a target for only a relatively small percentage of learners.

At the same time, native-speaker language remains the most widely favoured model, so much so that even to question it in that role can seem unnecessary. However, the vast majority of person-to-person encounters where English as a foreign language is the medium do not include a native speaker at all. Why, then, is what two native speakers **would** say if they were talking together be the criterion for what the non-natives **should** say when no native speaker is present? For simple vocabulary and Collocations the matter seems unimportant, but when we consider Expressions ('What we really say') a great deal more caution is required. Is it the case that the language used in native-speaker situations is always the language appropriate for intermediate learners? If not, why not, and by what criteria are we to choose language suitable for such learners? (See Activity 25, page 124). The question of what language is suitable for learners is a complex and emotive one, and needs careful analysis. A discussion of the issues involved should be an important part of teacher preparation.

The problem of a core lexicon is relatively straightforward if we confine ourselves to referential language; all native speakers of British English use *lift, catch the bus, railway station* in ways which are so similar we can treat them as identical. In this sense, there is a core lexicon of referential British English. Every individual has an additional lexicon related to each of the many sub-groups to which that individual belongs. But there are two major difficulties – the lexical items just listed are not standard in American English, and worse, no core lexicon of Expressions has even been attempted. Indeed, it is unclear whether or not such a thing could be identified and agreed upon. It would certainly produce heated debate if any diverse group of native speakers discussed it. Cries of *Well, that's not what I say* or *Well, I've never heard anybody say that* would undoubtedly be the order of the day.

Against this background, any consideration of a core lexicon of Expressions for learners needs to consider several factors:

Where and with whom are they likely to use their English?
What is their current general level and what is their target level?
Are there social restrictions on the language which make it unsuitable for EFL use?
Do the learners need ESL, in-country EFL or EFL in the learners' home country?
Is EFL in any fundamental way different from 'English'?

To my surprise I find myself answering *Yes* to the last question, which is the reverse of the answer I would have given until recently. I suggest four basic reasons to support my current position, each of which influences the kind of language suitable for the classroom:

1. L2 is relatively rarely used in intimate situations

L2 is more likely to be used with strangers than friends, while our most intimate relationships tend to be conducted in L1. Ironically, one of the exceptions to this generalisation is language teachers, who, more often than most, share intimate relationships in what is an L2 for one of the partners!

Native-speaker teachers must be conscious that what they themselves say to their friends is at best a limited guide to the language they should be teaching. This requires careful thought, as contemporary research on spoken English is almost invariably on native-speaker to native-speaker interactions. It is far from axiomatic that such observation is a wholly appropriate basis for the target language for EFL learners.

2. L2 often means limited background knowledge

In contrast with the previous point, L2 is often used with strangers; English in particular is often used as a lingua franca. In such circumstances the assumed shared background knowledge is very different from that in most L1 situations. It may, for example, involve assuming very little shared cultural background, but detailed shared professional knowledge, such as Japanese, Swedish and Argentinian experts talking during the coffee break at an international convention on cancer. This means L2 learners often need certain functions which are relatively rare in L1. Every learner in a multi-lingual class recognises the need for expressions such as *Do you have .... in your country? Do you know what .... is?* The area broadly described as *Establishing Common Ground* deserves increased attention.

3. Using an L2 is often itself a mark of education and social class

Most of us consciously self-censor our language; we do not use many of the L1 lexical items which we readily recognise. We avoid language with which we do not wish to be identified: dialect, teen-speak, swearing. Adequate exposure means we can often choose from a number of different ways of 'saying the same thing'.

The L2 user usually has comparatively limited exposure to the L2 and so has comparatively little direct evidence of the suitability or otherwise of particular Expressions. The learner's *Can you say ...?* question does not usually mean *Is ... possible English?*, but rather *Can I say ...?* The teacher has thus the responsibility to advise on the suitability or otherwise of particular expressions for particular learners at that stage of their learning, and the additional responsibility to help learners acquire the necessary framework to enable them to self-censor. As soon as learners have more than one way of saying 'the same thing', they need ways of choosing which are suitable in particular circumstances. A kind of neutral, acquaintance-to-acquaintance language is what is usually regarded as the core around which more complex choices are based.

We have moved from **possible** English to the more restricted **probable** English, and further limited that to what is appropriate in certain social circumstances. It was undoubtedly easier when we taught inaccurate but dogmatic grammar rules – *some* in positives, *any* in negatives and questions – without the confusion caused by the evidence of real language use, or concerns of how, when and where learners might actually use the language they were learning.

4. Defective but effective L2 is valuable

Most learners are, and will always remain, intermediate. Whatever teachers or 'the system' may say, these learners will see this not as failure to achieve near-native ability, but as success in acquiring a useful practical tool. For such learners a limited, and therefore flawed and inaccurate lexicon may, as well as being inevitable, also be perfectly adequate. With simple vocabulary, *talk* and *speak* are indispensable, but *whisper, mutter,* are more marginal. Which Expressions are indispensable and which are marginal? Learners need Expressions which are appropriate in as wide a range of situations as possible both linguistically (corresponding to *speak, talk*), and socially (in different countries/cultures, with native and non-native speakers).

This is another constraint on the language which is suitable for learners. A few may aspire to native-like language (including those who are, or intend to be, teachers of English), but for the majority their final linguistic goal is flawed intermediate English which, while being defective, can also be highly effective in achieving a wide variety of real-world non-linguistic goals: informing, travelling, selling, seducing. This has implications both for the Expressions they are taught, and, as I have discussed extensively elsewhere (*The Lexical Approach,* Chapters 10 – 11), for the teacher's attitude to error.

Lexical balance

The Lexical Approach suggests not only a larger lexicon, but also that teachers need to make conscious choices of how most efficiently to build learners' lexicons depending on the needs and circumstances of those particular learners.

In general, written text is content-rich, and correspondingly rich in adjective-noun, noun-noun and noun-verb Collocations, while informal speech more obviously carries pragmatic rather than referential meaning. Its relative lack of content means it is rich in socially important Expressions, but relatively light in collocational content. For ESL learners, or learners studying in Britain or another native-speaker environment, both elements are important, but for most strictly EFL situations – students in English classes in Europe or Japanese learners preparing for TOEFL – the emphasis should be decisively on Collocations, and Semi-fixed frames, with relatively few Fixed Expressions of the social kind. There is a danger, particularly for native-speaker teachers, of over-emphasising 'what we really say' for learners for whom such language is of less than immediate use or relevance.

Prototypicality

We have noted that frequency, and hence typicality, is not always the useful criterion we might assume it to be. On the other hand, prototypicality is, as we now see, much more powerful than has previously been recognised.

TASK

All of these are birds: *penguin, heron, robin, chicken, ostrich.* **Do you think they are all equally good examples of the concept 'bird'? If not, which do you think is the best example? And the worst?**
Can you think of a good example and a bad example of each of these categories: *jobs, buildings, colours?*

Until comparatively recently everyone assumed a category was a group of objects or ideas, all of which shared a list of characteristics. But in the task above you almost certainly selected *robin* as a better exemplar than *penguin* of the category 'bird'. All members of the category do not share all the characteristics (flight, wings, feathers etc.) and some are 'more typical than others'. Philosophy now talks of these 'best examples' as prototypes.

EFL grammar has often assumed that all examples of the present continuous or the first conditional were equally good examples, so classrooms were filled with examples which were easy to demonstrate or thought to be memorable: *I'm playing the piano. If I win a million pounds, I'll buy a private jet.* But prototype theory tells us that not all examples are equally good, and we should be looking for prototypical examples.

TASK

Consider these examples:

Set 1
1. John and Kate are waiting for their bags. Here are their bags. Their bags are coming.
2. Pressure is intensifying for the establishment of a Parliament in Scotland.
3. What can I get you?
   > Just an orange juice, please. I'm driving.

Set 2
4. Was that the phone?
   > Don't worry. I'll get it.
5. What are you going to have?
   > I'll have a gin and tonic, please.
6. Right, I'm off. I'll see you on Monday.
   > 'Bye. Have a nice weekend.

Examples 1-3 are all present continuous, but clearly not equally typical. (1) is typical EFL; it is an exemplification which in no way suggests a real occasion of use. (2) is natural, but has the feel of a one-off use; (3) is plausible used language, evoking a readily identifiable situation. Ironically, *I'm driving* is a Fixed Expression, a lexical item with immediately apparent pragmatic meaning and a highly frequent example of the present continuous; it does not, however, represent 'an action going on at the moment of speaking'. The prototypical example contradicts rather than supports a traditional EFL 'rule'.

Examples 4-6 are all prototypical examples, from used language, of *'ll.* It makes no sense, however, to ask about *shall* and *will,* short and long forms or even about 'the future'. Again, the examples are fine and contextually appropriate, useful and easy to understand, but they are not traditional EFL.

At the end of Chapter 2, we concluded that *Grammar becomes lexis as the event becomes more probable.* The best basis for L2 learners, as for L1 learners, is archetypical situations in which what is said is highly predictable. This means effective language courses need to make extensive use of highly lexicalised spoken language; immediately useful typical and prototypical examples which will be initially acquired lexically, and later converted into grammatical knowledge.

We have already seen that learners acquire most efficiently by learning wholes which they later break into parts, for later novel re-assembly, rather than by learning parts and then facing a completely new task, building those parts into wholes.

Why, though, should priority be given to the spoken language? We look now at that fundamental question.

The Existential Paradigm

Speech takes place in real time; between known participants in a particular place, so the most usual frame of reference to which the language is related, and by which it acquires meaning in use, is the place of speech – Here, and the moment of speech – Now. Speech is always related to the Here-and-Now frame, unless the participants explicitly agree on another frame, by saying, for example, *I was talking to a chap at work the other day and he was saying ...* . Writing, in contrast, is created to be read elsewhere or elsewhen, so its reference framework must be provided by other language of the text. This means writing must be much more explicit and include language which provides the frame of space and time reference; these factors mean writing does not have the immediate, situationally evocative prototypicality of much speech. The significance of this is taken up again in the last chapter.

The relative simplicity, accessibility, and value for learners of carefully selected spoken language becomes clearer if we consider some examples:

There you are! Where have you been? I've been waiting here for ages.
Have you seen my bag? I can't remember where I put it.
Oh, you've changed your hair. I like the way you've had it done.

I think I've missed the train.
> Don't worry, I'll give you a lift.
I'll have to go to the bank. I've left my wallet at home.
> Don't worry, I'll lend you some money till later.
I don't think I've met her before.
> Oh, I'll introduce you then.

These highly probable, spoken examples are the ideal basis for developing learners' grammatical awareness. The first set of examples clearly shows that the primary characteristic of the present perfect is its intimate connection with the moment of use. It is intrinsically a present tense. The traditional EFL contrast between present perfect and past simple was silly.

The second set shows that if we consider examples beyond the individual utterance an important relationship appears. It is common after I have indicated a problem with *I've...* , for you to offer help with *I'll ...* .

Only lexicalised spoken language provides such powerfully revealing examples, which evoke what we may call the grammar of situation sufficiently strongly. Neither de-contextualised, single-sentence examples, nor examples taken from written texts can provide these examples which are the basis for the native speaker's own acquisition of English. The importance of this insight is taken up again in the concluding chapter.

SUMMARY

Although this book is primarily concerned with methodology and classroom activities and exercises, the Lexical Approach suggests many changes to course content. These are both detailed additions and deletions and, more challengingly, involve a radical re-evaluation of the importance of well-chosen, situationally evocative spoken examples.

Chapter 10

Teachers and Teacher Training

Implementing the Lexical Approach has many implications for both the content and style of both pre- and in-service courses for teachers. Some relate directly to the lexical understanding discussed in Chapter 2, while others relate to the Lexical Approach as a whole, in which communicative power and successful language are valued above mere accuracy; acquisition, over which the teacher has no direct control, is valued, rather than formal learning; and the currently most-favoured methodological model (Present-Practise-Produce) is rejected, or at least very radically revised.

The Lexical Approach re-emphasises much that was put forward in the original Communicative Approach, most notably the centrality of meaning and activities which are explicitly purposive. In addition, recognition of the lexical nature of language means many activities are slightly modified to ensure a lexical, as well as, or rather than, grammatical focus to the activity. As Andrew Barfield has observed (see page 13), however, there is the ever present danger of trivialising by failing to acquire the necessary linguistic understanding to ensure effective implementation.

BACKGROUND

We look first at the issues in the wider theoretical framework of the Approach which will strongly influence the success or otherwise of attempts at implementation.

1. The nature of the subject

Every subject has principles, working methods and axioms which are different from other subjects, and are part of the very reason we consider that subject as a separate field, worthy of study in our education system.

Mathematics is concerned with the nature of proof; history with the evaluation of evidence; literary criticism with the primacy of the text, science with the relationship between hypothesis and experiment. If these subjects are taught by teachers who have not fully thought through the nature of their subject – why it is being taught and how it differs from what is being done in other classrooms in the same school – confusion, and even hostility, is inevitable.

TASK

In what ways is teaching a language different from teaching any other subject in the school curriculum?

What is the purpose of teaching a foreign language to school students? In what ways is this purpose reflected in the way it is taught on a day-to-day basis?

Do any of the activities which are typical of language classrooms actually fight against the main purpose of teaching the subject? If so, what changes are needed – in the exams, books, methods, classroom organisation, system of evaluation?

Linguists now describe how language is used rather than trying to say how it should be used. Varieties are (sometimes contentiously) described, but not condemned. The very existence of objectively valid norms is challenged and, without such norms, the concept of correctness becomes meaningless. Viewed from a sociological perspective, language is seen not as an end in itself, but as a means to an end, used to achieve non-linguistic purposes. In *The Lexical Approach* I argued that successful language is a wider and more helpful concept than formally accurate language.

Learning a language involves a small element of factual knowledge, but consists largely of procedural knowledge; it is not about knowing **how** to, but about being **able** to. This makes it sit uneasily in school systems which often test what students know, rather than what they can do. Language teachers need a sound understanding of the ways their subject differs from subjects which are predominantly knowledge-based if they are to feel personally comfortable, and confident when questioned or criticised by colleagues or representatives of 'the system'.

When people use language for real communication, they instinctively pay attention to only those mistakes which impede communication. Why, then, do language teachers ever attend to anything else? Correcting anything other than written work is explicitly anti-educational. It seems that teachers' image of themselves as teachers makes them do things in class which are directly contrary to everything we know about both language and learning. This absurdity should be openly faced on pre-service courses.

2. Teachers need confidence with real English, not just EFL

The best modern reference books are corpus-based; all modern descriptive studies are based on used language; natural texts are, and will be increasingly, more available via the electronic media. The language of EFL coursebooks has long been sanitised; they contain an idealisation from which many features of natural language have been removed. This may be pedagogically useful, but it can have the effect that non-native teachers feel uncomfortable with 'the real thing'. If teachers are to feel comfortable with materials which address what people 'really say' and the language resources which the internet will bring to their classrooms, they must be prepared during their training. In particular they must be prepared to handle unfamiliar or novel language without seeing it as a threat to their own knowledge, competence or status.

3. Teachers' attitude to novel or unknown language

Teachers and learners would like to be able to look up things about which they are uncertain: which is correct *strong/intense/severe illness? I'd rather you don't/didn't?* Clearly, reliable reference works which sanction Collocations and Expressions are needed but, although modern dictionaries pay ever more attention to such items, reference materials remain for the moment inadequate. Expressions may appear in dictionaries of idioms, but little attention is paid to the many utterances made of the most common words which are a pre-requisite for any kind of conversational fluency.

How, then, is the non-native teacher to answer *Can you say?* questions? Two important points need to be made: firstly, the native speaker and non-native speaker are different only in degree, not in kind. The native speaker has (usually) met more English than the non-native; if the native says *I've never heard/met that*, the evidence is probably stronger than if a non-native says the same thing, though even here we must ask whether an interested, linguistically aware non-native is really at a disadvantage over many linguistically insensitive native speakers. But even the most aware native speakers meet only a minute fraction of the language produced in their home environment: while writing this I heard an American politician on British TV News resign, saying he "did not want to be the victim of yellow journalism". I had never met the expression "yellow journalism" before and would confidently have said it 'didn't exist'; but it does and it is unsurprising to any American. We all need to remind ourselves frequently that *I've never heard it* is not a synonym for *It doesn't exist*.

Secondly, no teacher's knowledge can ever be more than partial; what matters is that the teacher's language is significantly better than that of the learners. Teachers in history and physics expect to have adequate rather than comprehensive knowledge of their subjects; unfortunately language as a subject lends itself to revealing on unexpected occasions what the teacher is uncertain about or simply does not know. This can be dealt with by reducing English to EFL, a regularised, pre-digested subject, of which the teacher can have comprehensive knowledge, but only at the cost of distorting English itself, or much more honestly and usefully, by openly acknowledging that this subject is boundless, and perfect knowledge is unattainable. If all teachers accept that, and share that uncertainty confidently with their students, the problem largely disappears. It can be further diminished if teachers learn to use appropriate language to guide learners: *I've never heard/met/come across that. I suggest you say/ use* ... is accurate and cautious but still clear and reassuring for learners. It is when teachers cover their insecurity by saying *You can't say ...* that they lay themselves open to embarrassing contradiction.

4. Ability to simplify their own speech

The Lexical Approach places great emphasis on the roughly-tuned input provided by the teacher when (s)he is talking informally to the class. A fundamental requirement is that teachers must be able to control, and most importantly, to simplify the language they use in class. The Lexical Approach values comprehensible input in the way outlined in Krashen's input theory, which says language is learned by understanding messages that the learner is interested in understanding, that the learner does not feel worried or threatened by, and that contain some unknown language which is understandable from the context. In such a theory, the ability to simplify is valuable because it is the way in which messages are made understandable.

Many teacher training courses, especially for non-natives, include an element aimed at developing the teachers' language skills, but I am not sure the ability to simplify is given the priority it deserves. It is not something we do frequently in our daily lives, so it needs to be practised.

5. Methodology based on a realistic timetable

The theoretical underpinning which supported the Present-Practise-Produce (P-P-P) paradigm is now largely discredited but its influence remains widespread. In broad terms, seen as M-M-M, it remains valid. Learners Meet, Muddle through, and (eventually, perhaps) Master some features of L2; but the period over which the process occurs may be weeks or even years. Formal teaching of isolated points may contribute to a developing understanding, but such points simply cannot be 'taught' in particular lessons. Dave Willis says: *However hard we work at it, we cannot predict what learners are going to learn at a given time.* This runs counter to much teacher training which tends to set very specific learning objectives for individual lessons, sometimes even particular activities in a lesson. Encouraging teachers to have defined objectives is clearly helpful; any suggestion that real and lasting learning occurs in a specific lesson is both theoretically indefensible and practically counter-productive, setting up wholly unrealistic and unrealisable expectations.

6. Holistic approach

The Lexical Approach takes a holistic rather than atomistic view of language. This applies to all aspects of content and methodology – it endorses Krashen's advocacy of Free Voluntary Reading; elsewhere in this book Jonathan Marks emphasises the importance of suprasegmentals rather than individual words or sounds in the teaching of pronunciation, and Mark Powell advocates response to whole texts, rather than traditional comprehension of details. Metaphor as an organising principle is based on gestalt understanding, rather than the accumulation of items in a list. In every area, the thrust of the Lexical Approach supports more holistic views and procedures.

As we have just noted, teacher training has tended to require teachers to know, or perhaps pretend to know, what learners are learning in any given lesson; moving to the holistic ideas implicit in the Lexical Approach means a radical change to this mindset.

LEXIS IN TEACHER TRAINING

We move now to implications directly related to the lexical nature of language.

7. Deep understanding of the arbitrariness of the sign

We discussed earlier the fundamental axiom of linguistics, the arbitrariness of the sign. Words, Collocations and Expressions are arbitrarily sanctioned by particular native-speaker communities. That is easily said and briefly summarised, but it lies at the heart of many individual responses teachers will make on a day-to-day basis. What is arbitrary cannot be explained; any apparent explanation is at best a waste of time; at worst it causes confusion later.

Why can you say *a close friend* but not *a near friend?*
Why can't you say *It's forty past three?*
Why can you say both *if I was you* and *if I were you?*
Why is it *He told me that* ... but you can't say *He said me that ...?*
Why does English have continuous forms when many other languages do not?
Why does French have *le* and *la* when English doesn't?

Good learners ask questions, and education encourages us to ask why, and to expect an answer. *Because that's how it is*, or *Because I say so* are unsatisfying, frustrating, even apparently incompetent answers. A corollary to this is that teachers must abandon many of the folk-linguistic 'explanations' they sometimes offer learners. Few of these are true, and most will confuse rather than help. What is and is not sanctioned as lexis is arbitrary. Teachers must know, understand and feel this, so they can gradually develop a similar understanding in their learners, without undermining the learners' confidence in either themselves or their teachers.

8. Memory load

The Lexical Approach draws attention to the sheer size of the mental lexicon and this poses a serious methodological challenge. Regular state school courses in Europe have aimed for a vocabulary over a full school career of 10,000 words; private language school teachers talk in terms of ten new words per lesson. These targets are simply not enough. We know from studies of L1 acquisition that children aged around seven may be acquiring 4/5000 words per year, which is more than 10 a day. That happens without them being directly taught vocabulary. The implication is clear – it is exposure to enough suitable input, not formal teaching, which is the key to increasing the learner's lexicon; most vocabulary is acquired, not taught, hence the endorsement of Stephen Krashen's recent book *The Power of Reading*.

Language teaching once restricted input, insisting on learners mastering one bit before they met the next. That practice is now discredited but its influence remains. Learners tend to want to 'understand every word', teachers to explain and laboriously practise a small number of supposedly important new items. Much communicative methodology emphasises learners' output, not input. All these factors militate against maximally efficient acquisition. Broadly, fluency depends on the size of the learner's lexicon, which in turn depends on the quality **and quantity** of input the learner has received. Again, this runs directly counter to what constitutes standard practice in many places.

Similarly, teachers have often tended to add to the burden by offering alternatives: *You can say ... but you can **also** say ...* . Recognising the increased memory load suggests teachers should think of excluding alternatives, rather than adding them.

9. Confidence with pedagogical chunking

The grammar/vocabulary dichotomy is deeply embedded in our way of looking at language; it is another radical change to direct attention to chunks rather than individual words and to accepting that many Expressions are best handled by consciously avoiding analysis of their internal structure.

Successful implementation of the Lexical Approach means teachers must feel confident looking at, analysing and making practical pedagogic decisions about language from a lexical viewpoint which will, for many, be new.

Traditionally, the texts in coursebooks have been read intensively, often squeezed dry of every 'new word'. The Lexical Approach suggests learners need to meet much more text, which is only partially or even superficially used for a specific purpose, as we do with texts of different kinds in our daily lives. This requires that teachers feel confident that they can identify the different kinds of lexical item, and that they have a readily accessible set of principles which allow them to guide learners, so they gain maximum benefit from the texts they meet both in and out of class.

Identifying lexical items is not always as straightforward as one might expect: one element of a partnership may be realised only pronominally; partnerships may occur across turn boundaries or both these features may occur together, burying the collocation even further. With many Expressions it is not a matter of them being Fixed or semi-fixed in some theoretical sense, but how they are best analysed and presented for a particular class.

10.   Choosing text-types

Throughout this book we use the word 'text' in the sense of any continuous natural piece of language, whether spoken or written. There is an important relationship between text-type and the kind of lexical item typical of the text. Fixed Expressions are obviously more likely in dialogue than in narrative writing, but the distinctions are much more complex than the obvious difference between speech and writing. Teacher training needs to help teachers develop an awareness of the relationship between lexis and text-type.

Almost any text-type may be appropriate for certain ESP students, but for the general EFL learner we may reasonably assume they may wish:

• To understand and take part in natural conversation, both with other non-native speakers, and perhaps as a special case, with native speakers.

• To tell a personal anecdote or funny story. Geoff Thompson notes: *people quite often tell stories in ordinary conversation (often very short ones) and they tend to use a lot of reporting [verbs] when they tell a story*. This endorses several of the points made when discussing target language in the previous chapter.

• To be able to give an oral presentation on a topic from their personal field, either for academic or business purposes.

• To read semi-specialised text written in an educated journalistic style.

• For a minority of usually more advanced learners, to write texts specific to their own field of study, employment or interest.

Clearly if these are the target text-types, examples of these must be used as classroom materials, rather than literary or narrative texts, although these may also be useful, either for general educational reasons, or to encourage imagination in the use of the target language. The main point is that the selection of appropriate texts for particular learning targets is more **linguistically** sensitive than has sometimes been recognised.

A full exploration of text-types is outside the scope of this book, but teacher training should at least make trainees aware of these types which exhibit widely lexically-different profiles.

Discursive Written Text

We find such texts in academic textbooks and serious journalism. Such texts contain many content-bearing words, particularly relatively unusual nouns, verbs, adjectives and adverbs, often in topic-specific collocations. In such texts, it is often possible to identify a small number of keywords, typically nouns, which recur throughout either the whole, or a significant section of the text. These topic-specific words are in an intuitive sense 'what the text is about'. Careful selection can produce dense, coherent summaries which reveal most of the content-bearing lexis. In a strong implementation of the Lexical Approach such text provides optimal input, particularly for older learners with specific linguistic objectives in, for example, a particular academic or job-orientated field.

Written summaries

Summaries exist as independently occurring texts, as synopses of plays, introductions to academic papers, as the first paragraph of many news reports or magazine articles, and in the extended contents of specialist magazines. They are invariably lexically very dense. Here is an example from the scientific magazine *Nature:*

> ### Quantum effects writ large
> *The magnetic dynamics of single crystals of a manganese cluster compound bear the signature of the macro-scopic quantum-mechanical effect. At certain values of an applied magnetic field, the rate of relaxation from one magnetization state to another is enhanced above the thermally activated rate by the process of quantum mechanical tunneling. These experiments show that the fundamentally non-classical quantum effects that occur in microscopic systems can also occur in highly complex macroscopic systems.*
> *Nature Issue 6596 September 96*

Such texts are ideal for inputting key lexis for ESP or EAP learners but such learners will also need other texts which display the more extended frames we discussed in Chapter 2.

Written Narrative

Discursive text tends to return to key lexis again and again; in this book *collocation, lexical perspective*, recur throughout the whole text. Narrative, by its very nature, moves from incident to incident, place to place, so that new lexical items replace old. Coherence is provided by linear time rather than a network of recurring lexical items. In general, narrative contains more 'new words', each used less frequently than the individual items in a discursive text of similar length.

We note in passing that, outside exam questions, few learners will ever need to produce written narrative. In contrast, most of us tell stories of what has happened to us or our acquaintances. Spoken narrative or anecdote deserves more attention than it often gets.

Adverts

Newspaper and other printed adverts tend to be lexically dense, but are rarely motivating as teaching materials. Two types of advert do, however, lend themselves to classroom activities – entertainment listings and lonely hearts columns. These provide largely ungrammaticalised, lexically dense input, but such text-types cover only a small area of the lexicon.

Informal conversation

Real conversational data exhibit the rather disconcerting quality of often being largely content-free. We tend to talk to each other rather than about anything. Conversation is frequently about building or maintaining relationships rather than exchanging information. This makes informal conversation a poor source of vocabulary in the narrowly-understood sense. It is, however, pervaded by a rich lexicon of prefabricated short phrases (*The thing is..., I know how you feel, Exactly.*) a knowledge of which is a pre-requisite for even basic conversational fluency.

Many EFL learners on a first visit to Britain or the States find their school learning of limited help when actually functioning in English. The vast difference between traditional EFL texts and natural informal spoken language accounts for this. A similar problem arises in reverse for many European learners. They communicate effectively in an international environment, using English as a lingua franca while, for example, travelling during their vacation, only to find their grades in written exams do not reflect the success they felt when speaking English. An adequate lexicon for writing English effectively can only be acquired from extended reading; listening and speaking alone cover only a limited area of a mature adult lexicon.

11. Lexical principles and texts

The question of what texts, even what kind of texts are most suitable as input for language learners is a contentious one, and one about which opinions have changed substantially over the years. Once upon a time the preference tended to be for 'good', often literary texts. In structural times, texts were usually specially written to incorporate the target structure – the story in *Kernel Lessons* remains a superb example of a text-type which fell out of favour as the textbooks claiming to embody the communicative approach preferred dialogue to prose, and so-called authentic text to specially written material. The Lexical Approach suggests we may need to revise our view of classroom texts again.

Different types of text provide different kinds of lexical input and a balance of text-types is needed, at least for general courses. A difficulty arises which is psychological and pedagogical rather than linguistic. Learners remain unhappy ignoring large numbers of unknown words which occur in a text. The teacher can, over time, wean learners away from this view but there is also value in using texts where a significant percentage of the text is directly useful to the learners. This causes problems if we wish to use naturally occurring texts.

The claim that only natural texts are appropriate for classroom use is logically confused, as its proponents also argue that texts are written and used for specific purposes. That is true, but since learners are using coursebook texts for the primary purpose of learning a language, not to read about rain forests or understand the workings of a market economy, it should be self-evident that some texts need to be written or adapted to take account of their language learning purpose. Applied linguists have long pointed out that authenticity does not inhere in text, but in the relationship between the user and the text, which means learners need at least some texts specifically designed for them **as language learners.**

If teachers choose alternative or supplementary texts appropriate for particular classes, it is essential that they have an explicit understanding of the principles upon which to base the choice of maximally useful texts together with techniques for lexical exploitation of the texts such as those outlined in Chapter 7. They need to consider the proportions of probable to possible language and to balance what is most typical or frequent, and therefore potentially most useful, with what is most novel and unusual and, therefore, potentially interesting.

A small number of text-types are collocationally dense, but many texts contain relatively long 'barren' passages, part of the essential structure of the text but not the target language needed by learners at that stage of their programme. Editing texts by crudely chopping the barren passages out produces an unsatisfactory mish-mash. It seems we need skilled writers who can re-cast some texts so that they are lexically enriched for the classroom. Choosing relatively long topical newspaper or magazine texts on grounds of interest is likely to prove frustrating to learners, unless teachers have selected the texts with great care and carefully highlighted specific passages for use in class, before they become bogged down in parts of the text which are of little use to the learners.

The Lexical Approach values both extensive and intensive reading, but makes a clear distinction between the two. Extensive reading, out of class and for pleasure, chosen on the basis of personal interest is essential to building an adequate lexicon. Intensive study, often of a very short text, or even a frame from a text as outlined by George Woolard earlier, also has an important role to play. Familiar techniques such as skimming and scanning, both of which are lexically based and emphasise using text for a specific purpose, need to be emphasised in teacher training so that teachers can ensure their learners get maximum benefit for language learning purposes from the texts they meet.

12. Implementing change for serving teachers

Change is threatening and implementing change is often painful. Systems, and especially education systems, are naturally conservative; those in charge of education have succeeded under the prevailing system; change to the system may threaten their own positions. Established teachers have a repertoire of standard techniques and lessons, as well as, most importantly, beliefs about learning, classroom procedures and their professional role. For senior teachers, expense on resources such as books or technology may need to be justified. The custodians of any education system often see themselves as responsible for handing on a received body of knowledge to the younger generation: they thus tend, typically through an examination system, to set conservative syllabuses. This means the most potent inertia frequently comes from examination systems which notoriously oppose change on the pretext of 'maintaining standards'.

Change is threatening because I know that, even if I don't like the present situation and I don't agree with certain things, I can at least **cope**. Change may mean I show my ignorance, make a fool of myself, lose face. Any attempt to introduce change, which does not take serious account of people's real anxieties in implementing their part of the overall change, is doomed to failure. Initial teacher training courses and in-service development courses need to tackle this issue sensitively, fully aware of the genuine threat implicit in any substantive change in the way one is used to working. Specific areas of anxiety in seeking to implement the Lexical Approach can be identified.

TASK

Which of the following:
a. do you think / have you thought?
b. can you hear a colleague saying?

I am confident with the old EFL grammar rules. I don't believe they were mostly wrong. I think they help – they helped me. Why discard what works?

I am not confident with lexical language (collocation or exactly what people do, rather than could, say) myself. You can't expect me to teach what I don't know, or what I do not feel confident about.

You say it will work better in the medium term but I, and my head teacher and the parents, want evidence of real progress in the short term. I have a responsibility to get my students through the exam.

I can't accept I've been doing it wrong for years; I prefer the devil I know to another fashion which I don't fully understand, don't fully accept and fear could change again tomorrow.

All of these are valid reservations which need to be both respected and answered. I hope this book provides reassurance that the changes implied in the Lexical Approach can be implemented without undue stress or conflict. A few points are worth re-emphasising:

You are being asked to advise students **more** on lexis and **less** on traditional grammar; the change in your thinking may be considerable, but the change in what you actually **do** in class is relatively small.

Start with very modest changes, nothing more radical than extending what you usually do with vocabulary to multi-word items, and when following up a text, drawing attention to new chunks rather than new words. Implement the new ideas step-by-step, gradually modifying what you do, rather than introducing wholesale changes.

Discuss the changes, briefly with learners, but also with colleagues and administrators. See it as experimenting; if you are convinced something doesn't work after trying it two or three times, revert to your earlier procedure. If the changes are successful you will carry your students and others with you without conflict.

Nobody is suggesting you ignore the demands of the examinations, even if those demands are absurd. But you don't have to teach for the exam all the time, and most exams have bad, better and good elements. Because reported speech **might** come up in one question in Paper 3 is a poor justification for defending the **entire** status quo.

Finally, nobody can change your teaching except you. Henry Widdowson has expressed concern that when teachers say *It works*, it sometimes stops them from asking if something else might work better. Teaching which is always the same, even if it was once alive and effective, cannot do other than become stale. But the stimulus to change, experiment and try new ways of doing old things, or doing new things must come from teachers themselves.

13. Familiarity with modern dictionaries

Any non-native teacher who relies on a 15-year-old edition of the *Advanced Learners* is quite simply out-of-date. 1995 was the 'Year of the Dictionary' in Britain; all the major ELT publishers produced a new dictionary or a radically revised edition of their main EFL dictionary. All are now, following Cobuild's ground-breaking example ten years ago, corpus-based. From our point of view, the most important thing is that they are now a superb source of reliable examples taken from used language.

Traditionally the coursebook has been seen as the primary source of input and the dictionary largely confined to a reference role and even then only in the narrow sense of looking up the meaning of unknown words. Implementing the Lexical Approach suggests a much more substantial role for an

English/English dictionary, and during training, teachers need to develop a range of techniques which they can pass on to learners to get maximum benefit from what is now potentially a major source of input.

Catherine Walters closes her survey review of the recent EFL dictionaries (*ELT Journal, Oct 96*) with these words, with which I wholly agree:

> *Teachers should remember that without first learning to use the dictionary skilfully learners will only have access to a small part of the information. All four publishers provide supplementary materials for learning and practising the techniques necessary to get the full benefit of their dictionaries. The extra investment involved in buying a class set of these materials and going through them with students will be money and time well spent.*

14. What would a lexical lesson be like?

Several correspondents, attracted by the theoretical position set out in *The Lexical Approach*, have written to ask *What would a lexical lesson be like?*, but, as we already emphasised, the Lexical Approach is not a new all-embracing method, but a set of principles based on a new understanding of language. While there is no such thing as 'a lexical lesson' in the way some correspondents would like, two characteristics are common to all the new, or newly-focused activities: firstly, attention is directed to larger chunks of language than has been the norm; instead of words, we consciously try to think of Collocations, and to present these in Expressions. Rather than trying to break things into ever smaller pieces, there is a conscious effort to see things in larger, more holistic, ways. Secondly, activities tend to unify the teaching of grammar, lexis and pronunciation; a chunk may be taught as a lexical item, a phonological unit, and as grammatical input. These two principles – holistic and unifying – are applied in many different ways.

These two principles conflict with much that is standard in contemporary teacher training, but this need not be so. Pre-service training often encourages trainees to set specific, often rather narrow, objectives for a particular lesson or activity. That is helpful to inexperienced teachers, but trainers must always then emphasise that these detailed, specific activities must always be used within a unifying, holistic framework. It is only when this wider perspective is lost that specific techniques inhibit rather than help.

15. Some central ideas

It is easy for teachers who are deeply involved in their own situation to forget that there is an enormous diversity of language classes: children playing in English, new-arrival ESL learners in the States, pensioners' evening classes, intensive one-to-one learners with a single highly specific objective, mature and highly intelligent EAP learners who need English for specific and sophisticated academic purposes, and also vast numbers of unmotivated learners on whom English is inflicted by their school system. With such diversity of classes, it is hardly surprising that even within the framework of a specific approach, there is a wide range of different, sometimes even mutually-contradictory, emphases.

I emphasise again that the Lexical Approach is not a revolution; revolutions inevitably fail. Its principles suggest many changes in content, methodology and attitude, which individual teachers can introduce in keeping with their own experience and suitability for their general situation and particular classes. At the same time, it is not sufficient, for example, to emphasise vocabulary rather than grammar; an old-fashioned vocabulary-building programme is no more lexical than a course based on audio-lingual practice in the language laboratory. The Lexical Approach must not become a new dogma; it is in no sense 'the' answer, but it is a principled approach, much more than a random collection of ideas that work, so it is worth listing a few central ideas without which teaching, however successful, cannot legitimately call itself the Lexical Approach.

If you are using the Lexical Approach you certainly **will:**

*   Consciously take every chance to expand the learners' phrasal lexicon.
*   Develop learners' awareness of word-grammar as well as sentence grammar.
*   Highlight Fixed Expressions and prototypical examples, so ensuring learners have maximum benefit from the language they meet.
*   Encourage accurate observation and noticing by learners, but without excessive analysis.
*   Use many different ways to increase learners' awareness of the value of noticing, recording and learning multi-word items.
*   Encourage learners to keep a well-organised lexical notebook.
*   Encourage lexical, but not structural, comparison between L1 and L2.
*   Help learners to hear and learn language in multi-word units.
*   Talk more informally, but in a carefully controlled way, with your class.
*   Tell simplified anecdotes (true or otherwise): increase carefully-controlled teacher talking time.
*   Take a global, holistic view of pronunciation.
*   Value successful language at all times, even if it is not formally accurate.

You will definitely **not:**

*   Ask learners *Are there any words you don't understand?*
*   Encourage learners to record many single *L1 word=L2* word items.
*   Worry about *ship/sheep*-style pronunciation problems of individual words.
*   Worry unduly about natural grammar errors, which disappear with exposure and time, not formal instruction and correction.
*   Indiscriminately teach 'what native speakers really say' to EFL classes where such language may be of limited use.
*   Throw away years of experience of good practice, only add a lexical perspective to that experience.

16. Some challenges to serving teachers

On a somewhat more contentious and demanding level, particularly for teachers working in a state school system, here are a number of challenges which would mean the full implementation of the Lexical Approach.

1. Stop using out-of-date grammar rules which, if you are honest, you have probably never really believed helped anyway.

2. Forget any inhibitions about possible defects in your own English, so you no longer need to teach what is 'safe' for you (grammar rules, written texts, all the old chestnuts that you have taught many times before) and move the focus of your attention to helping students understand and speak English.

3. Don't use the exams as an excuse for conservative teaching – reported speech 'because it's in the exam' – any more than absolutely necessary.

4. Develop a real linguistic curiosity. Do you come across new information about the language often? Do you find it intimidating or exhilarating?

5. Learn how to identify multi-word items; help your students to develop the ability to do the same.

6. Make sure you are fully familiar with the modern corpus-based reference books which offer so many helpful insights into English and which have only become available in the last few years, perhaps since you last undertook formal study.

7. Use these reference books regularly in class, and teach all your learners to do the same. A modern dictionary, with many thousands of corpus-based examples, is a valuable source of accurate, reliable and useful English, sometimes more useful than the language of the coursebook.

8. Pay more attention to fluency and communicative power and less to mere accuracy. This applies to all courses and learners, but it is a comparative, not absolute statement.

9. Remember the sheer size of the lexicon. Resist the temptation to be comprehensive; select out rather than in. Choose only what is maximally useful for your learners.

10. Teach the spoken language; make full use of new media available to you; increase the time you spend talking naturally to your learners. Most learners will never be better than 'intermediate', but nonetheless this is of great personal value to them. Value the ability to speak English, even a little, as a genuinely life-enhancing skill.

SUMMARY

Taking a lexical view of language will not, on its own, mean your students' English improves more rapidly than if you take a more traditional grammatical, or notional/functional approach. The Lexical Approach involves more than a lexical view of language; there are important methodological implications too. Traditional approaches have tended to restrict the amount of language to which students are exposed. Usually, it has been assumed that students must 'master' a particular language item before they 'go on' to the next item in the syllabus. Such a view runs counter to everything we know about both language and learning. Knowledge of a language develops as an organic whole; the appropriate metaphor is of a living plant, growing organically, rather than a building, constructed brick-by-brick. The Lexical Approach therefore implies greatly increased emphasis on listening and spoken examples for learners at all levels, and for literate learners, increased emphasis on extensive reading. They should listen and read extensively, consuming much larger quantities of material, but in less depth, than has been the norm. Modern media nowadays make this a realistic option. Teachers, course directors, school owners, and indeed national education systems need to wake up to the fantastic opportunities now available. In the modern world large quantities of up-to-date and individually appealing material can be introduced into language classrooms at very little inconvenience or expense.

The opportunities are there; the Lexical Approach continues to develop, and as discussed briefly in the final chapter, will continue to move towards a more unified view of lexis, grammar and phonology. For the moment, the challenge of implementing our present understanding of the Lexical Approach rests with administrators, schools and, perhaps most importantly, teachers.

Chapter 11

What Next?

The fundamental linguistic insight of the Lexical Approach is the greatly increased importance we need to give to two kinds of lexical item, Collocations and Fixed and Semi-fixed Expressions. Pedagogically both are important as, together with individual Words, they form complementary parts of the mental lexicon. Although there are great areas of overlap, it is broadly true that Words and Collocations convey referential meaning, while Expressions convey pragmatic meaning. The former are concerned with the speaker/writer's content, and the latter with the speaker/writer's intentions. This simple distinction helps direct our attention to theoretical problems, and thus to two glaring defects in current materials. One suggests an important modification in dictionaries, the other a radical change in grammar and an important methodological shift.

LEXIS IN DICTIONARIES

Why does the Lexical Approach, despite the undoubted strengths of modern EFL dictionaries, suggest that something more is needed? English/English dictionaries and their associated workbooks are immensely useful classroom resources for several reasons: they are full of excellent examples and categorise polysemous words in helpful ways, so they are a valuable source of potential input, particularly when coupled with a lexical Notebook. Anca Nemoianu, reviewing *The Lexical Approach* in TESL-EJ says:

> The emphasis on the teaching of collocating words, on the linguistic rather than the situational environment, with the dictionary as a learning (rather than just a reference) resource, and the identification of lexical chunks as a basic classroom activity, is novel and deserves our entire attention.

A good modern English/English dictionary helps learners and teachers develop a greater awareness of chunks. It offers a further, less obvious, advantage as research evidence supports what is intuitively plausible, namely that users of L2/L1 dictionaries tend not to develop paraphrasing skills, which are essential when you do not know a particular word. (This also implies that teachers who constantly 'help' learners by providing synonyms or, worse, translations of new words, are doing their learners a disservice in the medium term.) It also endorses the defining style of the Cobuild series of dictionaries which is based on the kind of paraphrase teachers use in glossing words in class.

Modern dictionaries provide ever better descriptions of English and are excellent at helping users de-code, which is the primary purpose for which learners use such dictionaries. The problem comes when the same dictionaries claim to help production, to sanction Collocations and Expressions. For this purpose, they remain of very limited use and the problems are intrinsic to the nature of current dictionaries.

Since such dictionaries are primarily designed to help the user to find the meaning of unknown words, they tend to "define" words, using simpler words. If you want the word *dispatch,* and only know the word *send,* you have no way of finding the more 'difficult' but more appropriate word. If you **suspect** the word you need is *dispatch,* further trouble surfaces immediately – the *Advanced Learners* is not untypical when it tells us:

dispatch *to send sb/sth to a destination for a special purpose*

To dispatch is to send; the dictionary suggests synonymy; which may be helpful if you want to de-code but positively misleads anyone who is seeking *le mot juste* for productive use, when writing an essay or report. Essential differences between words of similar meaning are lost because of the primary purpose of EFL dictionaries.

The problem is deeper. Dictionaries are, perhaps surprisingly, based on a naive view of vocabulary; simple dictionaries often assume synonymy, rather than similarity of meaning, so one word is defined by giving another with "the same" meaning; and the majority of even the most admirable dictionaries implicitly assume that one word can be **defined** in other words, but this is simply not the case. The difference between two words of similar meaning is in some cases **defined** precisely by their different collocational profiles. Until the dictionaries include lists of collocates to supplement the traditional definition, they will be of limited use for productive purposes.

Current dictionary entries contain a small number of examples, chosen on the basis of typicality, and thus frequency. Very strong collocations *(golden wedding / handshake / age)* are usually separate entries, included to aid de-coding. But the collocations which the learner typically needs for productive purposes, particularly writing, are neither the most frequent nor the strongest but medium strength collocations *(profit / output / turnover grew by 3%,* but *prices increased,* not **grew).* These are precisely the ones least likely to be accessible from the standard dictionaries.

The *Longman Activator* claims to be a productive dictionary, but rather than providing ready access to collocations, it seems to me to be most helpful if users simply browse under particular headings so that half-remembered lexis is re-activated for them. Ironically, the best of the dictionaries currently available for activating and suggesting collocations is, I find, one designed for native speakers and which combines dictionary and thesaurus entries on the same page: *Collins Concise Dictionary and Thesaurus* (1995 edition).

Some learners who have developed an awareness of chunks, particular short phrases made of the most common words of the language, report that they have found browsing in a large modern dictionary, in the long entries typical of common words, a surprisingly helpful way of building their mental lexicon. Browsing in this way activates and sanctions phrasal vocabulary which the learner may well not notice in formal study or in reading for pleasure. This represents a radical shift; learners have usually used dictionaries to de-code 'difficult' words, here they are using them to build their encoding possibilities using 'easy' words.

Implementing the Lexical Approach would be much easier if learners had access to a dictionary of medium-strength collocations, of the kind I have been working on recently and which will appear soon. *(Wordfinder, A Collocation Dictionary, published by LTP in mid 1997)*. This will contain only those medium-strength collocations about which learners are unsure and which they may therefore want to check. It is designed to re-activate half-known and half-remembered lexis and to answer those *Can you say ....?* questions about probable collocations.

When teachers are asked such questions they have two complementary resources at their disposal; firstly, their own knowledge and experience of English, but nowadays also access to the vast resources provided by corpora and computer concordance programs. To their (perhaps over-)tentative: *I've never heard/met/seen it*, they can now add *and it doesn't appear in the 20/150/800 examples in my computer data*. Non-native teachers are beginning to realise that what they have often seen as an Achilles heel – inadequate exposure to the target language – is now easily overcome for a comparatively modest one-off cash investment, and a regular, quick, easy and even enjoyable investment of time.

Lexicographers need vast quantities of data to ensure the comparatively rare words of English are adequately represented, but even a comparatively small corpus, easily available from the internet, is more than enough for a teacher who wishes to confirm the unlikelihood (remember, no corpus can confirm the impossibility) of a particular collocation or other pattern. My colleague Heinz Ribisch now marks university students' work while sitting beside his computer; it is a matter of a few seconds to check his intuitions against a corpus based on six or seven hundred thousand words of newspaper text, which can be downloaded free from the internet, and which, once coupled on the hard disk with an inexpensive concordance program, provides a more powerful and accessible reference than is yet available in printed reference works.

Such concordance programs, incidentally, are excellent for preparing exercises. Select, say, ten examples of two confusables such as *bring/take, speak/talk*, and print them so the lines are mixed. Most programs will blank out the 'search word' at a single keystroke, so the preparation of a discrimination exercise is almost instant.

While such technology is not yet available to every teacher, it is daily becoming more widely available and cheaper and cheaper. It is likely that this will soon more than compensate for the unavailability of reference books which license composition for learners and provide teachers with the objective support for which they have long expressed a need.

As for a reference book of Expressions, there is at the moment no British equivalent to *NTC's Everyday American English Expressions,* but the problems of a reference book for lexical items of this type are rather different, for while such a book is a valuable resource for teachers and materials writers, learners can hardly look up what to say under the constraint of real-time conversation and it is not clear how valuable simply browsing through such a listing would be.

Collocations, together with fully Fixed Expressions, suggest an important, but relatively modest extension to the traditional dictionary. In contrast, Semi-fixed Expressions suggest a much more radical re-appraisal of both grammar and methodology.

LEXIS AND GRAMMAR

The Lexical Approach received attention not only from language teachers, but also from applied linguists. Cheryl Boyd Zimmerman, for example, writes:

> The work of Sinclair, Nattinger and DeCarrico and Lewis represents a significant theoretical and pedagogical shift from the past. First, their claims have revived an interest in a central role for accurate language description. Second, they challenge a traditional view of word boundaries, emphasising the language learner's need to perceive and use patterns of lexis and collocation. Most significant is the underlying claim that language production is not a syntactic rule-governed process but is instead the retrieval of larger phrasal units from memory.

Her last statement is not strictly accurate. My position is not that language consists of prefabricated items, but that **much more** language than we have previously thought is stored and produced in this way. The section *Lexis is not enough* on page 41 may be short, but the importance of its content must be neither overlooked nor underestimated. The Lexical Approach claims that, far from language being the product of the application of rules, most language is acquired lexically, then 'broken down' or in Martin Bygate's term, syntactised, after which it becomes available for re-assembly in potentially new combinations. This suggests we need to make changes to the kind of input, particularly in the early stages of learning, which will be most appropriate and useful in helping learners to develop the ability to produce novel language on the basis on what is initially memorised as lexical intake.

Hearing only a few sounds of a real-world utterance may be enough for you to recognise exactly what was said. The actual language heard is only a small part of the information used to understand. Context, situation and global real-world knowledge mean that a very small amount of aural information is sufficient for us to identify what **must** have been said. How we do this has serious implications for the kind of input which is likely to be maximally useful to learners.

The Lexical Approach has encouraged us to see larger units of language and focuses attention on naturally occurring Expressions rather than rule-generated sentences such as these:

If you want to get away from modern life, you should go and live on a small
island in the middle of the ocean.
He tried to reach the shelf but he wasn't tall enough.
Perhaps one day your car will be stolen.

While all of these are possible, none 'rings true' as used language, yet all are from well-known grammar practice materials.

We have already seen that not all sentences in the language have the same status. Some, such as the above, are mere exemplifications at sentence level of supposed rules, while others, invariably drawn from used language and strongly institutionalised lexis are much more evocative of a whole situation or event. We need to replace sentential exemplifications with this situationally evocative language.

Grammar becomes lexis as the event becomes more probable. If we use lexical examples, particularly if they are two or three turns long, the input is much more likely to be situationally evocative. The way we understand what must have been said in many situations is often by recognising an Expression, rather than a single word. That is because such Expressions are precisely the multi-word labels for familiar situations:

I'm sorry, I didn't mean to make you jump.
It's the sort of thing you think will never happen to you.
There's a lot of it about at the moment.

It becomes increasingly clear that the best form of input is spoken language, based on situations in which the language is highly conventional, and the language correspondingly highly lexicalised. There is a strong case to be made for replicating this part of the L1 learning process for L2.

The relationship between L1 and L2 learning may be much debated but, despite important differences, the two must be more similar than different. This being so, it is a matter for amazement that although L1 acquisition is invariably based on huge amounts of listening, involving many repetitions of the same stereotypic and prototypical situational spoken language, L2 learning was for many years based on diametrically opposed criteria. It is very unlikely that an L2 is mastered in the classroom in ways which are so different from the way we all master our L1.

The shift to lexicalised situationally evocative language has considerable methodological implications too.

THE IMPORTANCE OF SPOKEN LANGUAGE

Spoken language is, as Jonathan Marks comments in Chapter 8, by its very nature, chunked by the user for the listener. It is also produced for communication in the Here-and-Now time and place of its moment of production. Finally, many of the situationally evocative events discussed above are frequently re-occurring, familiar events where we understand the language used, not simply by hearing the words used, but by reference to a wider top-down understanding of the whole event. These factors combine to make spoken language both easier and richer as input for the L2 learner. It is therefore with some surprise that we realise that for many years classroom input was strictly restricted and usually involved sentential exemplification based on written language. This methodology, based on structural criteria and the now discredited Present-Practise-Produce methodology, unquestionably makes language learning more difficult and less effective than using a rich diet of strongly lexicalised, situationally evocative spoken language. This means using larger units, ideally events lasting several turns, but at a minimum complete Expressions which are to be understood as initially unanalysed wholes.

After the first few lessons, in which learners may need considerable reassurance, using lexical input of this kind will mean fewer problems for learners as they deal with both receptive and productive language. Learners, for example, often have trouble understanding native-speaker speech delivered at natural speed; similarly, many have difficulty producing fluently, as part of the stream of speech, such elementary items as *it's, you're, it'd*. The reason is that they have been taught, explicitly or not, to **synthesise** larger units of language from smaller ones, while, as we have seen, natural language learning is based on **analysing,** breaking larger units down into smaller ones. It seems we can integrate lexis and grammar, and as a powerful bonus, phonology too, as we shall now see.

LEXIS, GRAMMAR AND PHONOLOGY

Studies of used language show us that informal speech usually consists of strings of unprocessed lexical items, not grammatically complex sentences. These strings are often delivered, as we saw in Chapter 8, as tone groups. Spoken text is inevitably chunked for the hearer while readers have to chunk the text for themselves, hence Roland Barthes' observation that 'when you read a text, you re-write it'. Reading involves re-creating the text, and for learners the inability to 'hear' the text correctly chunked may be a serious impediment to comprehension. Speech is a sequence of 'packets' in which lexical phrases are delivered as clearly delineated spoken units. Lexis, grammar and phonology converge in spoken language in ways which can only be poorly imitated by any written language. Listening is therefore fundamentally better input than reading for mastering the grammatical system of the language. (It is, after all, how most L1 grammatical knowledge is acquired.)

A comment made many years ago by my colleague Jimmie Hill continues to pose a challenge: *Grammar is what makes English a school subject.* He meant that specific content which can be tested, and 'making them think' are seen as the proper purposes of schooling. But ironically all of us acquire a sound basic grasp of L1, and many learn an L2, without formal instruction of any kind. Understanding and speaking a language involves procedural rather than content-based knowledge and is, in fact, not an intellectually demanding activity.

THE INTEGRATED APPROACH

Much language is acquired and remembered lexically. After several meetings, a lexical item is incorporated into learners' lexicons. With a sufficiently large lexicon, they break lexical items into pieces and gradually develop awareness of the possibilities of re-combining parts into new combinations; prefabricated lexis is the basis for analysis and later novel re-synthesis. This is essentially a holistic view which integrates lexis and grammar.

Equally, the importance of tone units, although discussed in this book, provides another fruitful area for further exploration as we move towards an integration of lexis and phonology.

Although the Lexical Approach gives great emphasis to the spoken language, and in particular to prototypical, situationally evocative examples, it is clear that this element of the Approach can usefully be developed further.

If we can identify situations which are easily recognisable across cultural barriers and in which the language is fully grammaticalised but strongly biased towards institutionalised Expressions, and if these are presented in natural spoken form, we have the exciting prospect of a holistic methodology in which the input brings together lexis, grammar and phonology.

It may be that by the time the Lexical Approach has been implemented, we shall have to turn our attention to the Integrated Approach.

Glossary

Acquisition A term popularised by Krashen for the unconscious intake of language, which is then available for spontaneous use. He presents it in opposition to conscious **learning** (qv). He claims – contentiously – that learning and acquisition are in no way related, and that it is only acquisition which is of permanent benefit to the learner.

Closed class Groups of grammatically similar words, such as relative pronouns, prepositions, or question words, where all the members can be listed and you cannot imagine a new one being added. Contrasts with open classes such as nouns, adjectives and verbs where new words are frequently added to the language.

Coherence All the factors, internal, textual and contextual, which mean the reader interprets different parts of a text as belonging to the same whole. It is an aspect of the way a reader interprets the text, in contrast to **cohesion** (qv) which is intrinsic to the text itself.

Cohesion The grammatical and lexical links in a text which make it seem a whole. It is an intrinsic property of the text. (cf **coherence,** qv)

Collocation The phenomenon whereby certain words co-occur with other words with more than random frequency: less formally called Word Partnerships, the concept is central to the Lexical Approach. Different kinds of collocation, and the differences between strong and frequent collocation are central to understanding the Lexical Approach.

Consciousness-raising Activities which concentrate on receptive skills, ensuring learners notice features of the **input** (qv) in ways which are most likely to help them turn it into **intake** (qv).

Context The totality of the event which surrounds the use of a particular piece of language. Context includes **situation** (qv), **co-text** (qv), and such factors as the relationship of the speakers, purpose of the text etc. The very width of the term makes it comparatively useless to us; we usually use more specific terms in seeking analytical principles within the Lexical Approach.

Co-text The language (but not other factors such as situation) which surrounds the language under analysis or discussion. (cf **context,** qv)

Corpus A collection of **texts** (qv) assembled to form the material for a scientific study of language. Corpus linguists describe the content of the corpus, perhaps confounding our preconceptions. Challenges to their work must be based either on the descriptive framework employed – usually a matter of academic hair-splitting – or, much more potently, the criteria used in the selection of the corpus material. Different corpuses may be constructed for different purposes and produce unexpected differences. Many contemporary corpuses have been designed for lexicographic purposes; while they always give useful information, it is a highly questionable article of faith that the evidence they reveal is equally suited to devising language teaching materials.

De-code Technical term for taking meaning from a piece of language, so the general term for what we do when we listen or read. (cf **encode,** qv)

De-lexicalised verb Most words even isolated from context carry definite meaning – *dog, accidental, produce*. This is as true of most verbs as other word classes. There are, however, a group of verbs in English which have little or no meaning outside the context of particular use: *to **have** nothing to do, to **take** your time, to **put** someone at their ease*. These verbs are components in a large number of multi-word expressions. Because of the wide range of patterns into which they enter, it is often more appropriate to think of these words as part of the grammar of English, rather than just as words in the lexicon. They are important in the Lexical Approach, as they provide an innovative organisational principle. The main de-lexicalised verbs are: *do, get, give, have, keep, look, make, put, take*.

Discursive Text The kind of content-bearing texts found in academic essays, textbooks, serious journalism etc.

Encode The mental process by which we express meaning in language, so the general term for what we do when we speak or write. (cf **de-code,** qv)

Equivalent Term used in this book for a word or expression in one language which corresponds in a contextually appropriate way to a word or expression in another language; loosely a 'proper' (as opposed to word-for-word) translation.

Fixed Expression A phrase or sentence which has an idiomatic **pragmatic meaning** (qv). Most totally fixed expressions (*Nice talking to you. You're kidding*) occur in speech, but the category overlaps **Semi-fixed Expressions** (qv).

Focus A grammatical term for the new information in a sentence, usually at the end of the sentence. It contrasts with the topic (qv).

Function A term to describe what the language user is doing by using a particular expression. Functions are usually expressed with ...*ing* forms of the verb *refusing/accepting an offer, playing for time*.

Headword The main word in a noun phrase which is qualified by the other words, e.g. *letter* in *a furious letter of complaint*, or *consultancy* in *management consultancy*. In the latter, both words are usually nouns, but in the combination *management* is used adjectivally to qualify the headword.

Idiom A multi-word lexical item where the meaning of the whole is not directly related to the meanings of the individual words. Traditionally used for colourful expressions such as *It was a storm in a teacup*, the term has a wider scope in the Lexical Approach, including common **Fixed Expressions** (qv) and **Semi-fixed Expressions** (qv) such as *I'll get it, I can't make (Tuesday)*.

Input Language the learner meets which can be turned into **intake** (qv). How input is turned into intake is the subject of Second Language Acquisition (SLA) research and remains highly contentious. What is broadly agreed is that learners need more, and more varied, input if they are to internalise (parts of) the structure of the target language and that learners need to meet the same item several/many times before it will be fully acquired.

Intake Language internalised by the learner in such a way that it becomes and remains available for productive use. To teachers' frustration, not all **input** (qv) becomes intake.

Intergrammar The learner's understanding of the systems of the target language at any particular stage of learning.

Interference The effect of learners' L1 on their perception of L2. The word carries negative connotations, and we prefer the neutral term **transfer** (qv).

L1/L2 L1 is a person's first language or mother-tongue; L2 is any second or foreign language.

Learning Often used loosely, as in *The history of language learning shows us that ... .* Used by Krashen to refer exclusively to conscious, explicit learning of rules etc. He uses it in contrast to unconscious **acquisition** (qv), which he (contentiously) claims is in no way related to learning.

Lexical item The concept of the individual word extended to the multi-word objects which are the fundamental units of the language. David Brazil (1995) suggested the definition: A lexical item is a word-like object representing a single sense selection.

Lexis A more general word than the common vocabulary. Vocabulary is often used only to talk of the individual words of the language; lexis covers single words and multi-word objects which have the same status in the language as simple words, the items we store in our mental lexicons ready for use. The implications of the differences between simple words and lexis are the subject of this book.

Matching A common exercise type where students re-arrange words, part sentences etc. by finding halves of a collocation or whole expression. Such material often tests rather than teaches, as learners need to recognise, and therefore already know, the whole phrases.

Meaning See **referential meaning** (qv) and **pragmatic meaning** (qv).

Modal The word class (qv) of auxiliary verbs which express the speaker's attitude to the factual content of a statement. The generally agreed modals are *can, could, may, might, shall, should, will, would, must*; some other verbs – such as *ought to, have to, need* – are included by some grammarians in the same class. The Lexical Approach suggests the modals should be lexically rather than grammatically treated, both theoretically and in the classroom.

Modality The way speakers show that what they say is to be taken as opinion, speculation, generalisation etc. rather than pure fact. It is realised both with the modal auxiliaries and lexically *(It looks as if ... , They tend to)*.

Mode Two are distinguished – the spoken mode and the written mode.

Noticing A key strategy in the Lexical Approach in which learners' attention is specifically drawn to lexical features of the **input** (qv) to which they are exposed.

Paradigm A way of showing a regular pattern in the language by presenting the information in a visual array. The best known are the verb paradigms *I am, You are* etc. Increased attention to word grammar in the Lexical Approach suggests more paradigms can be used to summarise patterns in accessible and (relatively) memorable form.

Person *I* is the first person singular, *you* the second person singular and so on. Noticing that certain Expressions are uniquely or strongly associated with a particular grammatical person both challenges some of the claims of traditional grammar and provides ways of generating useful expressions in the Lexical Approach.

Polyword A word-like item, representing a single sense choice, conventionally written as more than one word: *by the way, on the other hand*.

Pragmatic meaning The social significance of a piece of language; often usefully contrasted with referential meaning. A simple example is given under **referential meaning** (qv).

Random Volunteered Responses (RVR) A term used by Krashen in *The Natural Approach*. The teacher invites learners to offer responses, without naming individuals to answer specific questions. The responses may be used by the teacher, commented on, or simply (consciously and deliberately) 'ignored'. They are discussed in Chapter 3.

Receptive skills Listening and reading as opposed to the productive skills of speaking and writing. They were once inaccurately and unhelpfully called passive skills. Clearly, effective listening and reading are anything but passive; it is through these skills that every word we ever produce first becomes part of our individual mental lexicon. The Lexical Approach re-emphasises the importance of **input** (qv) and therefore of receptive skills.

Referential meaning Roughly what is being referred to, or talked about; the content of what the language user intends. Can be usefully contrasted with pragmatic meaning, roughly what the speaker (or writer) is doing, the social meaning of the language. In *Could you pass the pepper mill, please? pepper mill* is referential (typically Words and Collocations), while *Could you pass the ..., please?* is pragmatic (typically an Expression), here *Asking for something.* This simple broad distinction is helpful in looking at the language which typically expresses different types of meaning.

Scanning Looking through, rather than actually reading word-for-word, a text while searching for particular information, or the answer to known questions. Together with **skimming** (qv), two holistic and purposive ways of using a text which complement using the text as a source of specific language.

Semi-fixed Expression An item with one or more variable slots which must be filled by an item chosen from a relatively small group of items which share particular language characteristics. The category is not precisely defined, but lies between strictly **fixed expressions** (qv) and novel language produced by reference to generative grammatical patterns.

Sentence A tricky term although it seems simple. Traditionally, a 'complete thought' which starts with a capital letter and ends with a full stop, but this definition assumes written language and as soon as natural spoken language is considered the water becomes very muddy. Complete verbless items such as *Happy Birthday* are not traditional sentences; worse, educated speakers giving relatively formal lectures seem to pile phrase upon phrase with no regard for the traditional grammar of sentences. While this is only a problem for purists, linguists usually prefer the term *utterance* for a unit of speech. Sentences, particularly as presented in many EFL grammars, are often imagined, idealised language – they are possible language; utterances are not only probable, but have actually happened – examples of what David Brazil calls 'used language'.

Situation The place and circumstances in which some language is used. It combines with **co-text** (qv) to make the more general **context** (qv).

Skimming Looking quickly through a text to get a general idea of the content, usually before using it for a specific purpose. (cf **scanning,** qv)

Text A technical term for any piece of language chosen for study. Unlike the ordinary non-technical use, the term covers stretches of writing or speech, so that part of a lecture or conversation can be referred to as a text.

Text-type The simple distinction between spoken and written English is too crude to ensure a balance in materials; a wider range of text-types, which exhibit different lexical and grammatical profiles, is needed.

Tone unit A short stretch of speech containing a major intonation movement on a stressed syllable, *I'm sorry, I can't* is two tone units, while *I'm afraid I can't* is one.

Topic What a sentence is about, in the grammatical, not thematic sense. Usually the first words (traditionally called the subject) such as *The bus* in *The bus is coming.* Contrasts with the **focus** (qv). The terms topic and focus are particularly useful with sentences such as *What surprised me* (topic) *was how expensive it was* (focus).

Transfer The effects, both positive and negative, of the learners' L1 on their perception of L2. We prefer the term to the more common, but negatively connoted, **interference** (qv).

Turn The language spoken by one person in a conversation before another person takes over the conversation. A turn may be as short as a single word or as long as a complete passage, extending over several sentences or even, for example, a complete anecdote.

Utterance A single unit of meaning in speech. A more technical (and more useful and accurate) term than the familiar **sentence** (qv).

Vocabulary Usually used to refer to the stock of (single) words, usually imagined as having fixed meanings to be found codified in the dictionary. The Lexical Approach extends the meaning to the stock of lexical items, which we hope will one day be codified in lexicons which take account of this extended understanding of the real building-blocks of the language.

Word Perhaps surprisingly, a difficult term for many linguists; easy to agonise over *don't, isn't it*, etc. In this book the term is used in the naive sense of a thing which is surrounded by two spaces when it is written down. On this definition *don't* is one word, and *by the way* is three words. Notice, however, *by the way* is one lexical item, and *don't* is either part of the grammar of English, or can be treated as a single unanalysed item. This definition is not as innocent as it appears – lexically *don't/haven't* can be covertly shifted from their previously 'obvious' relationship with *do/have*.

Word class Formerly called 'parts of speech'. Words grouped according to their grammatical characteristics. The most common classes consisting of lexical words are nouns, verbs, adjectives and adverbs: the classes consisting of grammatical words are prepositions, modals, and conjunctions. Although the standard term is word class, many of the items are in fact multi-word lexical items (qv), such as *take off* (verb), *newly-built* (adjective), *in no uncertain terms* (adverb), *on either side of* (preposition).

Bibliography

The books and articles listed below have directly influenced some aspect of this book. Seminal works covering the general background are:

Lakoff, George and Johnson, Mark Metaphors We Live By, University of Chicago Press, 1980

Lewis, Michael The Lexical Approach, LTP, 1993

Nattinger, James R. and DeCarrico, Jeanette, S. Lexical Phrases in Language Teaching, OUP, 1992

Pawley, A. and Syder F. Two Puzzles for linguistic theory: nativelike selection and nativelike fluency, in Richards and Schmidt.

Richards, J. and Schmidt R. Language and Communication, Longman, 1983

Willis, D. The Lexical Syllabus, Collins Cobuild, 1990

The dictionaries referred to are:

Benson, M., Benson E., and Ilson R. The BBI Combinatory Dictionary of English, John Benjamins, 1986

Cambridge International Dictionary of English (CIDE), 1995 edition

Collins Cobuild English Dictionary (Cobuild), 1995 edition

Longman Dictionary of Contemporary English (LDCE), 1995 edition

Oxford Advanced Learners Dictionary (OALD), 1995 edition

Reference is also made to:

Collins Concise Dictionary and Thesaurus, New Edition 1995

Common American Phrases in Everyday Contexts, National textbook Company, 1994

NTC's Dictionary of Everyday American English Expressions, NTC Publishing Group, 1996

Readers interested in dictionaries may care to refer back to:

Alexander, Richard Fixed expressions in English, reference books and the teacher, ELT Journal Vol. 38/2 April 1984

More recent works which had particular influence on this book are:

Brazil, David Pronunciation for Advanced Learners of English, CUP, 1994

Brazil, David A Grammar of Speech, OUP, 1995

Brazil, David Designing an integrated pronunciation course, in Speak Out, Newsletter of the IATEFL Pronunciation Special Interest Group, No. 17, January 1996

Brown, Philip R. Lexical Collocation: A Strategy for Advanced Learners, in Modern English Teacher, Vol 3 No. 2 1994

Bygate, Martin Effects of task repetition: appraising the developing language of learners in Willis and Willis, 1996

Carter, Ronald and McCarthy, Michael Grammar and the Spoken language, Applied Linguistics, Vol. 16/2 June 1995

Channell, Joanna Vague Language, OUP, 1994

Coady, James and Huckin, Thomas Second Language Vocabulary Acquisition, CUP, 1997

Hoey, Michael, Patterns of Lexis in Text, OUP, 1991

Kövecses, Zoltan and Szabo, Peter Idioms: A view from cognitive semantics. In Applied Linguistics, Vol. 17/3 September 1996

Krashen, Stephen The Power of Reading, Libraries Unlimited, Inc., 1993

Lakoff, George Women, Fire and Dangerous Things, University of Chicago, 1987

Lewis, Michael Implications of a lexical view of language, in Willis and Willis

Lewis, Michael, Pedagogical implications of the lexical approach, In Coady and Huckin

McCarthy, Michael Vocabulary, OUP, 1990

Nation, I.S.P. Teaching and Learning Vocabulary, Heinle and Heinle, 1990

Norman, David, et al. Communicative Ideas, LTP, 1986

Odlin, Terence Perspectives on Pedagogical Grammar, CUP, 1994

Rudska, B., et al. The Words You Need, Macmillan, 1981

Skehan, Peter Second language acquisition research and task-based instruction, in Willis and Willis

Schmitt, Norbert and Schmitt, Diane Vocabulary notebooks: theoretical underpinnings and practical suggestions in ELT Journal, Volume 49/2 April 1995

Spears, Richard A. et al. Dictionary of Everyday American English Expressions, NTC Publishing Group, 1996

Swan, Michael Language Teaching is Teaching language, in IATEFL Annual Conference Report, 1996

Thompson, Geoff Collins Cobuild Guides, Number 5: Reporting, 1994

Walter, Catherine review of CIDE, Cobuild, LDCE, OALD in ELT Journal, Vol. 50/4 Oct 1996.

Willis, Jane and Dave, Collins Cobuild English Course, Student's Book 3, Collins, 1989

Willis, Jane and Willis, Dave Challenge and Change in Language Teaching, Heinemann, 1996

Yip, Virginia Grammatical consciousness-raising and learnability in Odlin

Zimmerman, Cheryl Boyd, Historical trends in second language vocabulary instruction in Coady and Huckin.

Most books published by LTP in recent years incorporate lexical exercises and activities. All of the following may be of interest to teachers seeking ways of implementing the Lexical Approach:

Build Your Vocabulary 1, 2, 3, John Flower ISBN 0 906717 76 0, 0 906717 7 79, 0 906717 78 7 The 1995 editions were revised to add extra work on Collocations and Expressions.

Financial English, Ian Mackenzie ISBN 1 899396 is much more than financial 'vocabulary'.

Lexical ideas are most fully developed in two books by my colleague Mark Powell:

Business Matters, Mark Powell A business course based on the Lexical Approach ISBN 1 899396 10 1 Teachers' Resource Book with many additional ideas and formats ISBN 1 899396 15 2 Cassette 1 899396 20 9
Presenting in English, Mark Powell A course which integrates lexis and pronunciation ISBN 1 899396 30 6 Cassette tape British English ISBN 1 899396 50 0 American English ISBN 1 899396 75 6

There are literally hundreds of suggestions for activities which have, or can easily be given a lexical focus in a book which, despite its title is a valuable resource for teachers of conventional classes:
One to One, Peter Wilberg, LTP, ISBN 0 906717 61 2

And finally a radically different reference book for anyone who wants to help learners with collocation:
Wordfinder – A Collocation Dictionary LTP, 1997, ISBN 1 899396 55 1